YEARS OF THE
50
Gibson
LES PAUL

50 YEARS OF THE Gibson LES PAUL

Half a Century of the Greatest Electric Guitars

TONY BACON

50 YEARS OF THE
Gibson
L E S P A U L

Tony Bacon

A BACKBEAT BOOK
First edition 2002
Published by Backbeat Books
600 Harrison Street,
San Francisco, CA94107
www.backbeatbooks.com

An imprint of The Music Player Network United
Entertainment Media Inc.

Published for Backbeat Books by Outline Press Ltd,
115J Cleveland Street, London W1T 6PU, England.
www.backbeatuk.com

Copyright © 2002 Balafon. All rights reserved. No part of this book covered by the copyrights hereon may be reproduced or copied in any manner whatsoever without written permission, except in the case of brief quotations embodied in articles or reviews where the source should be made clear. For more information contact the publishers.

ISBN 0-87930-711-0

Art Director: Nigel Osborne
Design: Paul Cooper Design
Editor: Siobhan Pascoe
Production: Phil Richardson

Origination by Global Graphics
Printed in Hong Kong by Colorprint Offset

02 03 04 05 06 5 4 3 2 1

CONTENTS

6	LES BEFORE THE PAUL
10	THE FIFTIES
42	THE SIXTIES
62	THE SEVENTIES
78	THE EIGHTIES
94	THE NINETIES
114	THE NOUGHTIES
126	REFERENCE SECTION
156	INDEX
160	ACKNOWLEDGEMENTS

In the years before the launch of the Gibson Les Paul in 1952, Les Paul had worked his way up to become the most famous guitarist in America. He first endorsed Gibson back in 1940 (ad, left), and had entertained US forces during the war. He'd played and been billed on a big Bing Crosby hit in 1945, and signed as a solo artist to Capitol. His first release, 'Lover', was a hit, showing off his New Sound, a marketing name for Paul's clever use of an early version of overdubbing to help him construct magical, multiple-guitar recordings. When he added vocalist Mary Ford in 1950 the hits got even bigger, with 'How High The Moon' providing a US number one in 1951.

Les before the Paul

LES BEFORE THE PAUL

When guitarist Les Paul and vocalist Mary Ford teamed up as a musical duo in 1950, they had already been married a year. Using Paul's groundbreaking overdub techniques, their records for Capitol featured multiple guitars and vocals to make a brilliantly fresh sound that also scored commercially. Between 1950 and 1954, 13 of their 20 singles went Top 10, with 'How High The Moon' and 'Vaya Con Dios' making number one in 1951 and 1953 respectively. They appeared frequently on the increasingly important new medium of television – the picture (left) shows them with their testbed Epiphone "clunker" guitars and TV host Ed Sullivan in 1951. They had their own TV networked *Les Paul & Mary Ford Show* from '53 to '55, as well as a weekly NBC radio slot. In short, by the early 1950s, they were very famous.

▲ Rear of "log" showing solid central section

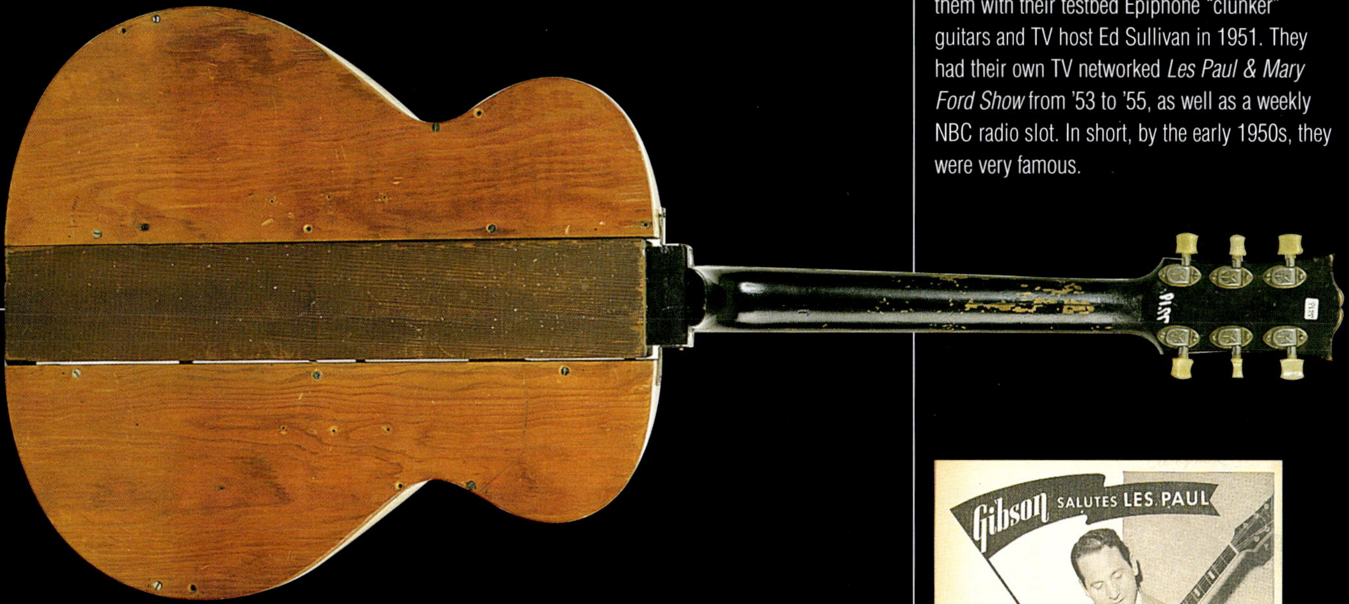

▲ Les Paul's 1940s "log" guitar

Les Paul's first guitar where he tried out ideas for a semi-solid body was this experimental "log". He put it together in the 1940s using parts taken from a Gibson (the neck), Larson Bros (fingerboard) and Epiphone (body), adding his own crude vibrato, pickups, and 4x4 solid central body section. Later in the 1940s he modified two further Epiphones for his semi-solid "clunkers".

Gibson acknowledged the success of Les Paul in this ad from early 1952 (above) which mentions the "wonderful new Gibsons now under construction for you and Mary". This was the first official notification that later in 1952 Gibson would launch its new solidbody electric guitar, the Gibson Les Paul Model. Note how the company made sure that the Epiphone headstock logo of Paul's "clunker" was just out of shot in the ad.

FIFTY YEARS OF THE GIBSON LES PAUL

Les Paul is not just the name on a guitar headstock. The man himself was born Lester William Polfus in Waukesha, Wisconsin, in the mid 1910s, and started professional life as a talented, teenage guitarist. By age 17 he was broadcasting on local radio stations, playing country as Rhubarb Red and adding jazz to his expanding repertoire. The kid had an apparently natural technical ability, which he applied to music as well as to making his own bits and pieces of instrumental and electrical gadgetry. Like a number of performers in the 1930s, the young Lester soon became interested in amplifying his guitar. He recalled later that in his early teens he'd managed to create a pickup out of a telephone mouthpiece and an amplifier from his parents' radio, allowing him to bring his guitar to the attention of the audience at a local roadhouse gig.

> Les Paul created on record a magical orchestra of massed guitars playing catchy instrumental tunes, and his first multi-guitar single was a big hit.

Around this time companies such as Rickenbacker, National and others began to sell the first commercial electric guitars, instruments with electric pickups and controls built into regular archtop acoustic guitars. By the middle of the 1930s the Gibson company had got into this market with an "Electric Spanish" guitar and amplifier, as had their biggest competitor, Epiphone of New York City.

Meanwhile, Lester Polfus had permanently adopted a suitably shortened version of his name – Les Paul – and for three years from 1938 led a jazz-based trio broadcasting out of New York on the Fred Waring show. It was at this time that he moved from an acoustic archtop model to one of Gibson's first electric guitars, the ES-300. Later he would visit the empty Epiphone factory at weekends to experiment with an instrument he called his "log". The nickname came from a four-by-four solid block of pine that he inserted between the sawn halves of a dismembered Epiphone body, with a Gibson neck and Larson Bros fingerboard, adding his own vibrato and pickups. He didn't play this one much – it was more of a testbed.

A little later Paul modified a second and third Epiphone, which he named his "clunkers", and he and vocal/guitar partner Mary Ford would use these semi-solid guitars regularly on stage and in recording studios through the early 1950s.

Other explorations into solidbody electric guitars were being made elsewhere in America at this time, not least by Rickenbacker, National, Bigsby and Fender, all in California. A solidbody electric was appealing to manufacturers because it would be easier to construct than an acoustic guitar, using a body or body-section made of solid wood to support the strings and pickups. For the player, it would cut down the annoying feedback produced by amplified acoustic guitars. A solidbody guitar reduced the effect that the body had on the instrument's overall tone – something that players of electric hollowbody guitars criticise – but the solid body had the benefit of more accurately reproducing and sustaining the sound of the strings.

Paul knew that Gibson was the biggest in the guitar business in the 1940s. After all, he'd appeared in the company's catalogues and ads as a famous player, both as Rhubarb Red and as Les Paul, and he'd played various Gibson guitars, including L-50, L-5 and Super 400 models (all acoustics) and that electric ES-300. So now he decided to try to interest them in his "log". Gibson was big, and undoubtedly successful. It had been founded in Kalamazoo, Michigan, in 1902, and had gained an enviable reputation among musicians for some fine, attractive and potent instruments, with Gibson mandolins in particular achieving wide popularity. The guitar had grown in importance during the 1920s and 1930s, and any company who wanted to succeed among guitarists needed to be seen as inventive and forward-thinking. Gibson certainly obliged with many six-string innovations, including the superb L-5 archtop of the early 1920s.

A controlling interest in Gibson was acquired in 1944 by the Chicago Musical Instrument Company (CMI) which had been founded some 25 years earlier in Chicago, Illinois, by Maurice H Berlin. Under the new deal, Berlin became the boss of Gibson's parent company. The manufacturing base remained at the original factory, purpose-built in 1917 at Kalamazoo, an industrial and commercial centre in a farming area, roughly halfway between Detroit and Chicago. The latter city was the location for Gibson's new sales and administration headquarters at CMI.

It was probably around 1946 that Paul took his experimental "log" to Berlin at CMI's HQ in Chicago to convince him to market such a guitar as a Gibson. No doubt with all the courtesy that a pressurised city businessman could muster, Berlin showed Les Paul the door. "They laughed at the guitar," he remembered.

OVERDUBBING THE HITS

Les Paul was becoming famous. He was a member of the original Jazz At The Philharmonic touring-and-recording "supergroup" organised by Verve Records boss Norman Granz, and during World War II had been in the Armed Forces Radio Service, operating out of their HQ in Hollywood and entertaining the troops. Among the singers he backed was Bing Crosby.

After the war Paul played prominent guitar on Crosby's number-one hit 'It's Been A Long Long Time' (1945), credited to Bing Crosby With The Les Paul Trio. It brought Paul to a much wider audience. Crosby showed a keen interest in new recording developments and from 1946 was an early user of tape-recording machines for his radio show. He encouraged Paul to build a studio into the garage of the guitarist's home in Hollywood, California.

It was in his small home studio that Les Paul hit upon some effective recording techniques – at first using discs, then tape. Paul's method was to build up multiple layers of instruments by using two recording machines. He would add new material to an existing recording at each pass of the tape and could vary the tape-speed to produce impossibly high and fast guitar passages. With this homegrown technology – and later with the facilities afforded by a single, modified tape recorder – Paul created on record a magical orchestra of massed guitars playing catchy instrumental tunes.

Les Paul and his "New Sound" was signed to Capitol Records, and the first multi-guitar single, 'Lover', became a number 21 hit in 1948. Jazzman Sidney Bechet had done a technically similar thing seven years earlier for his multi-instrument 'Sheik Of Araby', and singer Patti Page's hit 'Confess' later in 1948 used the same recording techniques. But it was Les Paul who made overdubbing his own, and more of the distinctive hits followed, many with Mary Ford. By 1951, Les Paul was just about the most famous guitarist in America.

"Carved top, great neck, cool sound, wild look ... this brand new Les Paul electric guitar really does have it all."

1950s

Freddie King ▸

11

FIFTY YEARS OF THE GIBSON LES PAUL

During the early 1950s guitarist Les Paul became a big recording star. After a long break to recover from a bad car accident he found even greater fame when he added vocalist Mary Ford to the act. He'd known Ford (her real name was Colleen Summers) since 1945, but they didn't hook up officially until 1949. Their marriage, Paul's second, took place in December, and the following year the duo released their first joint single, pairing 'Cryin' and 'Dry My Tears'.

Les Paul had developed a recording technique that was novel at the time. He could make multiple layers of instruments on record by cleverly using two recording machines, adding new material to the existing recording on each pass and ending up with a virtual orchestra of guitars. Signed to Capitol after leaving Decca, he'd had a hit with his first multi-guitar single for the label, 'Lover', in 1948. Guitars and now Mary's voice too were given the multiple recording treatment, and big hits followed for Les Paul & Mary Ford. 'The Tennessee Waltz' went to number six in the US charts in 1950, but it was 'How High The Moon' that struck gold for the duo, going to number one in April 1951.

Today it's perfectly normal and commonplace for musicians to build up recordings at home using multiple parallel tracks, whether on tape or disk, but back in the early 1950s it must have seemed as if some kind of witchcraft was being used. Like many at the time, *The Melody Maker*'s reviewer was mystified by the sound of 'High How The Moon'. "Beyond revealing that there are 12 guitar parts and nine vocal parts on it, and that Les works out his trick formula with the aid of a tape-recorder at home," wrote Laurie Henshaw in 1951, "Capitol refuses to divulge information it obviously regards as top secret." On a TV show in 1953, Paul suggested that the maximum number of dubs he could get on to tape with his scheme was 14.

More hits followed using the "trick formula". 'The World Is Waiting For The Sunrise' went to number two in 1951, as did 'Tiger Rag' the next year, and 'Bye Bye Blues' got to number five during 1953. 'Vaya Con Dios' was the duo's second number one, in 1953, while the same year 'I'm Sitting On Top Of The World' went to number ten, and 'I'm A Fool To Care' reached number six in 1954. The duo performed at a host of personal appearances and concerts, and were heard on NBC Radio's *Les Paul Show* every week for six months during 1949 and 1950. They starred in a networked TV series *The Les Paul & Mary Ford Show*, which began in 1953 and ran until 1955, filmed at their new luxury home in Mahwah, New Jersey. Les Paul & Mary Ford, "America's musical sweethearts", were huge 1950s stars.

FENDER'S SOLID FIRST

In 1950 a small California company that made amplifiers and electric lap-steel guitars launched on to an unsuspecting market the world's first commercially available solidbody electric "Spanish" guitar. This innovative musical instrument was originally called the Fender Esquire or Broadcaster, but soon was renamed the Fender Telecaster. Fender's burst of activity did not instantly convert guitarists everywhere to the new tones and the potential to play safely at higher volumes afforded by the new solidbody instruments. At first Fender's novel electrics were used by a handful of country players and western-swing guitarists, principally from areas local to the company's workshop in Fullerton, California. But slowly the word spread, and Fender's rise to the top of the electric guitar market had begun.

Such a success, even if modest at first, did not go unnoticed among other guitar makers. Valco of Chicago offered a cheap new single-pickup solidbody electric early in 1952 from both of its principal guitar brandnames – National, with the Cosmopolitan model, and Supro, with the Ozark. By the summer '52 music-trade show the other big two US guitar manufacturers had their new solidbody electrics: Kay offered the Thin Twin; Harmony the Stratotone. Over in Kalamazoo, Gibson too had their ears to the ground.

GIBSON RETALIATES

Ted McCarty had joined Gibson in March 1948, having worked at the Wurlitzer organ company for the previous 12 years. In summer 1950 he was made president of Gibson, replacing Guy Hart who resigned through ill health. McCarty recalled that Maurice Berlin, head of Gibson's parent company CMI, in Chicago, had appointed him expressly to improve Gibson's business performance, which had been suffering since World War II. The company had suspended most of its musical instrument production during the war, instead undertaking government electronics work for radar installations. This selfless activity earned Gibson three Army & Navy "E" Awards for productivity.

Gibson was finding it hard in the post-war years to get back into full-scale guitar production. McCarty's immediate targets when he joined were to increase the effectiveness of supervision in the factories, to bolster efficiency, and to improve and widen internal communication. "I went there on the 15th of March 1948," he remembered. "We lost money in March, we lost money in April, we made money in May, and we made it for the next 18 years that I was there." By 1950 Gibson's electric guitar line consisted of seven models, from the ES-125 retailing at $97.50, through the ES-140, ES-150, ES-175, ES-300 and ES-350, up to the ES-5 at $375. These were all archtop, hollowbody guitars of the f-holed, "amplified acoustic" type.

Then along came that Fender solidbody electric from California. McCarty remembered the reaction at Gibson. "We were watching what Leo Fender was doing, realising that he was gaining popularity in the west," said McCarty. "I watched him and watched him, and said we've got to get into that business. I thought we were giving him a free run, and he was about the only one making that kind of guitar with that real shrill sound which the country and western boys liked. It was becoming popular. We talked it over and decided to start out and make a solidbody for ourselves. We had a lot to learn about the solidbody guitar. It's different to the acoustic. Built differently, sounds different, responds differently." McCarty's recollection was that Gibson started work on its

> "Beyond revealing that there are 12 guitar parts and nine vocal parts on 'How High The Moon', and that Les works out his trick formula with a tape-recorder at home, Capitol refuses to divulge information that it obviously regards as top secret."

IN THE BEGINNING

1952-53 in context

Gibson launches its new Les Paul Model (52), known today as "the gold-top".

James Bond debuts (53) in Ian Fleming's first novel starring the spy, *Casino Royale*.

First H-Bomb is detonated (52) by the US down at Eniwotek Atoll in the Pacific. It makes a hell of a bang.

Bill Haley & His Comets get to No.12 in America with Crazy Man Crazy, arguably the first hit rock'n'roll record (53). Muddy Waters records Baby Please Don't Go.

Colour TV first demonstrated (53).

Muddy Waters with Les Paul gold-top ▶

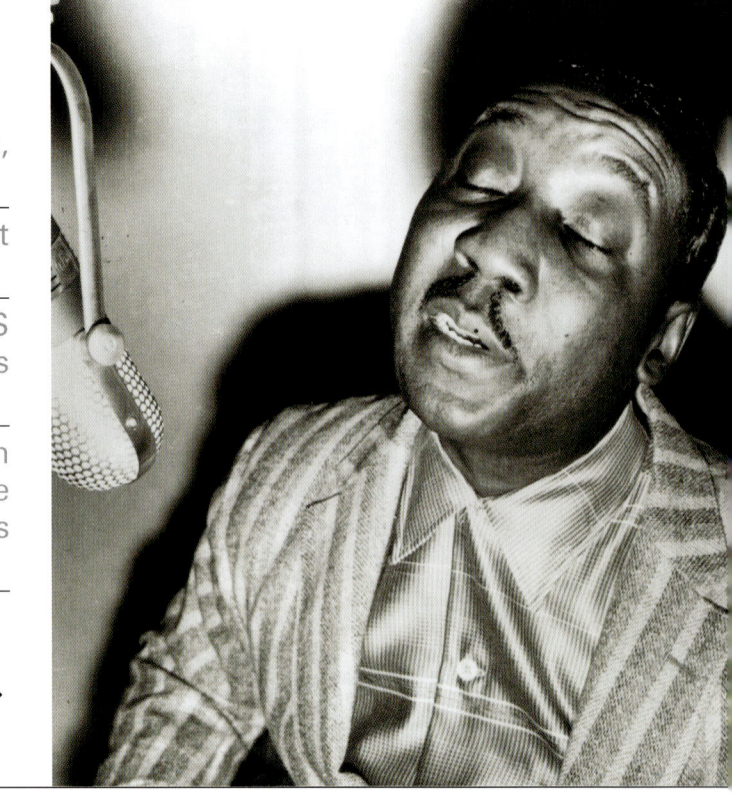

FIFTY YEARS OF THE GIBSON LES PAUL

THE FIFTIES

The first Gibson Les Paul solidbody electric guitar, known simply as the Les Paul Model then but now better known by its descriptive nickname "gold-top", first went on sale during 1952. This ad (right) was published in that first year, and shows Les Paul, the most famous guitarist in America at the time, proudly playing the instrument that bore his name. The early example of the gold-top pictured (left) may be a prototype; its black pickups were standard on other Gibsons at the time, but the production gold-top had white pickup covers, as can be seen on the main guitar and the left-hander shown below.

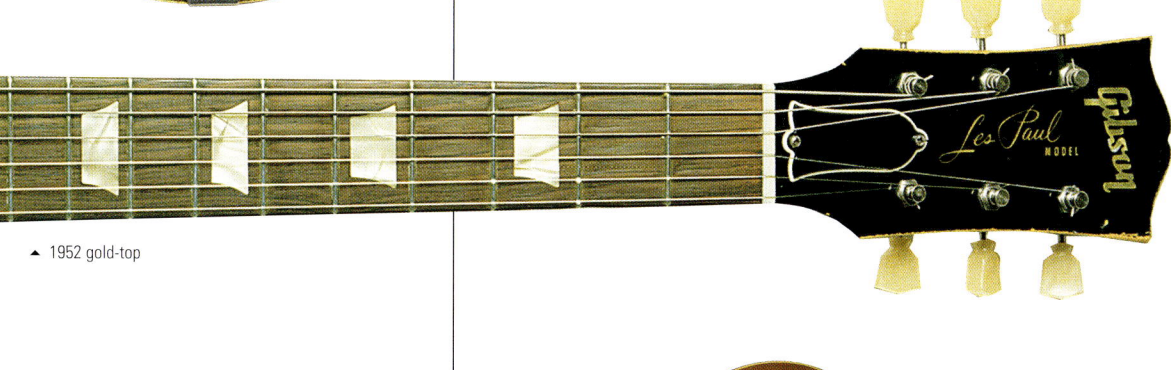

◄ 1952 gold-top

▲ 1952 gold-top

▲ 1952 gold-top left-hander

Guitarist Les Paul's only contribution to the design of the new Gibson solidbody was the long "trapeze" combined bridge and tailpiece fitted to the gold-top for a few years until more suitable units came along later. Left-handed versions like this one (left) have always been made in relatively small quantities, so this instrument is now considered an especially rare item.

FIFTY YEARS OF THE GIBSON LES PAUL

own solidbody guitar project soon after the appearance of Fender's Broadcaster in November 1950, and that he and the company's top engineers were involved in the project. "We designed the guitars," McCarty said emphatically. "And we started trying to learn something about a solidbody guitar. I was working with the rest of the engineers and we would sit down, like in a think tank, and we would talk about this guitar: let's do this, let's try that."

Exactly how many people at the company were involved in the design of the new instrument, which was to become the Gibson Les Paul, is unclear. McCarty thought there were at least four. "Myself, plus John Huis [McCarty's number two, vice president in charge of production], plus one of the fellows in charge of the wood department, and one of the guitar players in final assembly." McCarty also mentioned Gibson employees Julius Bellson and Wilbur Marker as being "in on the thing", and it's likely that Gibson's sales people were consulted at various stages through Clarence Havenga, the company's vice president in charge of sales. "We eventually came up with a guitar that was attractive," said McCarty, "and as far as we were concerned it had the tone, it had the resonance, and it also had the sustain – but not too much. As far as I can remember, to get to that point took us about a year."

An article early in 1952 in Gibson's local paper, the *Kalamazoo Gazette*, drew attention to the fact that the company had files bulging with instrument ideas that musicians had sent in. There were enough suggestions, the piece continued, "to create the combined pandemonium of a four-alarm fire, dog fight, curfew chorus, and mouse-frightened female". According to McCarty, the paper reported, "only a few of the ideas" were impractical. Presumably, somewhere in those files there still lurked Les Paul's idea for a semi-solid electric guitar, his "log" that he'd brought to the company years earlier. He'd been turned away then. But things were changing fast.

"We thought we had our guitar," said McCarty, "and now we needed an excuse to make it. So I got to thinking. At that time Les Paul and Mary Ford were riding very high, they were probably the number one vocal team in the United States. They were earning a million dollars a year. And knowing Les and Mary, I decided maybe I ought to show this guitar to them."

THE FELLOW WITH THE STRANGE LOG
Les Paul's recollections of the events that led to Gibson producing the Les Paul guitar are different. He said that Gibson first contacted him early in 1951, when Fender started making early examples of its solidbody electric. He remembered that Maurice Berlin, boss of Gibson's parent company CMI, told his second-in-command Marc Carlucci to get in touch with "the fellow with the strange log guitar" whom they'd seen briefly back in the 1940s. "They said to find that guy with the broomstick with the pickups on it," Paul laughed. "They came round right away, soon as they heard what Fender was doing. And I said well, you guys are a little bit behind the times, but OK, let's go."

Paul has said that after Gibson contacted him in 1951 about their interest in developing a solidbody electric, a meeting was set up at CMI headquarters in Chicago. Present were Berlin, Carlucci and CMI's attorney, Marv Henrickson, who also represented Paul. "They finalised their deal," Paul said, "and hammered out the specifics of the new guitar's design. Then, the research and development began in earnest."

LOUNGING WITH THE PROTOTYPE

McCarty's story of how he came to show the first prototype of the Gibson Les Paul guitar to Les Paul takes him away from the Gibson factory. Accompanied by Paul's business manager, Phil Braunstein, McCarty took the prototype to Paul and Ford at a hunting lodge in Stroudsburg, Pennsylvania, near the Delaware Water Gap park, probably in 1951 or early 1952. The lodge was owned by their friend, publisher Ben Selvin, and Paul had turned the living room into a studio, taking advantage of the quiet, isolated position of the building as an ideal recording retreat. On this occasion Paul and Ford were there to record together with Ford's sister Carol and her husband Wally Kamin. Carol Ford would sing harmony parts off-stage on the duo's live appearances to help recreate their multiple-recording sound, and Kamin played double-bass.

McCarty said that the purpose of the visit to the Stroudsburg lodge was to interest Paul in publicly playing the new guitar in return for a royalty on sales. Paul too recalled that the lodge was where he saw the first prototype of what became the Gibson Les Paul. McCarty remembered that Paul loved the prototype, saying to Ford, "I think we ought to join them, what do you think?" She said she liked it too. Neither McCarty nor Paul could remember for sure, but that prototype was probably very similar to the eventual production model, except that it most likely had a normal Gibson tailpiece of the period (as for example on a Gibson ES-350) with a separate bridge.

An agreement was reached that very night, said McCarty. He and Paul and Braunstein sat down and worked out a contract. First they decided on the royalty Gibson would pay for every Les Paul guitar sold. Paul said it was five per cent. The term of the contract was set at five years. McCarty remembered: "Braunstein, Les's business manager, said he wanted one extra paragraph in there, saying that Les Paul had to agree that he would not play any guitar other than a Gibson in public during the life of the contract. If in the fourth year he appeared playing a Gretsch, say, it would cancel the whole thing, he wouldn't get a dime." Braunstein explained that this was to save on tax commitments, and to assure money for Paul and Ford when their income from records and concerts might reduce in later years. McCarty said that there was also a clause in the contract stating that Paul should act as a consultant to Gibson. "We agreed that night," McCarty recalled. "We each had a copy, written out long-hand. Les could take it to his attorney and I could take it to ours, and if there were any questions then we would get together and work them out. But not a single word in that contract was changed. So anyway, I came back to the factory. Now we had a Les Paul model."

Paul said that he had a much bigger involvement in the design of the Les Paul guitar than McCarty's story of the development allows. Paul states categorically: "I designed everything on there except the arched top. That was contributed by Maurice Berlin. Mr Berlin told me he liked violins and took me by his vault to show

HIGH-END BLACK CUSTOM

1954 in context

Gibson starts to make an expensive Les Paul guitar, the Custom, as well as a budget model, the uncarved-body Junior.

Food rationing ends in Britain, long after the close of World War II. "Fast food" is first talked about in America.

Elvis Presley makes his first recordings.

Transistor radios go on general sale.

TV companies in the US make more money than radio stations for the first time.

Joseph McCarthy is discredited by the US Senate after his purge of "communists" in the State Department and elsewhere.

FIFTY YEARS OF THE GIBSON LES PAUL

THE FIFTIES

▲ 1954 Custom

▲ 1954 Custom, prototype pickups

▲ Keith Richards' painted 1957 Custom

The Custom was Gibson's marketing-led reply to the popularity of the original gold-top. By 1954, when the Custom was first marketed, a gold-top would have cost $225, so the Custom was pegged at $100 on top. And before you say, "I'll take 12 at that price," you may also care to know that the new Junior could be had for a mere $99.50. The Custom had an all-mahogany body, black finish, and fancier appointments, including gold-plated hardware. A rare prototype (below) has non-standard pickups; compare the stock example (left). The Custom was upped to three humbuckers in 1957, and Keith Richards used the one pictured (main guitar) with The Rolling Stones in the late 1960s, complete with personalised paint job. The two ads (below) feature the Custom and highlight Les Paul and Mary Ford's continuing 1950s fame.

FIFTY YEARS OF THE GIBSON LES PAUL

me his collection. And he said that Gibson had something that nobody else had, a shaper that could make a belly on that guitar, and it would be very expensive for Fender or whoever to make one like it. He asked if I'd have any objection to a violin top, and I said no, that was a wonderful idea. So then they introduced me to Ted McCarty, and we signed the agreement with Gibson." But McCarty was adamant. "I have told you exactly how it got to be a Les Paul. We spent a year designing that guitar, and Les never saw it until I took it to Pennsylvania."

Looking at photographs of Paul playing Gibson Les Paul guitars in the 1950s (and later) suggests that he continued to have his own ideas about what a solidbody electric guitar should be, usually contrary to Gibson's. Often his instruments were specially made with unique flat tops, where the production Les Pauls had carved tops. Paul nearly always modified his Gibsons in some way. As the diehard tinkerer said later: "By early '53 Gibson was shooting guitars to me all the time, and I was still cutting them up and modifying the pickups, bridges, controls and just about everything else."

After the deal was made between Paul and Gibson, the company requested that he change the logo on the modified Epiphone "clunker" models that he and Ford were still using on-stage (see pictures on page 7). "Gibson asked me if, until they made the Les Paul model for me, I would agree to play my Epiphone but put the name Gibson on it," explained Paul. "You could just pull off the Epiphone plates with a screwdriver, which I did. Then I suggested to Ted McCarty that he send me some Gibson decals, which we put on the guitars so they would say Gibson prior to the solidbody coming on the market."

> "Tiger Haynes, reported to be the premier colored guitarist, spent at least an hour on the Les Paul Model. We doubt Suite 4-V will ever be the same again."

The Les Paul was by no means Gibson's first guitar named for a musician. Today it would be called a signature model. Gibson's first signature instrument was the Nick Lucas acoustic flat-top, launched back in 1928. There are some parallels with the Gibson/Les Paul association. Lucas, touted as the "singing troubadour", was the first American to become a big star by making popular guitar-and-vocal records, notably his big hits 'I'm Looking Over A Four-leafed Clover' and 'Tiptoe Through The Tulips', though he also made some nifty guitar-loaded solo tracks like 'Pickin The Guitar' and 'Teasin The Frets'. Despite the signature model, Lucas continued to play his favoured Gibson L-1 flat-top.

Perhaps it will never be clear exactly who designed what on the original Gibson Les Paul model, but our view is that Gibson was responsible for virtually all of it. What is certain is that Paul's respected playing and commercial success plus Gibson's weighty experience in manufacturing and marketing guitars made for a strong and impressive combination.

The new Les Paul guitar was launched by Gibson in 1952, in the summer, priced at $210, which was about $20 more than Fender's Telecaster sold for at the time. (In today's money, you'd need to spend around $1400/£1000 now to match the buying power of $210 in 1952.) Early samples of the new guitar were shipped to Gibson's case manufacturer, Geib, at the end of April, and to Les Paul himself late in May. Some dealers began to receive stock in June.

The official unveiling of new musical instruments would usually be reserved for the annual convention of NAMM, the National Association of Music Merchants, which all the important music business people would attend. In 1952 it was held at the Hotel New Yorker in New York City from July 27th to the 31st. Gibson instruments were shown at the CMI exhibits in rooms 611 through 615. But Gibson also hosted a special pre-NAMM musicians' clinic at the nearby Waldorf Astoria on the Thursday and Friday before the convention, July 24th and 25th. The idea, reported *The Music Trades*, was that professional musicians, who couldn't officially attend the NAMM show, as well as local dealers, would have the opportunity to preview and play the latest Gibson instruments. "Especially Gibson's new Les Paul model electronic guitar," noted the trade magazine. The new GA-40 Les Paul amplifier was also shown. "Tiger Haynes, reported to be the premier colored guitarist, spent at least an hour on the Les Paul Model," the reporter continued, "and we doubt that suite 4-V will ever be the same again." Other guitarists who visited and tried the new Les Paul included a cross-section of sessionmen and jazzers such as George Barnes, Mundell Lowe, Tony Mottola and Billy Mure. "W.B. 'Doc' Caldwell demonstrated the tone and volume controls on the guitars," the report concluded, "and adjusted the new amplifiers to the tastes of the musicians."

Les Paul himself began using the new Gibson solidbody immediately, in line with his endorsement contract. He said he used one for the first time in June 1952, on-stage at the Paramount Theater in New York. Paul and Ford toured Europe that September, and a British musicians' newspaper noted the unusual new instruments that the "guitar boffin" and his singing partner were playing. "He'd brought his own special amplifiers," wrote the reporter, "four specially-made and surprisingly small guitars with cut-away shoulders to help with the high-speed treble, and plenty of spare tubes."

DESIGN ELEMENTS

Today, a gold-finish Les Paul model is nearly always called a gold-top thanks to its gold body face, and this is how we shall continue to refer to these guitars throughout the book. The new gold-top's solid body cleverly combined a carved maple top bonded to a mahogany base, a sandwich that united the darker tonality of mahogany with the brighter sonic "edge" of maple. Paul said that the gold colour of the original Les Paul model was his idea. "Gold means rich," he said, "expensive, the best, superb."

Gibson had made a one-off all-gold hollowbody guitar in 1951 for Paul to present to a terminally ill patient whom he had met when making a special appearance at a hospital in Milwaukee. ("They were pushing my amplifier along on a cart with wheels – Mary would sing to the people and I played the guitar," he recalled.) That presentation guitar probably prompted Gibson's all-gold archtop electric ES-295 model of 1952, and most likely was the inspiration for the colour of the first Les Paul model too.

Underlining the origin of the guitar from within Gibson, almost all other design elements of the first Les Paul have precedents in earlier Gibson models, although of course the solid body was a first for the company. The layout of two P-90

LES PAUL STUDENTS

1955-56 in context

Gibson add to the Junior model in their budget Les Paul line by introducing (55) the new matching two-pickup Special.

Underwater transatlantic phone cable linking the US and UK opens (56) for calls.

Disneyland is unveiled in Anaheim, Los Angeles (55), as out-of-work actors get used to wearing big black ears.

Chuck Berry makes his debut record on Chess (55). 'Hummingbird' is the last hit for Les Paul & Mary Ford in the US.

James Dean killed in car smash (55).

Les Paul plays a Les Paul at his home studio ▶

FIFTY YEARS OF THE GIBSON LES PAUL

THE FIFTIES

Gibson's cheaper Les Paul models, the Junior and the Special, were as you might expect simple, straightahead instruments, with uncarved tops and plain appointments. At the time they were intended for guitar-teaching schools (see Gibson's promo photo from the period, left) but have now become revered for their direct rock'n'roll spirit. The single-pickup Junior (main guitar) came in sunburst finish, the two-pickup Special (bottom) in a yellow/beige. The Junior in the same finish was called the TV model (below), apparently because the colour showed up well on black-and-white TV sets.

▲ 1957 TV

▼ 1956 Junior

▲ 1955 Special

FIFTY YEARS OF THE GIBSON LES PAUL

single-coil pickups and four controls (a volume and tone knob for each pickup) had been a feature of the previous year's L-5CES and Super 400CES models. The general outline of the single-cutaway body and the construction of the glued-in mahogany neck followed established Gibson traditions, while the crown-shaped inlays on the rosewood fingerboard had first appeared on a revised version of the ES-150 model first seen in 1950. Several Gibson acoustic guitars had already appeared with the Les Paul's particular string-length (the distance from nut to bridge saddle).

Unlike the prototype, the production Les Paul Model came with a new height-adjustable combined bridge-and-tailpiece. The part where the strings made contact was bar-shaped, and joined to this were two long metal rods that went down to anchor the unit at the bottom edge of the guitar. This device was without doubt designed by Les Paul, and was originally intended for use on archtop guitars. Gibson also sold it as a separate replacement accessory. The earliest gold-tops had a very shallow neck pitch – that is, the neck joined the body at a gentle angle. This was a mistake in the design. It meant that the strings were almost flat on to the body as they came off the neck. This precluded use of existing Gibson hardware, and so the new bridge/tailpiece was chosen as the only suitable item. But even this at its lowest setting would still have meant a string action that was too high, so Gibson had no choice but to adapt the bridge and wrap the strings around underneath it. This was contrary to the way the unit was designed to be used with the strings feeding over the top – as on some of Gibson's archtop, hollowbody electric models of the period including the ES-295 (1952) and ES-225 (1955).

This bridge arrangement on early Les Paul gold-tops meant that sustain suffered, intonation was inaccurate, and popular hand-damping techniques were virtually impossible. It was clearly unworkable, as Les Paul pointed out to Gibson. "They made the first guitar wrong," he remembered. "I don't know how many went out wrong that weren't playable. When they sent me mine, I stopped them, said this won't even play. They had run the strings under the bridge instead of over, and hadn't pitched the neck. They had it all screwed up."

ELECTRIC SALES
During 1953 Gibson dropped the original bridge/tailpiece unit – usually known as a "trapeze" because of the shape of the long rods – and replaced it with a new specially-designed single bar-shaped bridge-and-tailpiece unit that mounted on the top of the body using twin height-adjustable studs. *Down Beat* magazine's preview of Gibson's exhibit at the July 1953 NAMM show in Chicago noted the Les Paul's "new adjustable metal bridge and tailpieces". It was a more stable unit, and the strings now wrapped over the top of the bridge, providing improved sustain and intonation. Also, the guitar's neck pitch was made steeper. The result was a much happier and more playable instrument.

The original gold-top sold well in relation to Gibson's other models during these early years. In 1954 Gibson's historian Julius Bellson charted the progress of the company's electric instruments, both solidbody and hollowbody. Consulting records, Bellson estimated that back in 1938 electric guitars had made up no more than ten per cent of Gibson guitar sales, but that the proportion of electrics to the rest had risen to 15 per cent by 1940, to 50 per cent by 1951, and that by 1953 electric guitars constituted no less than 65 per cent of the company's total guitar sales. The buoyant Les Paul model must have helped considerably.

CUSTOM AND JUNIOR JOIN IN
In a move designed to widen the market still further for solidbody guitars, Gibson issued two new Les Paul models in 1954, the Custom and the Junior. As Ted McCarty described it: "You have all kinds of players out there who like this and like that. Chevrolet had a whole bunch of models, Ford had a whole bunch of models. So did we." The two-pickup Custom looked classy with its all-black finish, multiple binding, block-shaped position markers in an ebony fingerboard, and gold-plated hardware, and was indeed more expensive than the gold-top. Paul said that he chose the black colour for the Custom. "When you're on stage with a black tuxedo and a black guitar, the people can see your hands move with a spotlight on them. They'll see your hands flying."

The Custom had an all-mahogany body, as favoured by Les Paul himself, rather than the maple/mahogany mix of the gold-top, giving the new guitar a rather mellower tone. Paul insists that Gibson got the timber arrangements the wrong way around, and that as far as he was concerned the cheaper gold-top should have been all-mahogany, while the costlier Custom should have sported the more elaborate maple-and-mahogany combination. The Les Paul Custom was promoted in Gibson catalogues as "the fretless wonder" because of its use of very low, flat fretwire, different to the wire used on other Les Pauls at the time and favoured by some players for the way it helped them play more speedily.

The budget Junior was designed for and aimed at beginners. It did not pretend to be anything other than a cheaper guitar. The outline shape of its body was the same as the gold-top and Custom, but the most obvious difference to its Les Paul partners was a flat-top solid mahogany body. It had a single P-90 pickup, governed by a volume and tone control, and there were simple dot-shaped position markers along the unbound rosewood fingerboard. It was finished in Gibson's traditional two-colour brown-to-yellow sunburst, and had the wrap-over bar-shape bridge/tailpiece like the one used on the latest gold-top. The September 1954 pricelist showed the Les Paul Custom at $325 and the Les Paul Junior at $99.50. The gold-top meanwhile had sneaked up to $225.

In addition to its conventional P-90 at the bridge, the Les Paul Custom featured a new style of pickup at the neck. This unit was soon nicknamed the alnico, a reference to the *al*uminium-*ni*ckel-*co*balt alloy used for its distinctive rectangular magnetic polepieces (although alnico is certainly not unique to this pickup). It was designed by Seth Lover, a radio and electronics expert who had worked on and off for Gibson in the 1940s and early 1950s while he also did teaching and installation jobs for the US Navy. After several comings and goings, Lover rejoined Gibson's electronics department permanently in 1952.

Lover had been asked to come up with a pickup that would be louder than Gibson's P-90, and louder than the single-coil Dynasonic pickup used by Gretsch, a New York-based guitar maker and a competitor to Gibson. Gretsch's

BUCKING THAT HUM

1957 in context

Gibson begins using new humbucking pickups, adding them to a three-pickup Les Paul Custom and a revised gold-top.

Carl Perkins records his arrangement of Blind Lemon Jefferson's Matchbox (later among the Perkins covers by The Beatles).

On The Beach, a novel by Nevil Shute, is published. It's a chilling and horrific vision of worldwide nuclear devastation.

TV premieres include Wagon Train, Pinky & Perky, and Perry Mason.

A dog survives Soviets' Sputnik II orbits.

Carl Perkins: gold top and blue suede shoes ▶

▼ Paul McCartney's 1957 gold-top left-hander

A perfectly happy combination was the new humbucker-equipped gold-top, first sold during 1957 (example right). Gibson's twin-coil pickups were designed to shield extraneous noise, but also contributed a gorgeously warm, fat sound to the guitar. On reflection this is the gold-top's finest hour, although of course the previous versions with single-coil P-90 pickups also have their devotees. The same humbucker-equipped guitar would be given a more traditional sunburst finish in 1958, resulting in what is now considered the classic Les Paul instrument.

▲ 1957 gold-top

FIFTY YEARS OF THE GIBSON LES PAUL

THE FIFTIES

◀ 1954 gold-top

◀ Rear of "all-gold" version

Since the launch of the gold-top in 1952 the model had seen a few changes to improve playability. The first modification was to fit it with a one-piece bridge/tailpiece, like this 1954 example (far left), and then later a separate bridge and tailpiece, like the other examples on these pages. Some relatively rare 1950s gold-tops were treated to an all-around gold finish (back, left), with paint on the body sides and rear as well as the back of the neck and headstock.

Another rare left-handed Les Paul (above), this one owned by Paul McCartney. Like a number of players, McCartney has replaced the rather fragile original tuners with a sturdier set.

FIFTY YEARS OF THE GIBSON LES PAUL

unit was supplied by DeArmond, a pickup manufacturer in Toledo, Ohio. The reason for the rectangular polepieces of the new Gibson pickup was simple, remembered Lover. "I wanted to be different. I didn't want them to be round like DeArmond's," he said. "I don't like to copy things. If you're going to improve something, then I thought you should make it different. Also, by making them that shape I could put screws between for height adjustment. But that pickup was never too popular because the players would always adjust them up too tight to the strings. They'd get that slurring type tone and they didn't like that."

The Custom had another new piece of Gibson hardware fitted. It was the first Les Paul model to receive the company's Tune-o-matic bridge, used in conjunction with a separate bar-shaped tailpiece. Patented by McCarty, the Tune-o-matic offered for the first time on Gibsons the opportunity to individually adjust the length of each string, thus improving tuning accuracy. From 1955, it also became a feature of the gold-top model.

TOOTHPASTE AND TV
Also in 1955, Gibson launched the Les Paul TV, essentially a Junior but with a finish that the company referred to variously as "natural", "limed oak" and (more often) "limed mahogany". Surviving original TV models from the 1950s reveal a number of different colours, with earlier examples tending to a rather turgid beige, while later ones are often distinctly yellow.

Today there is much debate about where the model's TV name came from. As usual around Les Paul guitars, people speculate and come up with any number of theories – and all without evidence. One such theory says that the TV name was used because the pale colour of the finish was designed to stand out on the era's black-and-white TV screens. This seems unlikely, not least because pro players appearing on television would naturally opt for a high-end model. An ad that Gibson ran at the time, headed "Tennessee Ernie Stars With Gibsons", featured guitarist Bobby Gibbons from *The Tennessee Ernie Ford Show* on NBC television. Gibbons is pictured playing the most expensive Les Paul of the time – the Custom. It's hard to imagine him settling for a TV model.

Others say the guitar followed the look of fashionable contemporary furniture, where the expression "limed" was used for a particular look. Certainly Gibson promoted the Les Paul TV as being "the latest in modern appearance". There's also been a suggestion that "TV" might be a less than oblique reference to the competing blond-coloured Telecaster made by Fender. But in fact the name was coined to cash in on Les Paul's regular appearances at the time on television on *The Les Paul & Mary Ford Show*. This was effectively a sponsored daily ad for a toothpaste company, for which the couple signed a $2million three-year contract in 1953. Gibson reasoned that if you'd seen the man on TV, well, now you could buy his TV guitar. Following a reader's enquiry to *Guitar Player* in the 1970s, a Gibson spokesman confirmed that "the Les Paul TV model was so named after Les Paul's personal Listerine show was televised in the 1950s". So now you know the true story behind the Les Paul TV.

During research for this book, we interviewed many of the people working for Gibson today. One of those was Tom Murphy who, as we shall discover later, is renowned now for his work with modern Reissue guitars, especially those with "aged" finishes. Murphy's speciality is in refinishing and restoring old guitars. We asked him to name one thing he would enquire about at the 1950s Gibson factory, presuming he had the facilities of a time machine at his disposal. Murphy did not hesitate with his answer. "I'd watch them do a TV finish," he laughed. "I'd like to see the first day they ever tried it. I wonder what discussions took place to make them attempt that original beige colour? And when they went to the real yellow shade in '58, was it because someone said OK, enough is enough … paint it yellow!"

Also in 1955, the original line of Les Paul models was completed with the addition of the Special, effectively a two-pickup version of the Junior, finished in the TV's beige colour (but not called a TV model – a cause of much confusion since). The Special appeared on the company's September 1955 pricelist at $182.50. The following year Gibson added a Junior 3/4 model. It had a shorter neck, giving the model a scale-length some two inches shorter than the normal Junior. Gibson explained in its brochure at the time that the Junior 3/4 was designed to appeal to "youngsters, or adults with small hands and fingers".

LOVER BUCKS THE HUM

Meanwhile in the Gibson electronics department, run by Walt Fuller, the industrious Seth Lover started work on another new pickup. This one would turn out to have a far greater and lasting impact than his previous design. The idea was to try to find a way to cut down the hum and electrical interference that plagued standard single-coil pickups, Gibson's ubiquitous P-90 included. Lover contemplated the humbucking "choke coil" found in some Gibson amplifiers, installed to eliminate the hum dispensed by their power transformers. "I thought," recalled Lover, "that if we can make humbucking chokes, why can't we make humbucking pickups?" No reason at all, he concluded, and started to build prototypes.

The humbucking name comes straightforwardly from the ability of such devices to buck or cut hum. The design principle too is reasonably simple. A humbucking pickup employs two coils with opposite magnetic polarity, wired together so that they are electrically out-of-phase. The result is a pickup that is less prone to picking up extraneous noise, and one that in the process gives a fatter, thicker tone than single-coil types. Original humbucking pickups and the single-coil units of the day thus offered different sound characteristics, although today those differences have blurred as technology has developed.

Additional screening for Gibson's original humbucking pickup was provided by a metal cover, as Lover explained. "The cover helps shield away electrostatic noises from fluorescent lamps and so forth," he said. "I needed a material with high resistance so it wouldn't affect the high frequency response, and I

> "On a two-pickup guitar I set those new humbuckers with the screws towards the bridge on one pickup and towards the fingerboard on the other," said Seth Lover. "Would you like to know why I did that? For decorative purposes!"

CUTAWAYS FROM KALAMAZOO

1958 in context

Gibson discovers the joy of a double-cutaway guitar body, not only on Les Paul Juniors and Specials but also the ES-335.

Guitar-record heaven: Rebel Rouser from Duane Eddy, Summertime Blues by Eddie Cochran, and Link Wray's Rumble.

Campaign for Nuclear Disarmament (CND) is started in the UK with a protest march from London to Aldermaston.

Nautilus US nuclear submarine surfaces after passing under the North Pole.

First modem launched by Bell, allowing transmission of binary data by phone.

FIFTY YEARS OF THE GIBSON LES PAUL

THE FIFTIES

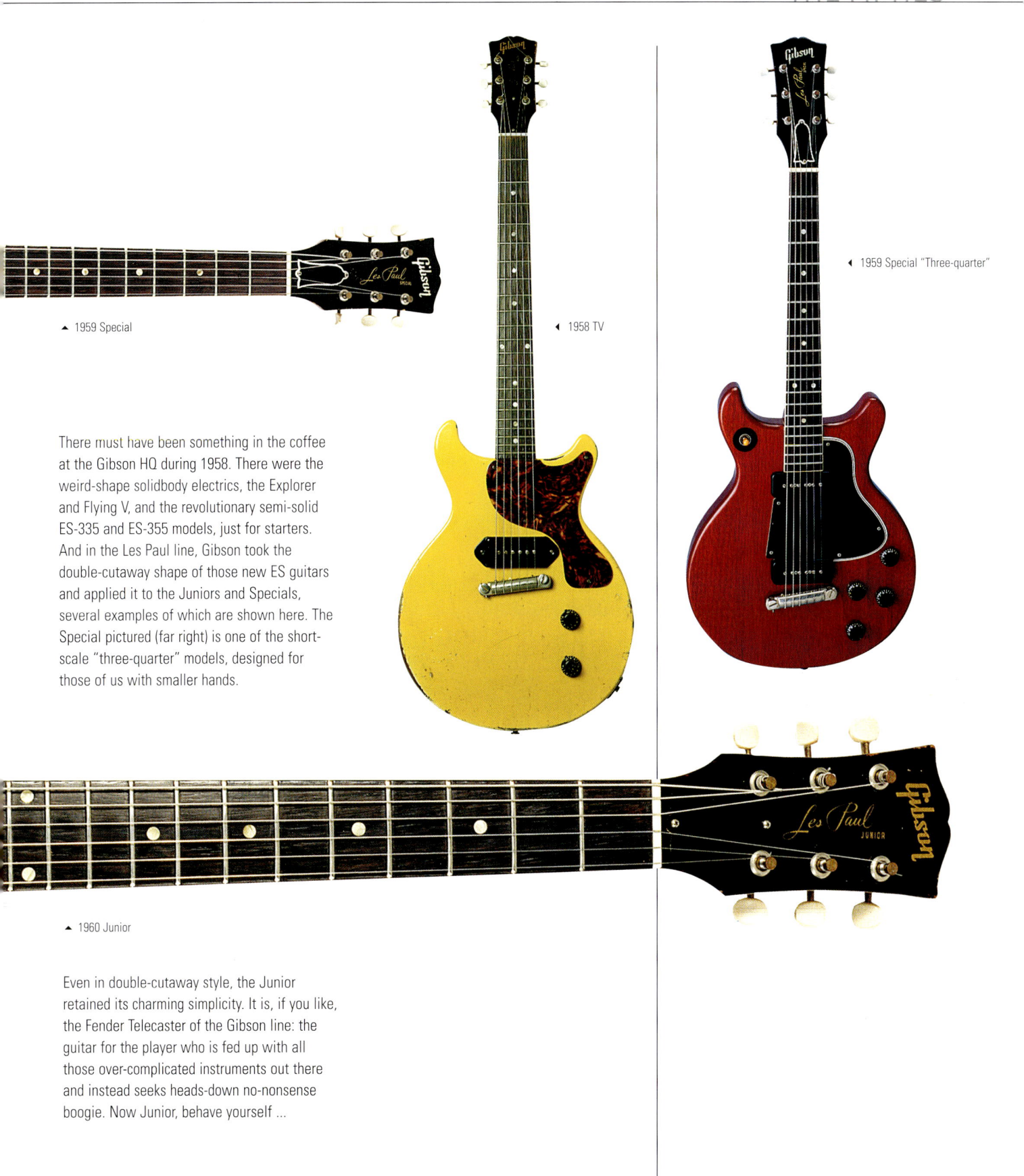

◀ 1959 Special "Three-quarter"

▲ 1959 Special

◀ 1958 TV

There must have been something in the coffee at the Gibson HQ during 1958. There were the weird-shape solidbody electrics, the Explorer and Flying V, and the revolutionary semi-solid ES-335 and ES-355 models, just for starters. And in the Les Paul line, Gibson took the double-cutaway shape of those new ES guitars and applied it to the Juniors and Specials, several examples of which are shown here. The Special pictured (far right) is one of the short-scale "three-quarter" models, designed for those of us with smaller hands.

▲ 1960 Junior

Even in double-cutaway style, the Junior retained its charming simplicity. It is, if you like, the Fender Telecaster of the Gibson line: the guitar for the player who is fed up with all those over-complicated instruments out there and instead seeks heads-down no-nonsense boogie. Now Junior, behave yourself ...

FIFTY YEARS OF THE GIBSON LES PAUL

considered non-magnetic stainless steel. But you can't solder to it. German silver [an alloy of copper, nickel and zinc] has high resistance, and you could solder to it, so I used that. The prototype didn't have adjusting screws, but our sales people wanted them – so that they would have something to talk to the dealers about. The screws were added before we went into production. For a two-pickup guitar I set the pickups in the guitars with the screws towards the bridge on the pickup nearest the bridge, and towards the fingerboard on the other. Want to know why I did that?" He laughed, and answered his own question. "For decorative purposes."

PATENTLY DEVIOUS

Gibson began to use the new humbuckers in the early months of 1957, and started to replace the P-90 single-coil pickups on the Les Paul gold-top and Custom during that year. The Custom was promoted to a three-pickup guitar in its new humbucker-equipped style. Players gradually came to appreciate that humbuckers and a Les Paul guitar made for a congenial mixture, and today many guitarists and collectors covet the earliest type of Gibson humbucking pickup. This is known as a PAF because of a small label with the words Patent Applied For attached to its underside.

Lover was not the first to come up with the idea of humbucking pickups, as he discovered when he came to patent the design (as assignor to Gibson). The filing office made reference to no fewer than six previous documents, the earliest dating from 1936. "I had a hell of a time getting a patent," Lover remembered, "and I finally got one with more or less one claim: that I'd built a humbucking pickup." Ray Butts came up with a similar principle around the same time while working with Gretsch, for whom he designed the Filter'Tron humbucking pickup. Lover's patent application had been filed in June 1955, and was eventually issued in July 1959. Which explains that PAF label. Or does it? The PAF labels appear on pickups on guitars dated up to 1962 – well after the patent was issued. Lover had a theory to explain this. "Gibson didn't want to give any information as to what patent to look up for those who wanted to make copies. I think that was the reason they carried on with the PAF label for quite a while." When they did eventually get around to putting a patent number on the pickup, Gibson also deterred budding copyists by "mistakenly" using the number for a bridge patent.

Some players say they prefer the sound of original PAF-label humbuckers. They consider later pickups to have a less good sound, apparently caused by small changes to coil-winding, magnet grades and wire-sheathing. Seth Lover could not recall any alterations made to his invention during the transition from those that had the PAF label to the later units that were stamped with patent numbers. "The only change that I'm aware of," he said, "is that from time to time Gibson would use gold plating on the covers, and I think if the gold plating got a little heavy then the pickups would tend to lose the high frequencies, because gold is a very good conductor."

The July 1957 Gibson pricelist details the Les Paul line as follows: Les Paul Junior (sunburst) $120; Les Paul Junior 3/4 (sunburst) $120; Les Paul TV (beige)

THE FIFTIES LES PAUL

$132.50; Les Paul Special (beige) $179.50; Les Paul Model (gold) $247.50; and Les Paul Custom (black) $375. Much of Gibson's later theme-and-variation of Les Paul designs was based upon these models. Sales of these original Les Paul guitars in general reached a peak in 1956 and 1957, with the Junior hitting a record-so-far 3129 units in '56. But famous musicians were still generally cautious of the relatively new-fanged solidbody electric guitar, although there were clearly a number of more adventurous players who recognised the musical benefits – as well as the fact that a guitar as flashy as a gold-top could make them look good too. Bluesmen like Muddy Waters, Guitar Slim, Freddie King and John Lee Hooker were seen pictured with Les Pauls, mostly gold-tops, during the 1950s, as were R&B surpremo Hubert Sumlin, guitarist with Howlin' Wolf, and rockabilly rebel Carl Perkins.

Among the most prominent of the new rockers using a Les Paul was Frannie Beecher of Bill Haley & His Comets. The group had introduced many record-buyers to the new rock'n'roll with 'Rock Around The Clock', a number one on both sides of the Atlantic in 1955. Beecher effectively became the first big-name official endorser of Les Paul guitars – after Les Paul himself, of course, although the popularity of Les & Mary's rather polite records was waning now that raucous rock was evidently here to stay. Beecher had played with western-swing groups and in Benny Goodman's big-band before joining Haley, following the death of original Comets guitarist Danny Cedrone in 1954. Beecher began the job with an acoustic archtop Epiphone guitar with added pickup, but it didn't take long for him to realise that his Epi wasn't up to the job.

"At the volume we had to play, I just couldn't do it," Beecher explained later. "Loud wasn't the word for it. Jeez!" Gibson then provided the band with guitars and amplifiers – Haley himself had an L-7, while Beecher played the top-of-the-line Les Paul Custom. "If there was anything wrong with it or I didn't like it," said Beecher, "I'd send it back and Gibson would send us another one." In return, Gibson used the band in ads in the 1950s. It was one of the first rock endorsement campaigns. "Bill Haley recommends that you see the magnificent Gibson line at your local dealer," ran the copy, with Beecher and his Les Paul Custom clearly visible at Haley's side. It was the model for decades of electric guitar promotion to follow.

> Frannie Beecher joined Bill Haley's Comets but soon realised his guitar wasn't up to the job. "At the volume we played, I couldn't do it," Beecher explained. "Loud wasn't the word for it. Jeez! Then Gibson sent me a Les Paul Custom ..."

A SPECIAL MISTAKE

In 1958 Gibson made a radical design change to three of the Les Paul models, and a cosmetic alteration to another. The Junior, Junior 3/4 and TV were revamped with a completely new double-cutaway body shape. Ted McCarty explained the re-design as a reaction to player's requests. "They wanted to be able to thumb the sixth string," he said, "but they couldn't do it if the only cutaway was over on the treble side. So we made them with another cutaway, so

BIRTH OF THE BURST

1958 in context

Gibson innocently change the gold-top's finish to traditional sunburst in an effort to boost faltering Les Paul sales.

Record companies release first stereo LPs in the summer. Meanwhile, John Lee Hooker remains defiantly low-tech as he records an unplugged album, *Folk Blues*.

Television sales boom, with sets now resident in over 75 per cent of US homes.

A new European "common market" is established by the Rome Treaty.

John Lee Hooker caresses a gold-top ▸

THE FIFTIES

Someone at Gibson decided to remake the gold-top with a sunburst finish in 1958. The gold paint was considered too garish, too wild, for the 1950s – at least that's what the diminishing sales figures suggested. Gibson had made sunburst-finish guitars for years, so it was no big deal to apply this much more sedate look to a Les Paul model. Gibson didn't call this new variant the Standard until 1960, but that's how most people now refer to it. Others affectionately name it "the burst". But whatever you want to call them, the 1,700 or so sunburst-finish Les Pauls made in 1958, 1959 and 1960 have become the most celebrated and sought-after electric guitars of the 20th century. They are rather good.

Jimmy Page has a beloved pair of sunburst-finish Les Paul Standards that he used throughout his time with Led Zeppelin, and below we picture his favourite of the two. Although the serial number disappeared long ago during some headstock repairs, the guitar is most likely of 1958 vintage. The back pickup is a replacement, as are the tuners. But so what? Ramble on ...

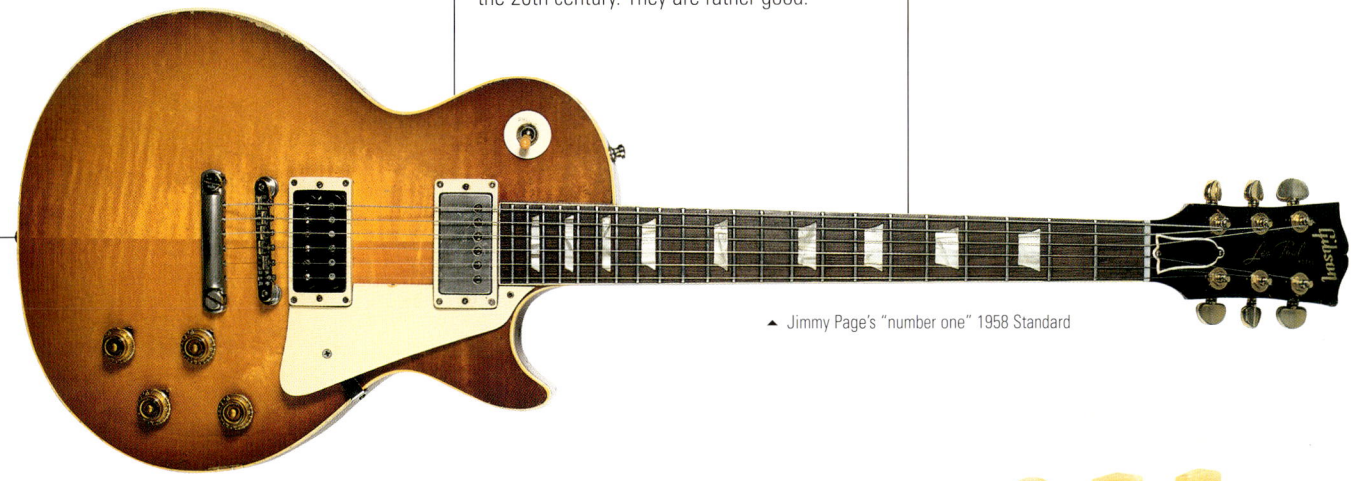

▲ Jimmy Page's "number one" 1958 Standard

▲ 1958 Standard

The look of an original Standard can hike the price, as of course would a detail such as prior ownership by Jimmy or Keith or Peter or ... dare we even suggest it ... Eric. The technical term is figure: pretty patterned wood is figured wood. You might also call it wave or curl or flame or anything else descriptive. The body of this '58 (left) has virtually no figure, but in its favour has nearly all the original colour, including oft-faded red. It's still a great Paul; it's still worth a bomb.

FIFTY YEARS OF THE GIBSON LES PAUL

they could get up there. We did things that the players wanted, as much as anything." The Junior's fresh look was enhanced with a new cherry red finish. The TV adopted the new double-cutaway design as well, along with a more yellow shade of TV finish. When the double-cutaway design was applied to the Special in the following year, the result was not an immediate success because of a design mistake. Gibson overlooked the fact that the cavity for the neck pickup in the Special's new body severely weakened the neck-to-body joint, and many a neck was snapped right off at this point. The error was soon corrected by moving the neck pickup further down into the body, resulting in a stronger joint. The new double-cutaway Special was offered in cherry or the new TV yellow. (However, and again causing much confusion later, the yellow Special was never actually called a TV model. TV models only ever have one pickup, just like a Junior.)

> The most attractive figured maple gives the illusion of rows of 3D hills-and-valleys going across the face of the timber. In extreme cases it can look dramatic.

WHY NOT TRY A CHERRY SUNBURST?
Sales of the Les Paul gold-top model in particular had begun to decline, so naturally the feeling at Gibson was that something needed to be done to stimulate renewed interest in this relatively high-price model. They decided that the unusual gold finish was at fault, figuring that some players found it too unconventional. So Gibson changed the look, applying a sunburst finish in a bid to attract new customers. The first two sunburst Les Pauls – known today as Standard models – were shipped from the factory on May 28th 1958, logged in Gibson's records simply as "LP Spec finish". The new look would last only until 1960.

Gibson had not used this colour of sunburst before. The regular sunburst finish that the company used resulted in a brown-to-yellow effect, as on the single-cutaway Les Paul Junior. But Gibson introduced a new cherry sunburst for the Standard. The maple body cap was now clearly visible through the finish. On gold-tops, the maple caps had always been hidden under the opaque gold paint. Now that the Standard showed off its maple through the virtually transparent sunburst finish, Gibson's woodworkers were a little more careful with its appearance, and would bookmatch the timber.

Bookmatching is a technique where a piece of wood is sliced into two, then opened out down a central join (like a book) to give symmetrically similar patterns on the wood's surface. Such a look – bookmatched maple, sunburst finish – had been used on a handful of Gibson guitars before, including a couple of solidbody electric steel models: the relatively broad-bodied Doubleneck Electric Hawaiian back in the late 1930s, and the more recent Royaltone, produced for a couple of years from 1950. Also, the backs of archtop hollowbody Gibson guitars were regularly made from carved bookmatched maple, often using spectacularly beautiful timber.

Some of the Les Paul Standards made between 1958 and 1960 also display some astonishing patterned maple. The woodworker's term for these patterns on the surface of timber is "figure". ("Grain" is something different, usually the lines in the wood that travel "across" any figuring.) Any tree can potentially provide figured timber, but it's actually an unpredictable fluke. Some trees will have it, some will not. It's caused by a sort of genetic anomaly in the growing tree that makes ripples or rays in the cells of the living wood. The visual effect of figure is also determined by variations in the colour and density of the tree's growth, the effect of disease or damage, and, significantly, the way in which the timber is cut from the felled tree. Quarter-sawing – which means cutting so that the grain is generally square to the face of the resulting planks – often provides the most attractive figured wood, sometimes giving the illusion of roughly parallel rows of three-dimensional "fingers" or "hills and valleys" going across the face of the timber. In extreme cases it can look dramatic.

Figured maple is also called many (non-technical) names, like curly, or fiddleback, or tigerstripe, but the most common word generally used among guitar people is flame or flamed. So a Standard might be said to have a flame top. Such figured timber is still highly prized at Gibson. "Flame can look like one thing on the raw billet and then turn out to be a totally different animal once it's carved," explains Rick Gembar, General Manager of today's Custom/Art/Historic Division. "I had one very established collector who had been talking about this 'holy grail' piece of wood he'd been hoarding for years. So I asked him to bring the wood in and offered to build him a Les Paul out of it. Sure enough, this piece of maple was highly flamed from top to bottom with beautifully spaced lines. It looked like what we would call a 'killer' top. We took it and started carving the dish for the top … and you could see the flame start to melt away. The depth of the flame is the key to whether or not it's going to remain figured during the entire process from board to guitar top."

PRICING THE BURST
Back at Gibson in the late 1950s, Les Paul Standards continued to come off the line. The quality of the maple used for their tops was never advertised or promoted by Gibson, because it was simply down to the wood that happened to be available, whether figured or plain. Indeed, no priority was given to the Standards. After all, Les Pauls had not been selling. The new-look Standards were almost an afterthought. If a good-looking one happened to come along now and again, well, that was a bonus. At the time, timber was cut and shaped in the 15,000-square-foot wing that had been added to Gibson's original 1917 Kalamazoo factory in 1945, just behind the famous chimney. From the guitars of the period that you see today, it's clear that Gibson's most impressively figured maple was reserved for the backs of archtop models. Nevertheless, some Les Paul Standards were astonishingly attractive. And some were extremely plain.

To some extent, Gibson's hunch about a different look for the guitar was proved right. They knew that sales of the gold-top had declined from a high of 920 during 1956 to just 434 in 1958, the year of the new Standard. After the revised model appeared, sales climbed to 643 in 1959, but they would dip again in 1960. Gibson then decided that the change of finish had not been enough, and that the only way to attract new customers was to completely redesign the entire Les Paul line. We'll go into this in more detail in the next chapter, which

THE MYSTICAL '59

1959 in context

Gibson continues with the sunburst Les Paul model, producing around 650 guitars this year that later become legendary.

Buddy Holly is killed in a plane crash in Iowa. The first electronic music synth is built by RCA in a large room in New York.

Howlin' Wolf and guitarist Hubert Sumlin look back on their great 50s cuts, not least the stirring Smokestack Lightning (1956).

Volvo's PC544 is the first car with a three-point seat belt system.

Fidel Castro comes to power in Cuba.

◂ Howlin Wolf guitarist Hubert Sumlin in the '90s

▴ Ex-Keith Richards 1959 Standard

FIFTY YEARS OF THE GIBSON LES PAUL

THE FIFTIES

Everything came together in rare synchronicity for the Les Paul Standards that Gibson made during 1959. The pickups are wound just so. The wood came from some inspired timber suppliers. The necks play like a dream. The little old ladies at the Kalamazoo production line still couldn't quite get the logos in the right place. As a generation of blues-rock players would discover in the decade to come, the 1959 Standard in particular is a Stradivarius among electric guitars. To play one is little short of guitar paradise. To lust for one is perfectly natural. To own one is to find out more about the lifestyle of the armed guard.

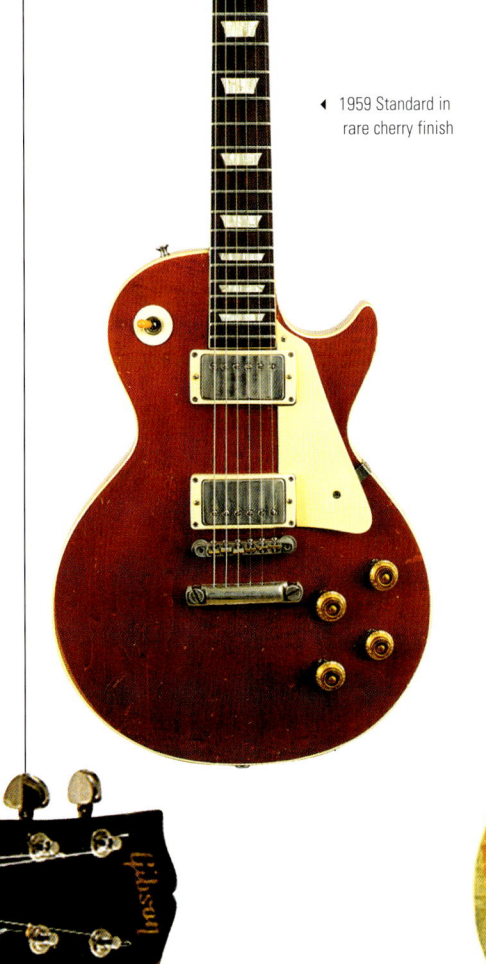

◀ 1959 Standard in rare cherry finish

◀ Gary Moore's ex-Peter Green 1959 Standard

Keith Richards acquired this '59 Standard (main guitar) on the Stones' first tour of the US, in June 1964. He used it until well into 1965, live and in the studio. It was the first star-owned Les Paul in Britain. Peter Green of Fleetwood Mac got his '59 (right) later in the 1960s. A handful of Standards were finished in cherry red (example, top right). The Standard's only appearance in Gibson sales literature was this 1960 catalogue (above).

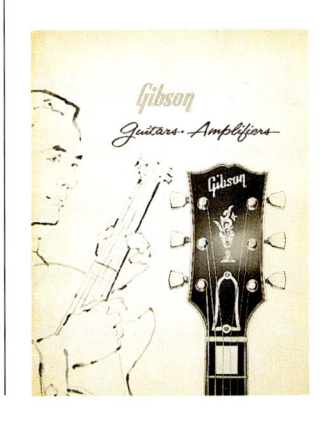

FIFTY YEARS OF THE GIBSON LES PAUL

covers the 1960s. The result of that decision was that the original sunburst Les Paul Standard was only produced from 1958 to 1960. Gibson's November 1959 pricelist offered the model at $280 (which, translated to today's buying power, is the equivalent now of about $1875, or £1350). Among players and collectors, the sunburst Standard has since become the most highly prized solidbody electric guitar ever. "Bursts", as these sunburst models are known, regularly fetch huge sums, presently around $25,000 and upward, far in excess of almost all other collectable solidbodys. The factor which above all determines the magnitude of their value is not usually at all related to the sound or playability of a particular example, but to the individual quality and visual impact of the maple top. Those with especially outrageous figure visible through the top's finish are rated most highly. Like collectable violins, some of the most celebrated "bursts" are even given names.

> The sunburst Standard has become the most highly prized solidbody electric guitar ever made, and "bursts" regularly fetch huge sums of money.

ZEBRAS, UNBURSTS, AND KILLER TOPS

There is another factor that can make Standards look different from one another today. The coloured paint used to create the sunburst effect can fade in varying ways, depending primarily on how a particular guitar has been exposed to daylight during its lifetime.

Some apparently sharp-eyed collectors even claim to be able to tell how long a particular guitar spent in a shop window or a smoke-filled club. In some cases the original shaded sunburst will have almost totally disappeared, leaving a uniform and rather pleasant honey colour on such guitars (now affectionately known as "unburst" examples).

A further cause for excitement among collectors – even some players – is the different coloured pickup "bobbins" that became evident years later with an Eric Clapton-led fashion for removing pickup covers. In the very late 1950s manufacturer Hughes Plastics and their distributor Eastman Chemical had run out of the black Tenite plastic they used in making Gibson's pickup bobbins. They substituted cream plastic for a while.

Today, some people insist that dual-coil Gibson pickups from the period with all-cream or cream-and-black ("zebra") bobbins are somehow better. The pickup's inventor, Seth Lover, was amused by the idea. "Yes, our supplier ran out of black material, but they did have cream. We were not going to stop production just for that," he laughed. "So we got some cream bobbins. I couldn't tell any difference one from the other – although I think cream was a better colour for winding the wire on to the pickups, because you could see the wire in there a lot easier than you could with the black." Gibson's Ken Killman said in 1973: "The coils are electrically the same."

Those who do get the chance to play Les Paul Standards, rather than consign them to bank-vaults as part of an investment portfolio, have noted a number of minor changes over the three production years: smaller frets in 1958, bigger during 1959-60; and a chunky, round-backed neck over the 1958-59 period compared to a slimmer, flatter-profiled version in 1960. But as one US guitar dealer puts it: "It seems like the top more than anything else will sell those guitars. If it has a killer top but it's beat to hell and refinished, it'll still sell for more than one that's plain. The high prices seem to be due to the fact that non-players are paying the most money for them, and often it seems that these people go solely for the look. I've seen them buy those guitars without even plugging them in. And they've missed some great guitars, because they've looked … and then said no, not interested. No top!"

And so the sunburst Standard has turned into one of Gibson's sleeping giants. Almost ignored at the time, the instrument has now become an ultra-collectable icon. Players and collectors came to realise that the guitar's inherent musicality, as well as its short production run – around 1700 were made between 1958 and 1960 – added up to a modern classic. As we'll discover in the next chapter, this re-evaluation was prompted originally in the middle and late 1960s when a number of guitarists discovered that the Gibson Les Paul had enormous potential for high-volume blues-based rock. It turned out that the Les Paul's inherent tonality coupled with its humbucking pickups – and all played through a loud tube or valve amp – made a wonderful noise.

"Wind it up through a stack and there's this great over-the-top sound that Les Paul never even dreamt of."

1960s

Eric Clapton, Cream ▸

43

FIFTY YEARS OF THE GIBSON LES PAUL

Considering all the Les Paul models as a whole, sales declined in 1960 after a peak in 1959. By 1961, Gibson had decided on a complete re-design of the line in an effort to try to reactivate them. The company had started a $400,000 expansion of its factory in Kalamazoo during 1960 that more than doubled the size of the plant by the time it was completed in August. It was the third addition to the original 1917 factory, other buildings having been added in 1945 and 1950. The new single-storey brick-and-steel building meant that Gibson's entire plant now totalled more than 120,000 square feet and extended for two city blocks at Parsons Street in Kalamazoo. Clearly they would be needing instruments that sold in big numbers to keep the new factory at peak performance.

> "My contract ended in 1962," said Les Paul, "right at the time that Mary and I decided to split. So Gibson could not make any more Les Paul guitars."

One of the first series of new models to benefit from Gibson's expanded production facilities was the revised Les Paul design, the SG ("Solid Guitar"). At first, these completely new instruments with their highly sculpted, double-cutaway design continued to be named Les Paul models, so guitars of this new style made between 1961 and 1963 with suitable markings are now known as SG/Les Pauls. But by 1963 the Les Paul name had been removed, and the models officially continued as SGs.

Ted McCarty, who was still president at Gibson, said Les Paul's name was taken off because the association had become less of a commercial bonus than it once had been. Paul's popularity as a recording artist had declined: he and Mary Ford had no more Top 40 hits on Capitol after 1955, and left the label three years later. They recorded for Columbia from 1958 to 1963, with little commercial impact.

But the main reason that Les Paul's name was dropped from Gibson guitars in 1963 relates to his divorce from Mary Ford. Their separation was noted in *Billboard* in May 1963. "Miss Ford is now living in California, while Paul is living in New Jersey," ran the news item, confined to the bottom of an inside page, under the headline "Les and Mary Say Bye-Bye". The couple were officially divorced by the end of 1964, and Paul retired from most playing and recording for about ten years from 1965. "The contract came due I think in 1962," recalled Paul, "right at the time that Mary and I decided to split." He said that he agreed with Gibson to wait until the divorce was over before starting further discussions. Paul did not want to sign any fresh contract bringing in new money while the divorce proceedings were underway, he said, "because [Ford's] lawyers would ask for part of it in the divorce settlement. So my contract ended in '62 and Gibson could not make any more Les Paul guitars."

Paul also said that he didn't like the design of the new SG/Les Paul models – and that this was another reason for the removal of his name from them. This was the explanation that was given prominence for a time. In 1982, for example, Paul told Tom Wheeler in *American Guitars*: "The first [SG/Les Paul] I saw was in a music store ... and I didn't like the shape – a guy could kill himself on those sharp horns. It was too thin, and they had moved the front pickup away from the fingerboard so they could fit my name in there. The neck was too skinny and I didn't like the way it joined the body; there wasn't enough wood, at least in my opinion. So I called Gibson and asked them to take my name off the thing. It wasn't my design."

Paul was pictured in various official Gibson promotional photographs of the 1960s with the SG/Les Paul models, and held one on the cover of his 1967 *Les Paul Now* album. *The Music Trades* magazine carried a report in summer 1961 of the gala banquet given at the close of the July NAMM convention, the trade fair for the National Association of Music Merchants. Star turn at the banquet was Les Paul & Mary Ford, and while the photo in the magazine clearly showed both Paul and Ford playing old-style single-cutaway Gibson Les Pauls, elsewhere in the same issue a Gibson ad headed "Solid Hit" had Paul and Ford promoting the new SG/Les Paul models ("ultra thin, hand contoured, double cutaway"). Paul, still under his Gibson contract, continued to play original-design Gibson Les Pauls on stage – but at the same time was used by Gibson to promote the new SG-style guitars.

Production of Les Paul models did increase slightly when the new SG designs were introduced during 1961. Output of all Gibson Les Paul models from the Kalamazoo factory settled at just under 6000 units every year for 1961, 1962 and 1963. Gibson's pricelist of September 1963 is among the last in the early 1960s to feature Les Pauls, and itemises three models: SG/Les Paul Junior (cherry) $155; SG/Les Paul Standard (cherry) $310; and SG/Les Paul Custom (white) $450. With the contract now expired, from 1964 until 1967 inclusive there were no guitars in the Gibson line bearing the Les Paul name, either on the guitars themselves or in the company's literature.

ALL CHANGE AT GIBSON

In the United States, sales of guitars in general – including acoustic as well as electric instruments – climbed throughout the early 1960s and hit a peak of about a million and a half units in 1965, after which the figure declined and fell to just over a million during 1967. CMI's sales of Gibson guitars and amplifiers hit a peak of $19million-worth in 1966, but then began to fall in line with the general trend, down to $15million by 1968.

In addition to this general decline in demand for guitars, Gibson's production was hit by a number of strikes in the 1960s, including a 16-day stoppage in 1966 which, said *The Music Trades*, resulted in a "turnover of skilled personnel" (they fired people) and "production efficiency at Gibson remained at relatively low levels throughout the year" (output was hit). Gibson was also not helped by a spate of bad local weather conditions, and matters were hardly improved when a trucking industry strike in the Chicago area "interrupted the flow of merchandise in and out of the company's distribution center".

A new home for Gibson's electronics department had been built in 1962, and a separate factory for making Gibson amps, strings and pickups was added in 1964. Guitar manufacturing remained at Parsons Street, Kalamazoo. Gibson president Ted McCarty and his number two, John Huis, left in 1966 after buying the Bigsby musical accessories company of California, which they re-established in Kalamazoo. In February 1968, after a number of short-stay occupants in the

A LATE BURST

1960 in context

A new decade – but still the old Standard at Gibson, as the sunburst-finish model makes its final (original) appearance.

Lady Chatterley's Lover, D.H. Lawrence's 1920s novel about the sexual shenanigans of Chatterley and her gamekeeper, is found not obscene by a London court.

Topping the charts on either side of the Atlantic is Cathy's Clown by The Everly Brothers; in the UK there's Apache by The Shadows, and in the US Marty Robbins and El Paso.

American U2 spy plane is shot down over Russia. The pilot, Gary Powers, is imprisoned, and then released some months later in exchange for a Soviet spy.

Two rock'n'roll deaths: Elvis leaves the army for a film career; Eddie Cochran is killed in a car crash in England.

Olympic Games open in Rome.

◀ 1960 Standard

▲ Paul McCartney's 1960 Standard left-hander

Gibson at this time was not the sort of company to let a model ride for years to see if its fortunes might change. As soon as the sunburst-finish Standard began to dip in sales, it was deleted from the catalogue. Indeed, Gibson stopped making all its original-design Les Paul models. It seemed as if the single-cutaway carved-top models were consigned to the history books. And so they would be – but without the emphatic full stop Gibson intended in the early 1960s.

FIFTY YEARS OF THE GIBSON LES PAUL

THE SIXTIES

Many Standards from the 1960 period have slimmer necks and appeal more to some players as a result. The three pictured here are fine examples, with Paul McCartney's leftie (main guitar) certainly the most famous. The other two '60s pictured on these pages exhibit especially pleasing figure, guaranteed to place them in the upper bracket of desirability. But let's not forget what these guitars were intended for. Who wants to squeeze bittersweet blues from their strings when they could be stuffed in a climate-controlled bank vault until 2060?

▼ 1960 Standard

FIFTY YEARS OF THE GIBSON LES PAUL

president's chair, Stan Rendell was appointed president of Gibson. Rendell had worked for CMI since 1963 and was vice president of manufacturing. He told his boss, Maurice Berlin, that he was tired of travelling so much between CMI's factories, including plants for Lowrey organs and Olds brass as well as Gibson. Berlin offered Rendell the chance to run Gibson – a challenge, as it turned out. "Mr Berlin said to me, you know, we're not doing too well with Gibson," remembered Rendell. "They had lost a million dollars at the factory for the two prior years." So Rendell was made president of Gibson, and faced the usual brief handed to incoming presidents: make sure you improve the company's fortunes.

Guitarist Bruce Bolen, born in England and raised in Chicago, joined Gibson in 1967 to organise and perform promotional shows and concerts for the company and, as he described it, "to be a representative player for Gibson". Gradually over the years he took on more responsibility, eventually getting involved in guitar design and marketing. Back in the late 1960s when he joined Gibson, Bolen too remembered a company in poor condition. "One of the reasons I was hired was because Gibson's electric sales were floundering," he said. "All we had in solidbody electrics were SGs, plus the archtop and thinline instruments, and they weren't selling all that well. The mainstay of the company at the time was the flat-top acoustics. So I was hired basically to go out and sell electric guitars."

He found that management at Gibson and its parent company CMI were generally unaware at the time of the growing interest among rock guitarists in the original pre-1961 Les Paul models. "I was just a punk kid, and most of the people there were in their 50s or older," Bolen recalled. "I don't think they had a great grasp on how important that guitar was becoming once again. The Mike Bloomfields, Eric Claptons … they'd found it to be something really precious that offered a sound that was very conducive to their form of music."

GOD MOVES TO SUNBURST
Starting around 1965 there was a boom in blues-based rock music, originating in Britain. Many white guitarists were at the core of this new musical movement, and some were naturally inspired by the guitars used by their black American influences. They discovered that a Gibson Les Paul overdriven through a stack – a powerful tube (valve) amplifier with multiple loudspeaker cabinets – produced a wonderfully rich, emotive sound that was well suited to this fresh musical setting.

The most notable member of the Les Paul guitar appreciation society was Eric Clapton. He told Dan Forte in *Guitar Player* in 1985 that the best Les Paul he ever had was a sunburst Standard, acquired around the middle of 1965 while playing with John Mayall's Bluesbreakers and stolen early in his career with Cream in 1966. "I bought [it] in one of the shops in London right after I'd seen Freddie King's album cover of *Let's Hide Away And Dance Away*," said Clapton, "where he's playing a gold-top. It had humbuckers and was almost brand new – original case with that lovely purple … lining, just magnificent. I never really found one as good as that. I do miss that one." Many, many Standards have since been hopefully offered as the famous ex-Clapton guitar, but no proof has ever accompanied such instruments. Clapton in fact played a number of Standards in the 1960s, probably three or four in total, as well as a three-humbucker Custom.

As a member of Mayall's Bluesbreakers, Clapton had played his Standard through a small Marshall combo amp to great effect on the group's *Blues Breakers* LP. This famous "Beano-cover" album came out in July 1966, and the rear of the sleeve pictured Clapton with his original Standard. Even though the photograph only showed part of the back of the guitar, keen-eyed Clapton fans could work out what it was. Some people argue today that this one image began the entire "vintage guitar" fashion, a trend based on the notion that old guitars are inherently better than new ones. Whatever the arguments, it was certainly Clapton more than any other musician who turned fellow players' ears toward the new sound of the old Les Paul guitars, not least when his innovative, sweet, flowing sound was introduced to the world on Cream's 1966 hit 'I Feel Free'.

In the US, Mike Bloomfield with the Butterfield Blues Band and then Electric Flag had a similar effect. Bloomfield said later that around the time he started using Les Pauls he noticed that British players had picked up on the guitar. When the Butterfield band played in the UK in November 1966 he saw Green and Clapton playing their Les Pauls. "I wondered to myself how they knew that this guitar had all the inherent qualities of sustain, volume and tone that was just better than any other possible rock'n'roll guitar at that time," said Bloomfield. "All of us, unbeknownst to the others, were playing the same model guitar."

BILLY G AND THE ICONIC BEANO COVER

Billy Gibbons, who would go on to do much for the popularity of Les Paul Standards in future decades with ZZ Top, recalled how his passion began. "It was the sound of blues music that we heard in the mid 1960s that really centred our interest," he told Chris Gill in *Guitar World* in 1997. "When I speak of blues from this period, it was not only American blues artists but the British interpreters as well. That draws us to one of the most recognisable icons of 1960s British blues, the *Blues Breakers* album, with Eric Clapton on guitar and the famous photo on the back cover showing Clapton playing a sunburst Les Paul and a Marshall amplifier. At the time I had been playing Fenders," Gibbons said. "The Les Paul was less than popular then. We suspected that double-humbucking pickups were the source of the Clapton sound. A friend of mine called and said he had an instrument with two humbucking pickups. It turned out to be a Flying V, but that was our first entry into the humbucking world."

The search for old Les Pauls grew ever more urgent as a queue of respected players formed to take up the ageing model. But Clapton certainly hadn't been the first to realise that the old, discontinued Les Paul models played so well. Keith Richards of The Rolling Stones was the first star guitarist to be seen with an old-style Les Paul. He acquired a Standard during the group's June 1964 US tour and used it into the following year (the guitar is pictured across pages 38/39, and in action on pages 2 and 50). Jimmy Page was playing a three-humbucker Custom by late 1964 when he was a busy session player on the London recording scene, and Jeff Beck was inspired to move from a Fender to a Les Paul Standard after seeing Eric Clapton play his with the Bluesbreakers in London. Clapton's replacement in Mayall's band, Peter Green, used a Standard (see page 39) to great effect in that group and also in Fleetwood Mac which he

SOLID GUITAR TIME

1961-67 in context

Gibson stops making original-design Les Paul models (61) and instead introduces a new body shape known as the SG.

Yuri Gagarin is first man in space (61).

President Kennedy is shot dead while electioneering in Dallas, Texas (63).

The Beatles play Ed Sullivan TV show on their first US visit (64). Later that year the Stones too appear on Ed's bash.

Lenny Bruce, comedian who assaulted such unmentionables as religion, politics, sex and race, dies (66) at age 40.

Monterey Pop fest (67): Jimi, Janis, Otis.

◀ Keith Richards with '59 Standard (see p38/9)

▼ 1961 SG/Les Paul Custom

With a brave new decade underway, Gibson redesigned its Les Paul line with body shapes sculpted, pointed and double-cutaway'd. The Custom (above) remained ahead, but with a whiter-than-white finish. Gibson's ads proclaimed the new look, with the example opposite, left, from Selmer, Gibson's UK distributor at the time. Everything pointed to a winner, although after just a few years Les Paul's name was removed and the guitars were renamed just plain "SG".

FIFTY YEARS OF THE GIBSON LES PAUL

THE SIXTIES

Some more SG/Les Pauls are featured here. The name is a bit of a mouthful, but is carefully chosen. At first, these were Les Paul models, and the logo was deployed to underline the connection. For the time being, Gibson still valued the association with the guitarist. The "SG" bit is Gibson's later official name for the model and, excitingly, stands for Solid Guitar. So these are the original SG/Les Pauls: SG shape, still with Les Paul markings. But then, for some tricky reasons that are all recounted in the main text of this book, the Les Paul name was removed from the instruments. Thus in 1963 the models became truly SGs. So if you talk about an SG, you mean a guitar of this design made from that point onward. If you talk about an SG/Les Paul, then it's one of these early versions. Got it?

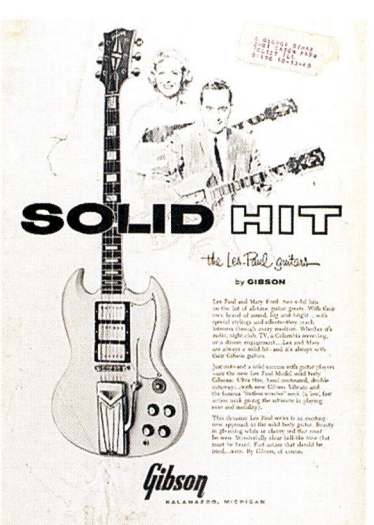

▲ 1961 SG/Les Paul Junior

▲ 1961 SG/Les Paul Standard

▲ 1962 SG/Les Paul Custom

FIFTY YEARS OF THE GIBSON LES PAUL

formed in 1967. Meanwhile, prices for secondhand Les Pauls had gradually begun to move upward, and reports began to appear in the musicians' press. One of the first to identify the trend was the British magazine *Beat Instrumental*, in summer 1966. "Les Paul Customs are in great demand!" shrieked a headline. "If you have a Les Paul Custom you want to sell, come to London and get a very good price for it from almost anyone. Rarest of the lot seems to be the three-pickup job which Jimmy Page uses. If you have one of these you are rich." Letters pleading for help began to appear, too. "I am having great difficulty in obtaining a Gibson Les Paul Custom guitar," wrote a *Beat* reader. "Have you any idea where I can obtain one? If you think this is impossible, perhaps you could tell me which guitar is similar in tone?"

While a Custom was specified, most guitarists would have been pleased to find any kind of original Les Paul guitar. The magazine replied: "The Les Paul Custom is a much sought after instrument. It is impossible to obtain a new one, and even secondhand models are very scarce. If you want one, then you will have to be very patient." They went on to recommend as an alternative one of the slowly growing band of Japanese-made copy guitars being imported to Europe and the US. These oriental "replicas" were of pretty poor quality at the time – but at least they looked similar and were available.

BECK'S BARGAIN BURST
The search for Les Pauls did not abate. In a news item later in '67, a reporter contemplated the sorry state of supply and demand. "So many people are interested in obtaining one of the almost legendary Les Paul guitars that we've done a bit of checking. Some guitarists insist that new Les Pauls can still be bought, but they're wrong ... so if you're offered a guitar, and told it's a Les Paul, be very wary."

Jeff Beck had bought his first Les Paul Standard early in 1966 when he was playing with The Yardbirds. When he spoke to a reporter later that year, Beck enthused about the Les Paul guitar as much as Les Paul the musician. "I want to do everything there is to be done with a guitar, preferably with a studio of my own. Les Paul did it, and the only reason he isn't recognised is because he doesn't record now, and the few records that are available are very old tunes. You can do anything with this instrument – simulate violin, sax, cello, or even sitar." Beck explained later that he first got a Les Paul for its sonic qualities. "Those guitars had a deep sound, and I really needed that power to help fill out the sound," he said. "There was a guy at Selmer's shop in Charing Cross Road in London, and he said he'd got a good one at home. It was a case of, well, meet me at so-and-so and I'll bring along the guitar. That sunburst '59 Les Paul cost me £150. It was my favourite Les Paul of all time, with a very distinct flame. It was bright and beautiful."

Gibson at last woke up to this interest and decided to do something about their deteriorating position in the electric guitar market – and specifically about the increasing demand for their old Les Paul guitars. Bruce Bolen, Gibson's "guitar-playing representative", remembered that one day soon after he started working for the company in 1967, vice president Marc Carlucci asked if he'd mind staying late that evening at the CMI headquarters in Chicago. "Marc told me they had someone coming in and wanted my opinion on what he had to show us. I asked who it was, and he told me it was Les Paul. Now when I was a kid, six years old, Les Paul was my first guitar hero," said Bolen, "so I was thrilled to have the chance to meet him. Gibson still wasn't too sure they wanted to reintroduce the Les Paul guitar. I was going: please!"

Les Paul's musical activities had been very low-key since the mid 1960s, but he had his first album for some time, *Les Paul Now*, released in 1967, and this meeting the same year marked the start of his new association with Gibson and the beginning of the reissue programme for Les Paul models. Paul's recollection of the circumstances was typically forthright. "I called Gibson and said hey, Fender's here bugging me and they want to make a deal, and my divorce is over. I asked if they wanted to make a deal. And Mr Berlin said it was odd that I should call, because they were striking all electrical instruments from the Gibson line. He told me the electric guitar was extinct. So I asked if he could meet me that Friday in Chicago. I said I wanted to buy him a cup of coffee. We stayed up for 24 hours, and I convinced him to go back and make the electric guitar."

Maybe Berlin really was thinking about "striking all electrical instruments from the Gibson line", but there's little evidence of such a move being contemplated. Certainly Gibson negotiated a new contract with Paul. The royalty agreed was five per cent of the "standard cost" of each Les Paul model – that is, the internal price at which Gibson sold the guitar to CMI, around a third of retail. Such a calculation meant that Paul would receive about $6.50 for each Les Paul model typically selling for $395 retail.

By the time Stan Rendell had become president of Gibson in early 1968 the decision to re-commence manufacturing Les Paul guitars had already been made by CMI management in Chicago, principally by Berlin and Carlucci. At the Gibson plant in Kalamazoo, Rendell and his team had their own difficulties. Rendell recalled the position when he joined Gibson. "We had all kinds of quality problems. We had production problems. We had personnel problems. We had union problems. We had problems that wouldn't end."

Rendell, the new broom, set to work. He developed a structure for supervision in the Kalamazoo factory, he instigated manufacturing schedules, improved inspection routines, installed a separate stock room, held regular meetings, and bought, as he puts it, "a ton of new equipment, all sorts of stuff. Mr Berlin said that in the first five years I was there, there were more new ideas, new machinery and new products than in the entire history of the Gibson company prior to that. We just had a ball. And if we didn't know how to do something, we found out."

Bruce Bolen, meanwhile, had a showstopper for his Gibson promotional concerts. He'd taken out on the road a prototype of the forthcoming reissue Les

> "That sunburst '59 Les Paul cost me £150," said Jeff Beck. "It was my favourite Les Paul of all time, with a very distinct flame. It was bright and beautiful. You can do anything you want with this instrument – simulate violin, sax, cello, or even sitar."

Paul Custom, as far as he can remember by very late 1967. "People were just falling apart about it. They couldn't wait to get one."

Gibson decided to re-introduce the relatively rare two-pickup Les Paul Custom, and the Les Paul gold-top with P-90 pickups and Tune-o-matic bridge. There was some initial discussion about making the Custom in white, like the SG/Les Paul Custom, but the sensitivity of white lacquer to contamination led the company to go with the "correct" black version. Gibson formally launched the two new models at the June 1968 NAMM trade show in Chicago. The company's pricelist from that month showed the two revived Les Pauls for the first time: the Custom was pitched at $545 and the gold-top ("Standard") at $395. Les Paul was at the NAMM show to promote the new guitars for Gibson by doing what he's always done best – playing the things. Bolen remembered: "I provided the rhythm section for Les, and it was the first time in years that he'd got on a stage. We had a lot of fun."

OKAY, YOU WIN ... LES PAULS AVAILABLE NOW

Gibson's press advertisement publicising the revived guitars, headed "Daddy of 'em all", admitted that Gibson had been forced to re-introduce the guitars. "The demand for them just won't quit. And the pressure to make more has never let up. Okay, you win. We are pleased to announce that more of the original Les Paul Gibsons are available. Line forms at your Gibson dealer."

Around the summer '68 NAMM show, production of the new Customs and gold-tops was started at Kalamazoo. Jim Tite of Gibson said at the time that production was expected to start in June. "The revival of these instruments answers a pressing need," he admitted. "It will soon be no longer necessary to search for used models that sell in auction for $700 to $1000 in the United States." Rendell said that the first run, which took 90 days to get from wood shop to stock room, was for 500 guitars: 400 gold-tops and 100 Customs. "And by the time we had that started, CMI wanted 100 a month of the gold-top and 25 a month of the Custom, and before we were finished with that we were making 100 Les Pauls a day. That's out of a total of 250, 300 instruments a day." Gibson clearly had a success in the making. The only mystery as far as many guitarists were concerned was why they'd waited so long.

An important change to Gibson's ownership occurred in 1969. The company's new owner, Norlin Industries, came into being in 1969 with the merger of CMI and ECL, an Ecuadorian brewery. ECL simply bought enough of CMI's publicly traded stock to gain control of the company. The Norlin name came from a combination of the first syllable of ECL chairman Norton Stevens's name and the last syllable of that of CMI founder Maurice Berlin. Norlin was in three businesses: musical instruments, brewing, and what was described loosely as "technology". The takeover was formalised in 1974 and Maurice Berlin, a man widely respected in the musical instrument industry, was moved sideways in the new structure, away from the general running of the company.

Many people who worked for Gibson at the time have said how, when the change of ownership occurred, there was suddenly a new breed of employee to be seen. The most common description – and indeed the most polite – is of a

Harvard MBA with suit, slide-rule and calculator at the ready. To translate, that's a Master of Business Administration graduate from the Harvard Business School, armed with the tools of his trade. Or, as one long-serving Gibson manager of the time put it, "I'd think about people, about machines, about parts ... and these new guys would 'solve' all the problems with a calculator. They had nothing to offer other than that they were looking for a place to invest their money and gain a profit. That was their motivation."

STUCK IN KALAMAZOO WITH THE NORLIN BLUES AGAIN

Gibson president Stan Rendell remembered that the new owners made a fundamental change to the way his business operated. "When they came in, they said we're going to change Gibson from a profit centre to a cost centre," he said. "Before, we sold guitars to CMI, which meant that we could make a profit at the factory. And with that profit we were able to buy machinery, improve the benefits to the employees, increase the rates of pay, everything that a company that makes a profit can do. But when they changed us to a cost centre we had no sales – they just paid our bills. And when they did that they destroyed the initiative. If someone runs up a bill, it's paid. So the person running up the bill doesn't have any incentive to not run it so high or not run it at all."

Many Gibson people from this period feel that there was a move away from managers who understood guitars to managers who understood manufacturing. Some of the instruments made during the period soon after Gibson was taken over have a bad reputation today. The new owners are generally felt now to have been insensitive to the needs of musicians. One insider remembered: "Up until about 1974 everything was hunky dory, and then it began to change. Too many people were doing too few things, too much money was being spent on too little, and it started to affect the infamous bottom line."

This air of retrospective uneasiness is mirrored in the case of two other American guitar-making giants that were also taken over during the period in question: Fender, by CBS in 1965, and Gretsch, by Baldwin in 1967. Clearly this was a sign of the times, as economic analysts advised big corporations to diversify into a range of different areas, pour in some money ... and sit back to wait for the profits. At any rate, Gibson was not alone in feeling the effects that the new management methods were causing.

The shift toward a "rationalisation" of production meant that changes would be made to some of the Gibson guitars built during the 1970s (and, to some extent, into the 1980s). Generally, these alterations were made for one of three reasons. First, to save money. Second, to limit the number of guitars returned for work under warranty. And third, to speed up production. The most common remark made about Gibson Les Pauls from the 1970s is a generalisation: many of them are relatively heavy when compared to examples from other periods. This was partly due to the increase in density of the mahogany that Gibson was buying, but also to a change in body construction that lasted from about 1969 to 1973.

Instead of the traditional maple-and-mahogany or all-mahogany construction, an elaborate multiple sandwich was developed (including, from 1969, the new Custom). This consisted of a maple top, with twin layers of mahogany underneath divided by another layer of thin maple. If you look at the side of a Les Paul made in this way you should be able to see the extra central strip of maple. Adding an extra piece of timber like this, with a contrary grain pattern, is known as cross-banding. Gibson's internal ECN (Engineering Change Notice) said that it was done to strengthen the body, to prevent cracking and checking. "It's a standard practice in the furniture industry," said Stan Rendell. "It ties the wood together." It may also have simplified Norlin's timber buying, because it meant that the thinner pieces of mahogany already earmarked for necks could now also be used for bodies. However, by about 1973 the cross-banding would be stopped. There were complaints from players and dealers about shrinkage around the obvious joins, but the extra labour costs involved in preparing the sandwich priced it out of existence anyway.

Gibson also changed the way they constructed guitar necks, from around 1969. The move was from the traditional one-piece neck to a stronger three-piece mahogany laminate, and on to three-piece maple around 1974, intended to give even greater strength. From about 1969 Gibson also added a "volute" to the back of the neck just below the point where it becomes the headstock, a sort of triangular "lump" that reinforced this notoriously weak spot. Another change made at this time to minimise problems in the same area came with a slight decrease in the angle at which the headstock tipped back from the neck. Such practical changes did nothing to enhance Gibson's reputation among those who liked the older guitars.

WHEN IS A HUMBUCKER NOT A HUMBUCKER?
The busy guitar design department at Gibson next changed the style and name of the recently reissued Les Paul gold-top model, meaning that the first type effectively only lasted a short time in production. In 1969 the Les Paul Deluxe took its place, and marked the first new name for a Les Paul model in 14 years. The Deluxe was prompted by calls from Gibson's marketing managers who were being told by dealers that players wanted the gold-top model with humbucking pickups rather than the single-coil P-90s of the reissue.

Jim Deurloo had joined Gibson back in 1958 as a factory worker, and worked his way up through the ranks. By 1969 he was heading the pattern shop at Kalamazoo, and was given the task of providing the planned Deluxe with humbuckers ... but without incurring new tooling costs. The only way he could do this was to fit a humbucking pickup into the space already being routed for smaller P-90s. He considered a few options, and eventually came up with the solution of using an Epiphone mini-humbucking pickup of a type that appeared on some Epiphone models of the time.

Gibson had acquired Epiphone and began producing guitars with the brand in Kalamazoo during 1958. According to Ted McCarty, who was president at the time of the purchase, Gibson thought that for the $20,000 asking price they were buying Epiphone's double-bass business. What they actually ended up with was virtually the entire company: guitars, parts, machinery and all. "We only discovered this when they shipped the whole thing back to Kalamazoo in a big furniture truck," said McCarty, who had to rent space in another building in

Eleanor Street in Kalamazoo so that Epiphone parts could be prepared before final assembly at Parsons Street. "I put Ward Arbanas in charge of it, and we made the Epiphone guitars just the way Epiphone made them, with every detail exact," claimed McCarty. Production of Gibson-made Epiphones was underway during 1958 – and by 1961 totally at Parsons Street. Many fine guitars were produced. But by 1969 the Epiphone line was being run down, because by then Epiphone prices more or less matched those of Gibson. Customers would naturally opt for the highly-rated Gibson, meaning a drop in demand for Epiphone. Something had to be done, and by 1970 Gibson took the decision to phase out US production of Epiphones, and instead applied the brandname to cheaper guitars imported from oriental factories. No proper Les Paul-style Epiphones would be made until the 1980s.

Back with the Gibson Les Paul Deluxe in 1969, Jim Deurloo managed to accommodate an Epiphone mini-humbucker by taking a P-90 pickup cover, cutting a hole in it, and dropping in the small Epiphone unit ... of which Gibson now had surplus stocks. The result pleased everyone: the look was relatively traditional, the pickup was a humbucker, and no extra tooling costs had been incurred. At first the Deluxe was only available with a gold top, but gradually sunbursts and other colours were introduced, and the model lasted in production until the mid 1980s. It appeared on Gibson's pricelist for September 1969, its year of introduction, at $425.

The gold-top model was, as you may remember, one of the two Les Pauls reissued in 1968, with P-90s and a Tune-O-Matic bridge. As we've seen, it was in effect dropped on release of the Deluxe in 1969. A new version was launched by Gibson around 1971, this time with the wrapover bar-shaped bridge/tailpiece like the one fitted to the second type of original 1950s model. It had narrow binding in the body cutaway, a characteristic of 1950s Les Pauls, prompting suggestions that Gibson was using up old bodies. This style of gold-top, still with P-90s, lasted for about a year, although it did not appear on the company's pricelists.

> The new maple-mahogany sandwich, the stronger three-piece neck, the lumpy "volute", the shallower headstock angle ... such practical changes did nothing to enhance Gibson's reputation among those who liked the older guitars.

GETTING DOWN WITH LES

As we've seen, Les Paul's ideas on guitar design did not necessarily coincide with what Gibson felt would be commercially successful. One of Paul's more out-of-step tastes was for low-impedance pickups. Today, low-impedance elements are more often used in pickups, thanks to improvements in the associated components, but back then Paul was largely on his own. The vast majority of electric guitars and guitar-related equipment was (and still is) high-impedance.

The chief advantage of low-impedance is a wide and all-encompassing tonal characteristic. This might appear at first to be an advantage, but in fact the tonal range offered isn't necessarily to everyone's taste. A disadvantage is that low-

WELCOME BACK

1968-69 in context

Gibson is forced to reintroduce a number of original-design Les Paul models after overwhelming demand from players (68).

Beatles among first to use new Moog synthesiser (69). King Crimson's debut LP uses another Beatle fave, the Mellotron.

In Vietnam Vietcong's big Tet Offensive attacks on Saigon (68) make victory by South Vietnamese and US seem unlikely.

Neil Armstrong is the first man on the moon (69). "We copy you down" means "Thank god for that" in NASA-speak.

Colour TV broadcasts start in UK (69).

◂ Robert Fripp, King Crimson, with trusty Custom

▲ 1968 Custom

▲ 1968 gold-top

FIFTY YEARS OF THE GIBSON LES PAUL

THE SIXTIES

▼ 1969 Personal

Finally, after Keith and Peter (below) and Eric and Mike and dozens of others proved the sonic efficacy of those early-design Les Pauls, Gibson reintroduced the original-type Les Pauls – and many would say they missed the obvious one. There was a P-90 gold-top, there was a two-humbucker Custom, but for the time being there was no sunburst Standard (two examples pictured, left). Then Gibson put out the Deluxe. It was sunburst. It had humbuckers. Only the wrong kind of humbuckers – mini-humbuckers. Oh well, almost there. On those original 1950s models Gibson had put Les Paul's name on their design. But in 1969 the roles were reversed as Gibson put their name on some of Les Paul's low-impedance designs: the Personal guitar (above), the Professional, and the Les Paul Bass.

◀ 1975 Deluxe

◀ 1970 Deluxe

FIFTY YEARS OF THE GIBSON LES PAUL

impedance pickups must have their power boosted at some point before the signal reaches the amplifier (unless the player is plugging the guitar straight into a recording studio mixer, as Les Paul would do). When Paul had gone to Gibson in 1967 to discuss the reissue of Les Paul guitars, he'd talked with great passion about his beloved low-impedance pickups, and how Gibson should use them on some instruments. Paul convinced Gibson to go ahead. In 1969 along came the first wave of Les Paul models with low-impedance pickups – the Les Paul Professional, the Les Paul Personal, and the Les Paul Bass.

> "A lot of rock'n'roll riffs and things go back to Les Paul," said Jimmy Page. "He's the father of it all. If it hadn't been for him, there wouldn't be anything, really."

The Personal was, as the name implied, in keeping with one of Paul's own modified Les Paul guitars, even copying its odd feature of a microphone socket on the top edge of the guitar. The Personal and Professional had a complex array of controls, and Gibson's instruction leaflet reinforced the impression that they were built with recording engineers rather than guitarists in mind. Familiar volume, bass, treble and pickup selector were augmented by an 11-position Decade control, "to tune high frequencies", a three-position tone selector to create various in and out-of-circuit mixes, and a pickup phase in/out switch. The Personal also provided a volume control for that handy on-board microphone input.

Both guitars required connection using the special cord (lead) supplied, which had a built-in transformer to boost the output from the low-impedance stacked-coil humbucking pickups up to a level suitable for use with normal high-impedance amplifiers. Predictably, with hindsight, the guitars were not a great success, and did not last long in the Gibson line. Terry Kath with Chicago was one of the few famous players ever seen playing one. Their sombre brown colour, achieved with a natural mahogany finish, could not have helped in an era when competitors were busily turning out simple guitars in bright colours.

The Les Paul Bass was the first Gibson bass guitar to bear Les Paul's name, and was similar to the low-impedance guitars. It featured two angled, black-cover pickups, but only the phase switch and the tone selector from the guitar circuitry. It too required a special cord, and similarly lasted only a short time in production. Gibson's pricelist from September 1969 listed the three Les Paul low-impedance models: Personal, $645; Professional, $485; and Bass, $465. Gibson also produced a special LP-12 combo amp and LP-1 amplifier, both with switchable high/low impedance that allowed the use of any standard cord. These were listed at $1110 for the LP-12 and $505 for the LP-1.

FRIPP OPENS UP, PAGE WINS A FIGHT
Toward the end of the 1960s, the fashion for original Les Pauls was showing no sign of letting up. Robert Fripp of King Crimson acquired his 1950s Les Paul Custom when he saw it in a London shop window during 1968. It was priced at £400. "The salesman was pretty loathsome," reported Fripp. "But we'd been given a loan and I had a briefcase with a very large sum of cash inside. I asked about a discount for cash and was refused. So I opened the briefcase and

showed the manager the money. I walked out with the Custom for £375. It remains to this day the finest Les Paul I've ever played, and I've played a few."

Jimmy Page had moved from his session-days Custom to a Fender Telecaster when he joined The Yardbirds, and he continued with the Tele in the early days of Led Zeppelin. But soon he acquired an old sunburst Les Paul Standard, and with the enormous rise in Zep's popularity into the 1970s Page became almost synonymous with the glories of overdriven humbuckers, and was often seen on stage with one of two favourite Standards. He acknowledged to Steve Rosen in 1977 that the Les Paul was always "more of a fight" than the Tele. "But there are rewards," said Page. "The Gibson's got stereotyped sound, maybe, I don't know. But it's got a beautiful sustain to it, and I like sustain because it relates to bowed instruments and everything, this whole area that everyone's been pushing and experimenting in."

Like Jeff Beck earlier, Page also had praise for Les Paul the musician. He asked if his interviewer had heard the hit single Paul had made back in 1945 with Bing Crosby, 'It's Been A long, Long Time'. "He does everything on that, everything in one go," Page enthused. "He sets the whole tone, and then he goes into this solo which is fantastic. I've traced a hell of a lot of rock'n'roll, little riffs and things, back to Les Paul. He's the father of it all. If it hadn't been for him, there wouldn't have been anything, really."

> "Humbuckers ... single cut ... check that flame ... whack it right up ... OK, let's get down!"

1970s

Jimmy Page, Led Zeppelin ›

63

In 1970 Gibson launched a very peculiar instrument, the Les Paul Jumbo. It was a flat-top acoustic guitar with round soundhole and a single cutaway. It had a low-impedance pickup installed in the top and a row of body-mounted controls – volume, treble and bass, that 11-way Decade control from the Personal and Professional models, and a bypass switch designed to cut the tone controls from the circuit. Very few Jumbos were made, and it's not difficult to see why. It made a final appearance on Gibson's November 1971 pricelist, at $610.

Les Paul himself in a 1971 interview hinted at another unusual acoustic, an amplified nylon-strung model that he called the Gibson Les Paul Classical Guitar but which never reached production. Years later Gibson did produce a guitar along similar lines, the 1981 Chet Atkins CE. Paul also spoke in that '71 interview of developing a special acoustic pickup that we would today call a piezo, and suggested combining it with a regular magnetic electric pickup to "give the player both types of sounds". Here again was the avant-garde Les Paul in action, for he was clearly describing the modern acoustic/electric "hybrid" guitar – which would not appear until the 1990s.

Gibson made its second attempt at a line of low-impedance solidbody Les Pauls in 1971. First, the body size of the Professional/Personal style was scaled down virtually to that of a normal Les Paul, and it was given a contoured back. Second, the still-necessary impedance transformer was shifted into the guitar itself, with a switch provided on the guitar for low-impedance or regular high-impedance output. Third, the guitar's name was changed to Les Paul Recording (and the bass version to the Les Paul Triumph Bass). Gibson's pricelist for June 1971 showed the Recording at $625 and Triumph Bass at $515; this second wave of low-impedance models lasted until the end of the decade. Bruce Bolen thought that their lack of success was down to Gibson not grasping what players really wanted. "The high end was so clean on those guitars," he said, "that they just didn't have enough harmonic distortion to relate to the rock players."

THE ART & SCIENCE OF GUITAR COLLECTING
As the 1970s went on, more guitarists were finding that older instruments often seemed more playable and sounded better than new guitars. Some players of acoustic guitars had felt this for a while, and a small number of specialist dealers had grown up in the US since th°e late 1940s to cater for the demand. Harry West in New York and Jon & Deirdre Lundberg in California had been among the first. But now older electrics, too, were being sought, and 1950s Les Pauls were near the top of many a wish-list. Norman's Rare Guitars, established in California during the mid 1970s, was one of the newer dealers specialising in the vintage requirements of rock players. Norman Harris was in no doubt about why so many guitarists were taking up older instruments. "You simply cannot compare what I have to offer with what the big companies are mass producing today," he boasted in 1976.

Steve Stills of Crosby Stills & Nash had amassed a collection of some 70 guitars by the middle of the decade. Touring with his solo band at the time he needed two dressing rooms: one for himself, another for the 17 guitars that accompanied him. Included were two double-cut Specials and a Standard. He was an old-guitar evangelist. "I don't think they've built anything new that's worth a damn since 1965," Stills told *Guitar Player* in 1976. "It's all mechanised." If the image of Clapton with his Standard on the '66 *Blues Breakers* album really had started the vintage-guitar trend, then it was this quote from Stills that popularised the notion that it was somehow only old guitars that were worthy of attention by "real" players.

Steve Howe of Yes was another famous player-collector in the 1970s. Like Stills, the British guitarist acquired dozens of guitars because he craved new sounds. Touring the US regularly with Yes gave him the opportunity to buy instruments from dealers who were busily supplying the growing demand. Howe would visit Silver Strings in St Louis, Pete's Guitar in St Paul, Mandolin Bros or Manny's in New York, Gruhn Guitars in Nashville, adding guitars to his collection – like the 1956 Les Paul Custom he bought from Gruhn for $800 in 1974.

George Gruhn wrote the first serious magazine piece about this new trend in *Guitar Player* in 1975, grandly titled "The Art and Science of Guitar Collecting". Writing as both a shrewd businessman promoting demand for his wares and an obsessive collector hungry for detailed information, Gruhn emphasised the desirability of old Les Pauls in the article. "There are currently more people looking for Les Pauls than for any other electric guitar," he reported. And the 1958-60 Standard, he said, "is today probably the most sought after of the Les Pauls, and has become the standard by which other guitars are judged, at least on the current market."

Gibson itself had reflected the interest in its own history with an amateurish but eagerly devoured booklet, *The Gibson Story*, in 1973. The company was of course in the business of selling new instruments, but noted briefly that some players had "requested the opportunity to purchase certain previously discontinued models" and pointed to its recent limited-edition reissues meant to address such demand, including the Les Paul Custom 54. The first published attempt to sort out the various Les Paul models and their dates of manufacture came in Tom Wheeler's *The Guitar Book* in 1974. Further detailed studies would follow later with André Duchossoir's *Gibson Electrics* (1981) and Wheeler's *American Guitars* (1982).

> "The musical world now accepts concepts like The Guitar Player Who Has Collected The Most Oldest Guitars In The World (some of which have been played by dead guitar players who were actually musicians)."
> Frank Zappa, 1977.

Of course, it wasn't long before a kind of backlash had hit the more extreme forms of guitar lust and the dangerous associated disease of collectoritis. The punks of the later 1970s were portrayed as an antidote to the excesses of out-of-touch rock stars who destroyed hotels for fun and amassed rare guitars by the store-load. But one of the old guard itself was also able to criticise the growth of the vintage-guitar fashion. The ever-cynical Frank Zappa poked fun at the trend when in 1977 he wrote a typically playful "brief version" of the evolution of the guitar's use in pop music. "[The] musical world has reached a point of sophistication," wrote Zappa, "that accepts concepts like The Super-Group, The

MY IMPEDANCE IS LOW

1970-73 in context

Gibson's low-impedance Les Pauls include Recording, Jumbo, and Triumph Bass (70).

Microprocessor, the essential computer component, is patented by Intel (71).

Allman Brothers release the classic *Live At Fillmore East* (71); that October, Duane Allman is killed in a motorcycle accident.

Watergate scandal (72) as five caught trying to bug Democrats' Washington HQ.

Skylab is the first US space station (73).

Dead: Noel Coward, Maurice Chevalier, Memphis Minnie, J.R.R. Tolkein.

◀ Duane Allman relaxes with a gold-top

The new Les Paul Recording model, like the one shown here, seemed aptly named. Les Paul was as much known for his fine guitar playing as his exploits as a pioneer in the early years of sound-on-sound and multi-track recording. His ideas for a guitar more suited to the recording studio than the live stage turned into the Recording model, and as you can see it was suitably festooned with switches and knobs. This tended to put off many guitarists, for whom the fewer controls the better.

FIFTY YEARS OF THE GIBSON LES PAUL

THE SEVENTIES

▼ 1972 Recording

Paul Kossoff (1950-1976) came to prominence in Free, especially through their hit single All Right Now (1970). Kossoff (above) was a passionate Les Paul player, able to say in a handful of notes what many would waste dozens attempting.

◀ 1970 Jumbo

New models such as the Recording and the Bass (see catalogue above) and the existing Personal and Professional used low-impedance pickups. Today, low-impedance elements are used more often in pickup design. Back then, however, most were high-impedance. But low impedance offered wide tonal range, longer cable runs, and noise reduction. Les Paul thought guitarists would want to share with him these advantages. Generally, they did not. None of the low-impedance Les Pauls survived the decade – including the bizarre and now rare flat-top-electric Jumbo (right).

FIFTY YEARS OF THE GIBSON LES PAUL

Fastest Guitar Player In The World, and The Guitar Player In The World Who Has Collected The Most Oldest Guitars In The World (some of which have been played by dead guitar players who were actually musicians)."

DECADE SWITCHES AND ANNIVERSARY PAULS
Gibson's final fling with low-impedance pickups was reserved for the company's thinline electric guitar design, a shallow, semi-hollowbody style of guitar that had begun with the company's classic ES-335 in 1958. That instrument had a central block of timber inside the otherwise hollow body on which to mount the pickups and bridge. It reduced any tendency to feedback and gave the guitar a musically useful blend of solidbody and hollowbody tones. It was in 1974 that the new two-pickup Les Paul Signature guitar was launched, alongside the single-pickup Les Paul Signature Bass, both in thinline style. Bruce Bolen said, "The Signature was basically an asymmetric 335, although it didn't have the full centre block like that model." What it had was a smaller block below the bridge, which made it more like Gibson's ES-330 model.

Some of the Signature's controls were similar to those found on earlier low-impedance models, but the 11-position Decade control had shrunk to a three-position switch and lost its name. The Signature had a pair of jacks (sockets), one on the side of the body for normal high-impedance output, the other on the face of the body for connection to low-impedance equipment such as a recording mixer. A similar facility was offered on the final version of the Recording model. The gold-finish Signature models never fired players' imaginations, despite their luxurious image, and by the end of the 1970s had gone out of production. Gibson's February 1974 pricelist showed the Signature at $610 and the Signature Bass at $540.

It occurred to Gibson in 1974 that it was 20 years since the first Les Paul Custom had appeared, so they celebrated by issuing a Custom with a Twentieth Anniversary inlay at the 15th fret, in place of the normal blank position marker. This was the first Gibson anniversary model. The only precursors in the electric guitar market were Gretsch's four Anniversary models of 1958, issued to celebrate that company's foundation 75 years earlier. The 20th Anniversary Les Paul Custom established a marketing trend, and a number of special anniversary-edition Les Paul models have appeared since. As one ex-Gibson man put it, "Whenever it was time for an anniversary, we made one."

By now Gibson employed around 600 people at its Kalamazoo factory, producing some 300 guitars a day. Demand for new guitars had increased during the early 1970s, and as a result the management of Gibson's parent company, Norlin, decided to build a second factory in Nashville, Tennessee, many hundreds of miles to the south of Kalamazoo. No doubt several factors affected Norlin's choice of site, but one that was probably high on their list was the fact that Tennessee was a "right to work" state. In other words, unions existed but employees could choose whether or not to join. Michigan – and indeed a good deal of the north-eastern United States – had much stronger unions and established closed-shop arrangements, meaning obligatory union membership along with generally higher wages and insurance rates. Recent strikes at Gibson had cost Norlin dear. So the new plant of 100,000 square feet at Nashville was constructed not only with increased production in mind, but also with a view to decreasing costs through advantageous labour deals.

Work began in 1974 on the new facility, five miles to the east of Nashville, and the factory eventually opened in June 1975. Training a new workforce took some time. Stan Rendell, still Gibson president at the time, recalled that a limited number of people were transferred from Kalamazoo to Nashville in supervisory positions, but that no workers made the move. "So everybody there had to be hired and trained," he said, "and that takes time. I think a Les Paul guitar took on average eight or ten man-hours of labour. So if you're going to make, say, 100 guitars a day you would need maybe 125 or more direct-labour people – and that's without all the support personnel. It takes time to train the management, the workers, everybody. So we shipped some key people down there."

NASHVILLE PLANS
The original intention was to keep both the Kalamazoo and Nashville factories running, and that the new Nashville plant would produce only acoustic guitars. Rendell said that trying to build acoustics and electrics in the same factory was a bit like trying to build trucks and cars in the same place. They need different kinds of attention at different stages in their fabrication.

"The real challenge," he said, "was to schedule a flow of work through the factory so that everybody was kept busy. For example, the amount of work needed to finish an electric guitar is tremendous, whereas with an acoustic guitar about all you've got to do is put on strings and machine heads. So the types of guitars flowing through final assembly at any one time make a big difference to the workload. What I wanted to do was to try to specialise and remove the flat-top acoustic guitars out of the mainstream at Kalamazoo, and get a group of people who lived and breathed nothing but acoustic guitars at Nashville."

Unfortunately, the new acoustic project allocated to Nashville was the Mark series of models, some of the least successful of Gibson's flat-tops. The guitars were fraught with technical and construction problems. As one ex-employee puts it rather bluntly, "The Mark series was a fiasco." After this failure, management decided to transfer to Nashville the production of the bulk of the Les Paul line, by far the most successful Gibson solidbodys at the time. Ken Killman, manager of the company's Customer Service department, said in 1975: "During the early 1960s we couldn't sell solidbodies at all. Now the Les Paul range is the largest seller of the lot."

Kalamazoo had always been what is known technically as a "soft tool" factory. This means that the machines and fixtures used to make the guitars could be modified and adapted at will, as circumstances dictated. In other words, things could be changed easily. Nashville started life as a "hard tool" facility, which means that it had a lot of heavy machines and fixtures on which the settings were never changed. So it was that the character of the two factories that Gibson ran during the remaining years of the 1970s and into the early 1980s was quite different. Nashville was set up to produce very large quantities of a handful of individual models, where Kalamazoo was more flexible and had the potential to

SIGNATURE SOUND

1974-75 in context

Gibson first markets the semi-solid Les Paul Signature models (74).

Vietnam War finally ends (75) as South surrenders. Around 58,000 Americans died, over a million South Vietnamese and about 750,000 from North Vietnam.

Bob Marley & The Wailers record (75) classic *Live!* album at London's Lyceum.

Barcodes first used (74) for product pricing.

Patty Hearst, the teenage daughter of publisher Randolph Hearst, is kidnapped by the Symbionese Liberation Army (74).

McDonald's introduce "clamshell" pack (75).

Bob Marley with his modified Les Paul Special ▶

▼ 1976 Signature

The semi-solid style of electric guiutar had been invented by Gibson back in the late 1950s with the ES-335 family, so it must have seemed natural to apply the design to the new low-impedance series, and to tie it more closely to the Les Paul lines by treating the instruments to a gold finish. But again, the relative complexity of controls on the Signature guitar and bass left them in the cold.

FIFTY YEARS OF THE GIBSON LES PAUL

THE SEVENTIES

◀ 1980 Pro Deluxe

◀ 1975 Signature Bass

A Signature Bass (near left) appeared alongside the guitar version, but it too failed to excite much interest. About the only famous player to take up the four-string version was Jack Casady, ex-Jefferson Airplane bassman who stumbled on a Signature while seeking a more acoustic-like tone. Gibson's Epiphone line today boasts a Casady Signature. Another new model in the Les Paul line of the mid 1970s was the Pro Deluxe (far left), in effect a Deluxe model with single-coil P-90 pickups and ebony fingerboard.

T. Rex had a slew of UK hits in the early 1970s, awash with Marc Bolan's simple and effective pop guitar. Bolan (1947-1977) often used a Les Paul live. It probably started life as a Standard or gold-top, but Marc had it refinished in an opaque orange, possibly to look like the colour of hero Eddie Cochran's Gretsch. It also suffered a couple of neck changes after breaks; pictured (below) is the guitar in its mid-1970s Custom-neck phase.

FIFTY YEARS OF THE GIBSON LES PAUL

specialise in small runs. Nashville was therefore the obvious choice to produce the highest-volume models in Gibson's solidbody line at the time – the Les Paul Custom and Les Paul Deluxe – along with various other solid models.

As if to highlight the contrast between the two plants' capabilities, Gibson introduced two new Les Paul models in 1976. First was the Pro Deluxe, effectively a Deluxe with P-90 pickups and an ebony fingerboard. It was produced in large quantities at Nashville.

The other was The Les Paul, which had first been seen at the 1975 NAMM show. It was a spectacular limited edition notable for its use of fine woods for virtually the entire instrument. Many parts that on a normal electric guitar would be made from plastic were hand-carved from rosewood, including the pickguard, pickup surrounds, backplates, controls and truss-rod cover. Raw bodies and necks of attractive maple, including the back, and an ornate ebony and rosewood fingerboard were produced at Gibson's Kalamazoo factory. Further work on the multiple coloured binding, abalone inlays and handmade wooden parts was continued at the workshop of freelance luthier Dick Schneider, about a mile from the factory in Kalamazoo. Schneider worked on The Les Pauls together with his brother Donnie and Abe Wechter from Gibson.

SCHNEIDER'S HANDMADE PARTS

Very few of The Les Pauls were made, and while an unfortunate four-figure misprint in Gibson's own records precludes an exact total, it's likely that there were well under 100 produced between 1976 and 1979, with most made during the first year. During the model's life, Schneider moved away from Kalamazoo, and some later examples of The Les Paul were therefore produced entirely at the Gibson factory. As the limited stocks of Schneider's handmade wooden parts ran out, so normal plastic items were substituted, as well as less ornate binding. Each example of The Les Paul had a numbered oval plate on the back of the headstock. Bruce Bolen remembered flying to Hollywood to present number 25 to Les Paul, just prior to the 1977 Grammy Awards ceremony where Paul and Chet Atkins received a Grammy for their *Chester & Lester* album. It was 25 years since the first Gibson Les Paul guitar of 1952.

"That instrument, The Les Paul, was a fun project," remembered Rendell. "They were gorgeous guitars, the wood was so beautiful. I remember saying nothing to CMI about it until we had it done. We showed it at NAMM and I remember Les Propp, president of CMI at the time, asking how much we were going to charge for the guitar. Well, I said, it's 3000 bucks. And he choked," laughed Rendell. That tag put The Les Paul at four times the cost of its nearest Les Paul rival on the 1976 pricelist – but not far from what some players were paying for Gibson's old Les Paul Standards.

Despite ventures like The Les Paul, it seems that there had not been quite enough "fun projects" to maintain Stan Rendell's interest as president of Gibson, and in November 1976 he resigned. After a number of short-stay presidents, Marty Locke would move over from CMI's Lowrey organ business to head up Gibson in 1980. During the mid to late 1970s Gibson indulged in more theme and variation within the Les Paul line, but there was little innovation. The company could hardly have failed to notice the continuing interest in older Les Pauls in general and the Standard in particular. Duane Allman had used a gold-top and a Standard with The Allman Brothers before his untimely death in 1971, while Duane's bandmate Dickey Betts had several 1950s Pauls, and came to prefer a Standard for slide and a gold-top for regular lead work.

LUSTING FOR OLD LES PAULS
Toy Caldwell of the Marshall Tucker Band decided not to take his old Les Pauls on tour after losing two to thieves on the road. He opted instead for a two-year-old stock model fitted with 1950s humbuckers for live work, reserving his more precious instruments for the studio. As the values of vintage guitars increased, this would become a practical necessity for some. On the other hand there was Joe Walsh, with The James Gang and Barnstorm, who was an especially enthusiastic original-Standard fan. "I can't live with anything but a Les Paul," he said in 1973. He persuaded others too by distributing Standards to many player friends and acquaintances, not least Jimmy Page who was using Walsh's gift to great effect in the world-dominating Led Zeppelin (see this one pictured on page 35).

Mick Ronson with David Bowie, aka Ziggy Stardust, played a recent Custom but had it stripped to reveal the maple top, and Marc Bolan in T Rex too had his Les Paul refinished. Southern-boogie star Charlie Daniels had an original '58 Standard, and while he told a 1970s interviewer that he didn't particularly care about the date of manufacture, he added: "It just happens that most guitars that sound good and play good are old ones."

But the Les Paul Standard was still not officially part of the current Gibson line. Nonetheless, the model was available as a special order. Roger Matthews of Gibson said in 1974, "We are producing a Les Paul Standard model which could be related to the instrument produced in the latter part of the 1950s. The limited edition that is now in production has the large humbucking pickups and is available in [sunburst] finish." One of the first to prompt this sideline at Kalamazoo was a guitar dealer called Strings & Things who were based in Memphis, Tennessee. They ordered a small number of Standards with custom specs that allied them a little more closely to the 1950s originals.

At last in 1976 Gibson officially added the Standard to its pricelist, at $649, as a straightforward sunburst model with two humbuckers, but still ignoring the precise requirements of vintage fans. Some players were prepared to pay as much as $2500 for one of the original 1958-60 sunburst Standards. It's interesting to note that to match that in today's buying power you'd need to spend $7800 now. But to actually buy a good one of those Standards today, you'd need at least $25,000. This is what is known as a good investment. Meanwhile, right down at the low end of Gibson's market in the 1970s, oriental

> Joe Walsh was an especially enthusiastic Standard fan who would distribute them to many player friends and acquaintances, not least Jimmy Page who was using one of Walsh's gifts to great effect in his world-dominating band, Led Zeppelin.

FANCY AN ARTIST?

1976-79 in context

Gibson introduces the most expensive Les Paul so far, "The Les Paul" (76).

Three Mile Island US radiation leak (79).

Apple II is first pre-assembled personal computer (77), the same year that Paul Allen and Bill Gates set up Microsoft.

Peter Frampton's new *Frampton Comes Alive* is biggest selling live LP ever (76).

"I Love New York" campaign starts (77).

Dead: Howlin' Wolf, Lowell George, Sid Vicious, Elvis Presley, Maybelle Carter.

JVC introduces new VHS format (76) for domestic video tape.

◂ Peter Frampton comes alive with his Custom

▾ 1978 The Les Paul

The Les Paul (above) was a luxurious limited-run model made from the best timbers Gibson could find at the time, while the 25/50 Anniversary guitar (right) apparently celebrated Les Paul's 25-year association with Gibson and his 50th year in the music business. Complex electronics were featured in the Artist (opposite, left), and the Artisan (opposite, right) had Martin-like fancy fingerboard inlays.

FIFTY YEARS OF THE GIBSON LES PAUL

THE SEVENTIES

Punk brought a new spirit to rock in the 1970s, simpifying the music and re-affirming its basic drive and excitement. Johnny Thunders (far left, with Les Paul Junior) had done much to pave the way for punk guitar-playing while a member of The New York Dolls in the early part of the decade, happily combining garage and psychedelia. Thunders (1952-1991) later formed The Heartbreakers. Much of the old-guard of rock were dismissive of or simply mystified by punk, but Pete Townshend of The Who (with Les Paul Deluxe, near left) was widely cited as an influence by the new boys, and seemed more naturally in tune with punk's aggression.

◀ 1979 Artist

◀ 1982 Artisan

▼ 1979 25/50 Anniversary

FIFTY YEARS OF THE GIBSON LES PAUL

makers were providing well-priced copies of many classic American guitar designs, Gibson Les Pauls included. Some of them were cheap both in price and quality, but brands such as Ibanez were beginning to produce good instruments. Indeed, by the end of the 1970s the label "Made in Japan" was no longer the sign of an also-ran. Ibanez, Yamaha, Aria and others had turned the oriental guitar into a well made, competitive instrument on the world market.

Ever more aware of the value of its own history, Gibson intended its new 25/50 model to celebrate Les Paul's 25th year with Gibson (presumably it was planned for 1977) and his 50th year in the music business. There was plenty of the silver and gold associated with those anniversaries in the guitar's chrome and gold-plated hardware, while Chuck Burge in Gibson's R&D (research and development) department designed the special intricate inlay in pearl and abalone on the guitar's headstock. The instrument bore a three-digit edition number on the back of the headstock as well as a standard serial number, and Les Paul was presented with number 001 at a party given in his honour by Gibson on its launch in 1978.

> Bob Marley favoured a Special among one of the tightest bands of the 1970s, The Wailers, but punks too used the bare power of the flat-bodied Les Pauls.

Despite its relatively high price (around $1200) the Kalamazoo-made 25/50 sold well, bringing into sharp focus for Norlin the ready market for more costly Les Paul models. Management was also swayed by the opinions of Gibson's salespeople about what the market wanted. An example from this period was the figured-top Les Paul KM model, also made at Kalamazoo and one of a series of six otherwise uninspiring instruments made for a southern sales region.

JUNIOR IN BAD COMPANY SEEKS SPECIAL PISTOLS

Gibson also reissued single and double-cutaway versions of the Les Paul Special in the mid 1970s. Many players were wallowing in the rock'n'roll glory of old Juniors and Specials, the straightforward uncarved-top models that Gibson had at first intended as beginners' models. Original 1950s examples were plentiful and nowhere like as expensive as the now hallowed Standards and Customs, with price tags as little as $75 if you were lucky. But it was the raw sound of the P-90 pickups and the responsive playability of the guitars that appealed as much as any financial advantage they offered.

Leslie West with his classic early-1970s rock trio Mountain had directed the attention of many a player to the little Junior he drove so hard. One such was Mick Ralphs who developed a masterful vibrato on his Junior, playing with Mott The Hoople early in the decade and then the generally more raucous Bad Company from 1973. Reggae master Bob Marley favoured the two-pickup Special for his electric work among one of the tightest bands of the 1970s, The Wailers, but it was the punk explosion later in the decade that saw still more players discovering the bare power of the flat-bodied Les Pauls.

In the US, Johnny Thunders paved the way with his Junior in The New York Dolls. In Britain, Mick Jones of The Clash also came to love the power of his Junior, and Steve Jones of The Sex Pistols could often be seen with a Special. In fact, Jones was hardly the typical punk thrasher, having a refined taste for his chosen weapons, all of which were Gibsons. As well as the Special, Jones was fond of a white Les Paul Custom and another in sunburst with a Bigsby, and found room too for an occasional foray with a Firebird and an SG Standard.

FLICKING THE SYNTH SWITCH
Tim Shaw joined Gibson in 1978, having worked in California and in Kalamazoo as a guitar repairer and maker. His first few months with the company were spent in Gibson's pickup plant in Elgin, Illinois, but by early 1979 he was working with Bruce Bolen in R&D at Kalamazoo. Together with Chuck Burge and Abe Wechter, Shaw built prototypes and artists' instruments and worked on new designs. One of the first prototypes he was involved with became the Les Paul Artist, a model that used a system of active electronics originally developed for Gibson's RD models.

Synthesisers were becoming big business in the late 1970s and Norlin figured that if Gibson were to hook up with one of the synth field's most famous names, Moog, it might re-capture some of the ground that guitars were apparently losing to the new keyboards. Gibson's resulting RD line was issued in 1977, but did not prove popular. Many guitarists disliked the RDs' active circuitry, which could be harsher than regular tone controls. This proved a major factor in the downfall of the series. However, Gibson believed the radical styling of the RD models was more to blame, and that the solution was to transplant the technology over to some traditional guitar designs.

"In 1979 Gibson decided to expand the RD concept into two of their more mainstream series, the ES and the Les Paul," Shaw explained. "We had to re-design the circuit board, because the original RD board is too big for almost anything. So we transferred the circuitry into two boards, which still meant we had to take a lot of wood out of the Artist guitars. But something I didn't fully appreciate until later was that guitar players are really conservative folks, and nobody really wanted a Les Paul that did all that. Somebody once said that with one of those Artists you were a flick of a switch away from total disaster."

The Artist hobbled on to 1981, when it was quietly dropped. A happier project was the Les Paul Heritage Series, one of the first conscious attempts to try to make Les Pauls in a way that many people thought was no longer possible at Gibson. Chuck Burge began to build prototypes in 1979, but we'll meet the production models in the next chapter.

"That '59 vibe can't be beat. Bottle it in a brand new guitar, and you'll have lines around the block."

1980s

Slash, Guns N'Roses ›

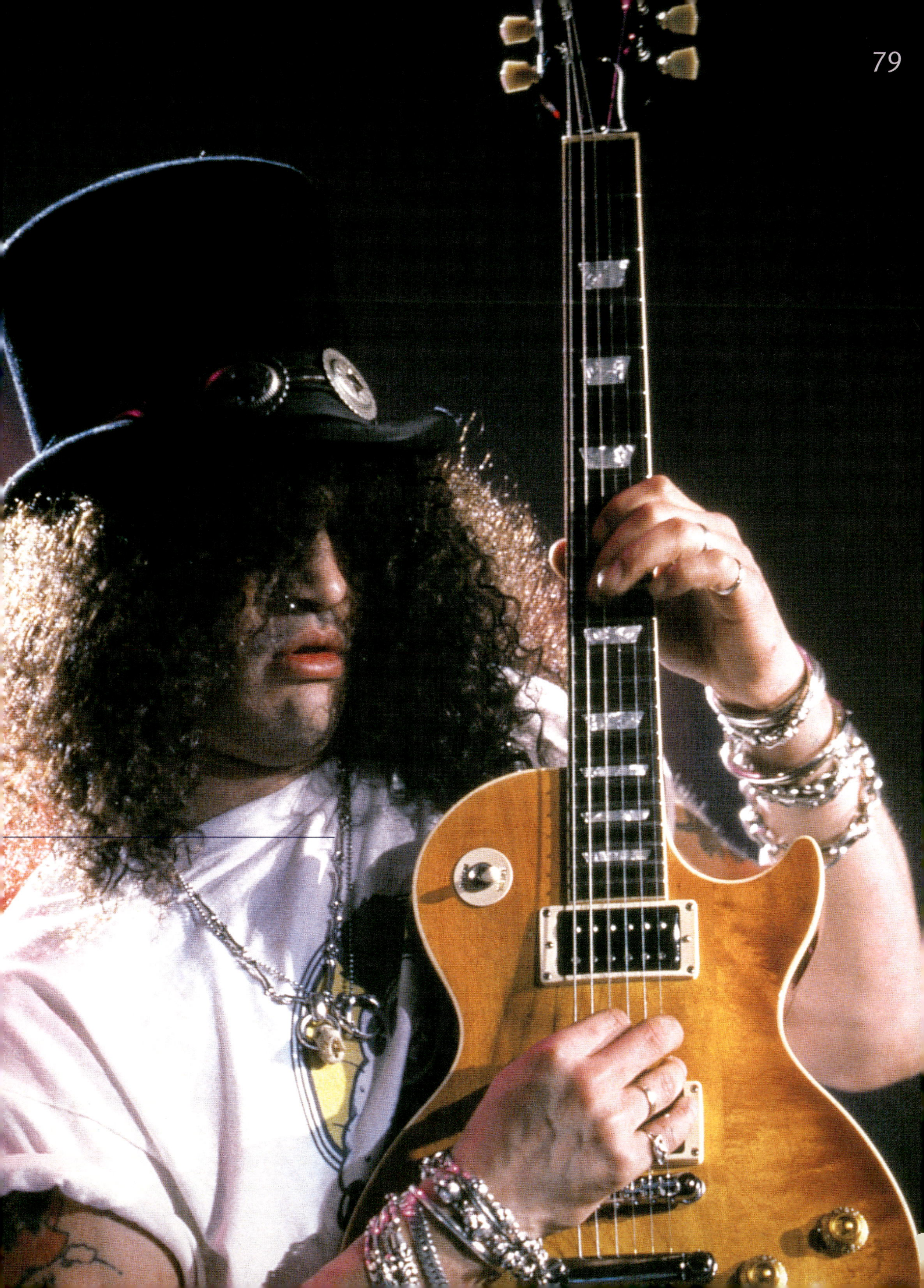

FIFTY YEARS OF THE GIBSON LES PAUL

As we discovered during the last chapter, in the 1970s some US dealers who specialised in older instruments began to order from Gibson's Kalamazoo plant selected Les Pauls with "vintage correct" appointments. Since the onset of Gibson's new Nashville factory in 1975 the original Kalamazoo plant had leaned more heavily toward shorter, specialised runs of guitars. Jim Deurloo, by the early 1980s plant manager at Kalamazoo, remembers dealers such as Leo's of California, Jimmy Wallace of Texas, and Guitar Trader of New Jersey ordering special vintage-style Les Paul Standards. These dealers and their customers were looking for features such as an exact old-style carving shape and a particular neck feel, as well as a number of small visual details – and Kalamazoo provided an approximation.

A typical ad for these dealer specials came in Guitar Trader's May 1982 newsletter. "Guitar Trader and Gibson Guitars announce the ultimate Les Paul reissue," claimed the blurb, alongside a repro of the original Standard entry from Gibson's 1960 catalogue. A list of features followed: "Dimensions as per 1959 model shown; 'painted-on' serial number; original style bridge; two-piece highly figured tops personally selected by our luthiers. These instruments will be produced in strictly limited quantities at the original Gibson factory in Kalamazoo, MI, and represent a special investment value."

Guitar Trader added that if you ordered your "59 Flametop" immediately for summer '82 delivery they would install original 1950s patent-applied-for pickups, subject to availability. The price (with case) was $1500. In the same newsletter, Guitar Trader was happy to offer an original 1959 Standard with "tiger-striped curly maple top" for $7500. By the end of the year Aerosmith's Brad Whitford was pictured taking delivery of his Guitar Trader Flametop. "Hasn't felt this good since '59," he reckoned.

BACK TO THE HERITAGE

Jim Deurloo recalled that dealer specials like the Guitar Trader instruments were selected from the production line at Gibson, but were custom-built to some degree. "It was at a time when we weren't making a vintage looking instrument," he said. "We were making what was in the catalogue at the time, and not the guitar with the washed-out top. I remember that Guitar Trader selected each top, and they were very picky about the colour."

Meanwhile, during 1979 Chuck Burge in R&D had started building prototypes for the new Heritage Series Les Pauls. Tim Shaw remembered, "They were our first stab at asking questions like: What's the best this guitar ever was? Are we building it like that now? And if not, why not? Management didn't want to hear that at first, so we fought tooth and nail to do it." The R&D team used a 1954 pattern sample to provide the carving of the Heritage's body top, and they changed the neck construction to three-piece mahogany. They also disposed of then-current production oddities such as the volute below the back of the headstock, and moved a little closer to older pickup specifications. Pretty figured timber was selected for the tops of these new Heritage Series Les Pauls.

Bruce Bolen, head of R&D by then, managed to persuade Norlin to put the vintage-flavoured Heritages into production – not as standard Les Pauls, however, but rather as separate, premium items, touted as "limited editions" and not included on the company's general pricelist. Launched in 1980, the first two models in the Heritage Series were the Standard 80 and the Standard 80 Elite, the latter with an ebony fingerboard, one-piece neck, and even fancier quilted-figure top. A year later the Standard 80 Award was added, with gold-plated hardware and block fingerboard markers. The various Heritage models lasted in production for just a couple of years.

Whether as a direct result of the influence of the Heritage models or a general awareness of market demands, Gibson began to move away from some of the production quirks it had brought in during the 1970s. For example, the volute was removed, and gradually there was a change back to one-piece mahogany necks. In 1982 Kalamazoo put out the limited-run Les Paul Standard 82, distinguished from the Heritage Standard 80 primarily by its one-piece neck and the fact that it was made in Kalamazoo. The regular July 1980 pricelist showed six basic Les Paul models: Deluxe $799; Standard $849; Pro Deluxe $889; Custom $899; Artisan (a sort of decorated Custom) $1099; and Artist $1299.

According to some of the employees at Gibson, it seems likely that by about 1980 Norlin had decided to sell Gibson. A later report in *The Music Trades* magazine said that by 1981 Norlin Industries had incurred "excessive debt through substantial losses in its music divisions" and that this forced the sale of its profitable technology and beer divisions in 1982. As well as Gibson and Gibson Accessories, Norlin's music divisions included Lowrey organs, Moog synthesisers, and a "Band & Orchestral" division. As an example of Norlin's falling income, Gibson sales fell 30 per cent in 1982 alone, to a total of $19.5million, against a high in 1979 of $35.5million. Of course, Gibson was not alone in this decline. The US guitar market in general had virtually imploded, and most other American makers were suffering in broadly similar ways. Their costs were high, economic circumstances and currency fluctuations were against them, and Japanese competitors increasingly had the edge.

Norlin's overall losses in its music divisions were high, according to a 1982 message to shareholders from chairman Norton Stevens. "The operating loss was $11million before a goodwill write-off of $22.6million," he said. Norlin had "lean music businesses whose break-even has been reduced significantly in the last few years," continued Stevens, putting a brave face on the company's position. He claimed that Norlin's objective was "to put our capital base to work for growing future earnings". By 1984 Stevens was off the Norlin board after a hostile takeover that year by Rooney Pace.

Norlin relocated some of its sales, marketing, administration and finance personnel from Chicago to Nashville around 1980. All the main Gibson production was now handled at the Nashville plant, while Kalamazoo as we've

> By the end of 1982 Aerosmith's Brad Whitford was taking delivery of one of Guitar Trader's special-edition Flametops, a $1500 Standard built to order at Gibson's Kalamazoo plant. "Hasn't felt this good since '59," reckoned Whitford.

BACK TO THE HERITAGE

1980-82 in context

Gibson's first nod to the enduring appeal of its vintage Les Paul guitars comes with the Heritage Standard 80 models.

John Lennon murdered in New York (80).

MTV goes on air (81); the visual in pop is never more important. Ace Frehley leaves Kiss (82) and invests in make-up remover.

Post-It Notes by 3M go on sale (81).

AIDS is named (82) and a year later the cause is discovered: the human immuno-deficiency virus, or HIV.

CD players first sold (82), at first made only by developers Philips and Sony.

◀ Ace Frehley, Kiss, makes up with his Custom

FIFTY YEARS OF THE GIBSON LES PAUL

THE EIGHTIES

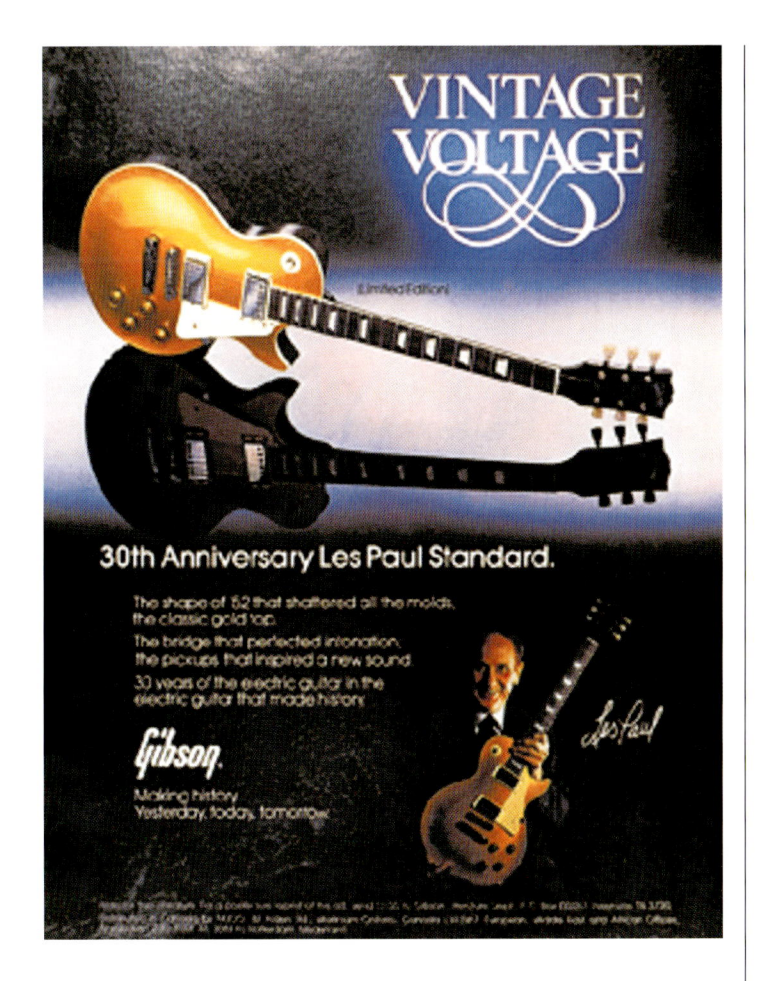

The importance of old Les Paul models among players and collectors was gradually dawning on Gibson as the 1980s got underway. The company had already started to mark birthdays of key models, and continued the publicity in 1982 with the 30-year-old gold-top (ad, left), even if the Anniversary model itself centred on the more desirable '57-style instrument with humbuckers. More significant was the Heritage Standard Series of 1980 (main guitar). Some of the constructional oddities of the 1970s were disposed of, and the vibe if not the fine detail pointed to the revered '58-60 Standard. But clearly this is where Gibson's modern programme of reissue Les Paul models begins.

Evidence of a less focused Gibson operation came with the Spotlight Special of 1983 (below), an odd limited run designed to use up some bits and pieces lying around the factory – including a central walnut block and some spectacular pieces of figured maple for the outer body parts.

▾ 1980 Heritage Standard 80

▾ 1983 Spotlight Special

FIFTY YEARS OF THE GIBSON LES PAUL

seen had become a specialist factory making custom orders, banjos and mandolins. Plant manager Jim Deurloo told André Duchossoir in 1982: "The plant is now mainly manufacturing specific models that we call custom shop editions, built in small runs of 25 to 100, sometimes more. Kalamazoo is more of a giant custom-job shop, and we are proud of our heritage and workmanship."

CLOSING KALAMAZOO

In July 1983 Gibson president Marty Locke informed Jim Deurloo that the Kalamazoo plant would close. The last production at Kalamazoo was in June 1984, and the plant closed three months later, after more than 65 years of worthy service since the original building had been erected by Gibson. It was an emotional time for the managers and workers, many of whom had worked in the plant for a considerable time.

One employee said that people there knew the closure was inevitable. "You added it all up, and the Kalamazoo factory was falling apart, a very old building, steeped so heavily in tradition and history. The Nashville plant was brand new, in 17 acres, a very beautiful facility. What it boils down to is that the business could not support the two facilities, and there was really only one choice." This same observer noted too that the business would, of course, now be easier to sell with just the Nashville plant and its more amenable labour relations and lower costs.

Tim Shaw also recalled those last years. "Jim Deurloo, to his great credit, had fought a hard battle to keep Kalamazoo open, and he lost," said Shaw. "But when the announcement came down, he got the entire factory together and said look, they've made the decision to close this place. You people have been with the company for a long time, he said, and I'm very sorry that it's worked out this way. But you're all professionals, you've worked here a long time, you have a heritage to be proud of, and as we downsize and as we close I want you to remain professionals. Basically, Deurloo told them to go out there and smile. And I think to a large part, they did. But it hurt every time you looked around on a Friday and 30 to 60 people would disappear. I think Deurloo did all that was humanly possible in terms of keeping morale up and trying to set a tone in a very professional framework."

Some of the key people were offered positions at Nashville. But Deurloo, together with Marv Lamb, who'd been with Gibson since 1956, and J P Moats, a Gibson employee of equally long standing, decided to leave. They rented part of the Kalamazoo plant and started the Heritage guitar company in April 1985. They continue that business today, with a line of 27 models. As Marv Lamb puts it, "We all grew up building guitars and we didn't know too different. We could have searched for another job, but we wanted to do what we know how to do best."

Although the emphasis at the Nashville plant was on large runs of a small number of individual Gibson models, this had to change gradually as it adjusted to its new role as the company's sole factory. A good if unusual example came along in 1983 when Nashville produced the $1299 Spotlight Special, a limited run designed to use up various components. It was exactly the kind of job that Kalamazoo would normally have done. Walnut had been left over from production of two discontinued models – The Paul and The SG – and a number of narrow pieces of curly maple were picked out from some unused timber stock. Nashville managers combined these elements and adapted some headstock veneers and dark binding from a Chet Atkins model. The resulting concoction was the Les Paul Spotlight Special, its body displaying a distinctive centre stripe of walnut between two maple "wings" through an antique natural or antique sunburst finish. In fact, this 1983 model seems to mark the start of an official Custom Shop at Nashville. It carries a Custom Shop logo on the rear of the headstock, and an edition number showing "83" for the date plus a three-digit serial. Records indicate that a little over 200 were made.

AT LAST, THE NEW OLD REISSUE
Also in 1983, Gibson finally produced an official early-style Standard and gold-top. The company was now well aware of the continuing demand up at the monied end of the market for vintage Les Pauls. The Heritage Series had turned out to be only a half-hearted attempt at a proper reincarnation of the most celebrated old Les Pauls. The new Les Paul Reissue Outfits were the next steps – backward and forward at the same time. They came in Curly Maple Top or Gold Top, and when they appeared on pricelists in 1985 were priced at $1599 and $1299 respectively. Regular production models retailed for $999. There was some way to go before detail-conscious customers would be happy with the Reissue models, but Gibson had at least made a start.

Another new model for 1983 that would have a long and important life in the Les Paul line was the Studio. Gibson decided it needed a cheaper Les Paul and, as one person involved in the design puts it, "We stripped off the gingerbread." Primarily this meant no binding on the body or fingerboard, giving the instrument a basic, straightforward look. Bruce Bolen remembered an unsuccessful meeting to try to come up with a name for the model, which he had to leave to visit a recording studio. "A little lightbulb came on in my head, and I thought let's call it the Studio. What could be more closely associated with Les than a studio?" By the mid 1980s Bolen had become vice president of marketing and R&D at Gibson. He left the company in 1986, after 19 years' sterling service.

The Les Paul Studio first appeared on a 1983 pricelist at $699, which made it $300 cheaper than any other carved-top Les Paul at the time. Still in the line today, the Studio would go through several changes after its launch. It started with a body of normal size but, unusually for Gibson, the timber was alder. However, aesthetic problems associated with the type of lacquer used prompted a quick change to Gibson's established maple/mahogany combination. This new body was around an eighth of an inch thinner than other Les Pauls, which led to a reduction in production costs and weight.

Around 1986 some Studios began to appear with ebony rather than rosewood fingerboards – which, on the face of it, seemed a luxurious feature for such a relatively cheap guitar, though lower-grade ebony was used (as well as rosewood, depending on availability). The earlier Studios also have dot fingerboard markers, generally reserved for Gibson's cheaper models, but around 1990 the fancier "crown" type was adopted, a marketing decision to give the guitar a little more visual appeal. A version with bound neck and body, the Studio

ISSUING THE REISSUES

1983-87 in context

Gibson try to revive past Les Paul glories with a reissue gold-top and Standard (83).

Space battle scenes in *Last Starfighter* movie (84) created entirely on computer.

Michael J Fox returns to 1955 in *Back To The Future* movie (85); inexplicably does not stuff the DeLorean with Les Pauls.

Challenger space shuttle explodes (85).

ZZ Top meld crunching Les Pauls, slabs of pop, sharp dressed beards, and synth grooves for classic *Eliminator* album (83).

Prozac anti-depressant first licensed (87).

◀ Billy Gibbons, ZZ Top, at the Pearly Gates again

FIFTY YEARS OF THE GIBSON LES PAUL

THE EIGHTIES

1990 SG/Les Paul Custom

1987 Standard Reissue

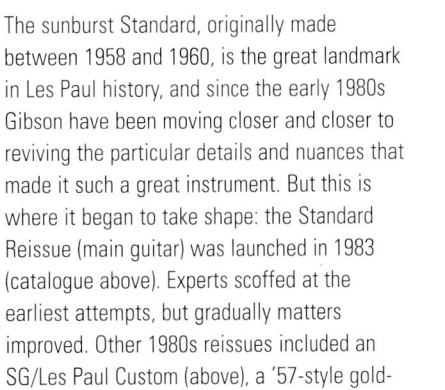

The sunburst Standard, originally made between 1958 and 1960, is the great landmark in Les Paul history, and since the early 1980s Gibson have been moving closer and closer to reviving the particular details and nuances that made it such a great instrument. But this is where it began to take shape: the Standard Reissue (main guitar) was launched in 1983 (catalogue above). Experts scoffed at the earliest attempts, but gradually matters improved. Other 1980s reissues included an SG/Les Paul Custom (above), a '57-style gold-top, and various Juniors and Specials.

FIFTY YEARS OF THE GIBSON LES PAUL

Standard, came along for a couple of years from 1984, while a similarly shortlived variant was the Studio Custom with gold-plated hardware.

Alert readers may recall that Norlin had put Gibson up for sale around 1980. By summer 1985 a buyer had finally been found, and in January 1986 Henry Juszkiewicz, David Berryman and Gary Zebrowski completed their purchase of the entire Gibson operation. They paid an undisclosed sum, now generally considered to be about $5million. By this time Norlin's main business was in printing. Gibson was the last part of its once-large musical empire to be sold off.

Juszkiewicz, Berryman and Zebrowski had met while studying at the Harvard Business School in the late 1970s, since when Juszkiewicz had been in engineering and investment banking, Berryman in accountancy, and Zebrowski in marketing. Also, crucially, Juszkiewicz was an enthusiastic guitarist who loved Gibson instruments: "He's a fan," as one Gibson employee put it. The three had gone into business together, teaming up in 1981 to turn a failing Oklahoma electronics company into a successful operation. When they bought Gibson in 1986 Juszkiewicz became president and Berryman vice-president of finance and accounting, while Zebrowski continued to run their electronics business. The most immediate effect of the new ownership was that a lot of people were fired, including the plant manager, the quality control manager, and many others. One could hardly expect this to have been a popular first move. "It was pretty scary," admitted one insider. "But Henry got what he was after. If you judge it on results, he brought the company back from the dead."

Juszkiewicz explained to a reporter early in 1986 that he was, as he described it, in the process of "restructuring Gibson's production operation". He said that the new Gibson set-up would be extremely aggressive in developing and introducing new products, and insisted that they would be more creative in merchandising and marketing than Gibson had ever been, with a more competitive pricing policy.

"It turned out well," Juszkiewicz said later. "But I pretty much knew that it would be two years of sheer hell." As far as the ever-popular Les Paul models were concerned, Juszkiewicz said that he inherited a poor relationship between Gibson and Les Paul himself. "Les obviously had a proprietary interest in the success of his guitars, and they'd killed them, so he was pretty annoyed. Les lives in New Jersey, and [New Jersey-based maker] Kramer were constantly seeing him. He even did an MTV video saying how nice Kramer guitars were. So I established a rapport with Les early on, and that seemed to solve the problem. I listened to what he had to say. He wanted to see a lower-cost Les Paul instrument in our imported Epiphone line, for example, and we ended up doing that a few years into the business."

There were several changes to the roles of some key guitar-design people around the time of the change of ownership. Tim Shaw moved from the Custom

> **Heavy Les Pauls? One mahogany block might weigh five times that of an identically sized piece, depending on the minerals drawn into the wood as it grows.**

Shop and R&D to an international role for the company, travelling often to Korea to help expand Gibson's Epiphone lines. He would leave Gibson in 1992, after 14 years' service with the company. J T Riboloff joined Gibson in 1987, moving to Nashville from his home in California where he had operated as a guitar maker, repairer and restorer. He was hired for the Custom Shop, and soon became involved in work on new designs.

OLD LADIES DON'T MEASURE UP
The new Reissue models, effectively an attempt to recreate more accurately the old-style Standard and gold-top, had been in production since 1983, driven by the persistent demands of customers seeking perfect duplication of the hallowed 1950s instruments. "When I went to Gibson in '87 the Les Paul Reissue was basically a Standard with a flame top," said Riboloff. "Slowly but surely they let us get away with a little more." One of the many problems associated with Gibson's Reissue programme – and there will be much more to come on this subject in the following 1990s chapter – has always been to determine exactly which details to duplicate. Simply put, there is no such thing as a definitive 1958-60 Standard.

Tim Shaw calls to mind the infamous Gibson "old ladies" who did much of the hand-work in the factory at the time of those praised models. "They used to hand-sand the old ones a little bit differently every time," he said. "It used to tickle the hell out of me with all these people saying oh, the placement of the Gibson logo has to be *right here*, and the Les Paul Model logo *exactly there*. And I'd say well, those women who put the decals on – you think they measured? No, they didn't!" Shaw went on to ask himself an obviously unanswerable question. "What's the correct specifications of an early Les Paul?" He laughed, concluding with another question. "Who knows?" Who indeed.

One aspect of Les Pauls that leaves less room for argument than vintage details is their weight. Some are, without doubt, heavier than others, but generally speaking a Les Paul is a heavy guitar, and examples from the late 1970s and early 1980s include some of the heaviest. Gibson was determined to do something about this. The weight is due principally to the relative density of available mahogany.

Riboloff outlines the real extremes. "You can have two pieces of mahogany the same size," he said, "and one might weigh five pounds, the other 25 pounds. The difference is due to the amount of minerals drawn into the wood as it grows, especially silica. Of course we didn't use that extremely heavy stuff. That became fixtures. It's very useful for little wooden mallets," he laughed.

The new owners of Gibson had inherited an earlier attempt to cut down the weight of the mahogany. Since about 1982 Nashville had drilled a series of small pockets into the mahogany section of Les Paul bodies, uncharitably called the "Swiss cheese" effect by some observers. Of course, once the maple top was in place those holes were invisible, except perhaps to touring musicians with a keen interest in airport X-ray systems. "I don't think it made a bit of difference to the sound," said Tim Shaw concerning the Swiss cheese. "The holes were too small to act as resonant cavities." Gibson's new president, Henry Juszkiewicz, also considered the drilled bodies irrelevant to the guitar's sound. "It didn't make any

ANNIVERSARY FRETS

1988-89 in context

Gibson addresses backache problem of Les Paul players with the Studio Lite (88).

Billboard magazine starts rap chart (89).

Scriptel offer a system (88) for inputting data to computer by writing on its screen

The Pixies make a dark, harsh, menacing classic, the *Surfer Rosa* album (88).

New presidents: Bush Senior elected in US (88); Gorbachev in Soviet Union (89).

Berlin Wall falls; in China, 5000 die and many are arrested as students in Beijing demand political reform (89).

Joey Santiago of The Pixies, with black Paul ▶

▼ 1989 35th Anniversary

The more expensive model from the original line of Les Pauls, the black Custom, had been largely overlooked by Gibson in their 1980s reissues, apart from an early attempt as the Black Beauty 82. But the 35th Anniversary Les Paul of 1989 (above) recalled the Custom's birth in '54 – even if the model itself was based on the three-humbucker '57-style Custom.

FIFTY YEARS OF THE GIBSON LES PAUL

THE EIGHTIES

◀ 1992 Studio Lite

Steve Clark (below) played his last show with Def Leppard in late 1988 at the close of a mammoth 14-month world tour. His Les Paul-fuelled work had brought the band from early UK successes to international fame with the superb Pyromania album of 1983. But early in 1991 Clark was found dead, at the age of just 30. The '87 catalogue (above) shows the continuing Standard Reissue.

Meanwhile, over at the Gibson factory in Nashville, designers had been trying to find a way of reducing the sometimes oppresive weight of Les Paul models. The Studio Lite model offered some relief. At first it had a Fender-styled contouring to the back of the body to lighten the load, while the later version shown (left) has balsa wood inserts to reduce the weight of the body.

FIFTY YEARS OF THE GIBSON LES PAUL

difference to the tonal characteristics of the model," he said. "The critical part of the body to the sound is the bridge area. If you do something up where the toggle switch is, say, it won't make any difference to the sound. The maple top is solid, of course, and a lot of the tonal characteristics come from that. So we were making a better guitar: it was more comfortable, and still sounded good."

Another attempt to deal with the Les Paul weight problem came in the form of a new model called the Custom Lite, introduced in 1987. It had a contoured back that was pure Fender in style. The timber lost in this sculpting cut the weight and made the guitar more comfortable. At first it was priced higher than the normal Custom, presumably as a result of extra production costs – in 1987 the basic models were pitched at $1170 for the Custom and $1249 for the Custom Lite – but was gone from the line by 1989. A year earlier Gibson introduced a similarly contoured version of its Les Paul Studio model, the Studio Lite, with an '88 list showing the Studio at $909 and the Studio Lite at $974.

> As the shredders lined up for their superstrats, Guns N'Roses redefined hard rock, with Slash out front unleashing his blues-laden licks on a Gibson Les Paul.

WHERE HAVE ALL THE LES PAULS GONE?

Changes in fashion among guitar-players and guitar-makers had not been kind to Gibson during the 1980s. Some of the key musicians who had been allied closely to the original Les Paul had moved on to other models. At a charity benefit show in London in 1983 Jeff Beck, Eric Clapton and Jimmy Page played together on stage. Beck was seen playing Fender Stratocasters. Clapton too played a Strat, and for one song he strapped on a lovely Gibson Firebird. Page mainly played a Fender Telecaster, although he did use his Les Paul Standard briefly. Beck and Clapton would go on to work with Fender and produce signature models a few years later.

The new guitar-making trends of the 1980s were moving away from the Les Paul style of solidbody. There were also loads of odd-shaped axes about, and some mad, brief fads for "headless" guitars, as well as misguided attempts at synthesiser hook-ups. Fender's Stratocaster was the flavour of the decade, and an offshoot, the so-called superstrat, attracted many of the high-octane players who might otherwise have seemed potential naturals for a Gibson Les Paul.

The superstrat was largely developed by US maker Jackson from the Stratocaster. It offered more frets, deeper cutaways, a drooped pointy-shape headstock, altered pickup layouts, a high-performance vibrato system, and bright graphic finishes. In many ways it was the antithesis of a Les Paul Standard, and it came to define the mainstream rock guitar of the 1980s.

Jackson and the related Charvel brand attracted important 1980s players, not least the highly talented Eddie Van Halen. But Ibanez too had a highly visible line of superstrats, especially the RG series, and did much to popularise the style. Key 1980s guitar heroes Steve Vai and Joe Satriani opted for Ibanez models and helped to design new instruments.

In a 1989 interview, Satriani summed up the way many players and makers were trying to synthesise the best of several instrument styles into a new kind of

THE EIGHTIES LES PAUL

guitar. "I've tried to get the ultimate Strat sound and the ultimate Les Paul sound from one guitar," said Satriani, "but it's like a jinx."

Of course, some players kept the faith. You would hardly expect such a passionate Les Paul fan as Joe Walsh, for example, to switch allegiance. He'd joined The Eagles in '76 until they disbanded in the early 1980s. In 1988, Walsh still defined his all-time favourite guitar set-up as a vintage Les Paul through a pair of Fender Super Reverb amps. "I'm partial to a '59 or a '60," he told *Guitar Player*. "It depends … '58s are fun too. Les Pauls just really make it for me. I do also love Strats and Teles, though."

When Gibson stumbled on old hand Gary Richrath of REO Speedwagon, who still relied on an enviable collection of old Les Pauls, they got him to endorse the company's attempt to jump on the superstrat bandwagon, the US-1 model. The resulting 1987 ad displayed Richrath among his vintage collection of seven Standards, a gold-top and two Customs, but holding the incongruous looking US-1. Gibson was experiencing a problem that has never been too far from the company's door ever since. Players want Gibson to be traditional, to make good versions of what they'd always made. But if the company tries to innovate or to run with new trends, well, that's just un-Gibson, and not to be tolerated. The US-1 did not last long in the Gibson catalogue.

SLASH THE SAVIOUR

Among all the new shred players lining up for their new superstrats, along came Guns N'Roses to redefine hard rock – and, no doubt to Gibson's delight, guitarist Slash used mostly Les Pauls on which to unleash his aggressive blues-laden licks. He'd been influenced to take up Les Pauls by Jimmy Page and Joe Perry. As Guns N'Roses began to sell millions of albums, Slash assembled a fine collection of guitars, including vintage Les Pauls. But the guitar he was most often seen with on stage was a regular 1980s Standard.

Gibson tried to entice Slash to have special models built and to endorse a signature model. "They offered to make me a Les Paul model to my specs, and that included a thinner, low-profile neck with bigger frets," he said in *The Guitar Magazine*. "But I wasn't happy with the sound. In 1989 they approached me to do a Slash model which included gold hardware and a heavy bookmatched flametop with translucent colours. They were going to be marketed, and ideally I would use them on stage, but again I wasn't happy with the sound." Gibson would eventually produce a small run of Slash Les Pauls in 1997, with an Epiphone-brand version following shortly afterward.

As a difficult decade for Gibson drew to a close, a June 1989 pricelist showed eight basic Les Paul models: Junior $913; "Junior II" (actually a Special) $913; Studio $1089; Studio Lite $1154; Standard $1263; Custom $1586; Custom Lite $1569; gold-top Reissue $1879; and Standard Reissue $2779.

"Call it grunge, rock, punk, whatever – good music is good music. But a great guitar is sex."

1990s

Stone Gossard, Pearl Jam ▸

95

We've already noted several times that Les Pauls are not the lightest guitars in the world, and how Gibson has tried various remedies to make them lighter. For a while in the 1990s an apparently unlikely wood provided a solution for one model. Matthew Klein had joined Gibson's small Custom team in 1986, bringing with him some intriguing experience of balsa wood. He'd built for his own amusement a balsa-body Les Paul, discovering that it sustained well and sounded fine unplugged. Balsa has good resonating qualities and, despite a popular misconception, is certainly not cheap. And at about four pounds, Klein's Les Paul was a lot lighter than some Gibsons that were clocking in at up to 11 pounds thanks to the increasing density of available mahogany.

News of Klein's balsa experiments reached Billy Gibbons of ZZ Top, who promptly ordered from him four white Explorer-shape balsa instruments (two guitars, two basses) for the group's 1985 *Afterburner* world tour. Klein skinned them with thin spruce to help hold screws and prevent paint cracks. "It was like a spruce and balsa sandwich, the filling being the balsa," he said. The guitars worked well on-stage, playing and sounding good – and were virtually half the weight of regular models. Klein supplied ZZ Top with further balsa guitars – this time Super 400-style with Firebird headstocks – for their *Recycler* tour. Then Klein joined Gibson, and with his Custom colleagues Mike Voltz and Phil Jones began considering the application of balsa to Gibson models.

BALSA, SUPERSTRATS, AND BASSES
The first result from the new Gibson team was the maple-skinned-balsa US-1 superstrat-style guitar of 1986, but this turned out to be too difficult to produce and was dropped by 1991. Balsa was then used in the body wood mix of the Chet Atkins SST model, launched in 1987, and three years later was applied to the Les Paul's weight problem. The existing Les Paul Studio Lite was modified to incorporate balsa inserts. Gibson renamed balsa as chromite, derived from the first word of its Latin names, ochroma pyramidale and ochroma lagopus. The new balsa-enhanced Studio Lite of 1990 was given a normal flat back and a slimmer neck compared to its previous incarnation, and lost a couple of pounds in weight. A roughly D-shaped cut-out in the guitar body left the bridge and tailpiece connected to the back, with the space around filled by balsa, which Gibson bought cut to the required dimensions. The model lasted until 1998 – and the balsa experiment was gone from the Les Paul line.

Another attempt at producing a lighter Les Paul came along in 1995 when a model with hollowed "tone chambers" inside was introduced, the Bantam Elite. The chambers were reminiscent of the sort of thing used in Guild's Nightbird of the late 1980s, or even Gretsch's semi-solid Jet models of the 1950s. Washburn soon objected to the use of the Bantam name, which it already used for a guitar, so it was quickly renamed the Florentine Standard or Florentine Plus, the "Plus" as usual indicating a fancier figured top. The Florentines too were gone by 1998, but Gibson did adopt a hollow-body Les Paul for its lower-cost Epiphone brand – the Custom-style Elite in 1996, and the Standard-like ES a few years later.

With the double-cutaway solidbody MIII model of 1991, Gibson launched a radically styled guitar with circuitry more flexible than normal. J T Riboloff in the

Custom Shop had come up with the original MIII idea, and at first planned a two-pickup guitar. Management pointed to the popularity of the superstrat's humbucker/single-coil/humbucker arrangement, and the MIII dutifully appeared in this three-pickup form. "My intention was to get every selection of the Stratocaster and every selection of the Les Paul from a five-way switch," said Riboloff of his ambitious idea. Unfortunately, Gibson's customers felt the design and the electronics of the MIII guitar were too "un-Gibson" and did not rush to buy the instrument.

So it was that the wiring was adapted into two Les Paul models, the Classic/MIII (1991) and the Studio Lite/MIII (1992), in a move reminiscent of the marriage of RD circuitry and Les Paul Artist ten years earlier. Riboloff feels that the Studio Lite was better suited to the MIII sound, the tone of the lightweight body sitting well with the expanded sonic possibilities of the circuitry. The Classic/MIII was dropped in 1992; the Studio Lite/MIII lasted a further two years. The original M-III guitars (and the later Steinberger trem-equipped M-IVs) had all gone from the Gibson catalogue by 1997.

A fashion among some bass players for 1950s-styled instruments prompted Gibson to add three Les Paul basses to the catalogue in the early 1990s: the Deluxe Plus Bass (1991), the Special Bass (1991) and the Standard Bass (1992). They were designed primarily by Gibson's Phil Jones, and were the first bass guitars to carry the Les Paul name since the Triumph Bass and Signature Bass of the 1970s. The new basses came in a variety of finishes and hardware styles, and in 1993 several five-string versions were added, with active circuitry and a re-styled headstock absorbed into the designs. The models were gone from the line by 1995, although the Standard Bass was reintroduced during 1999.

REISSUES: THE STORY SO FAR
Gibson's first official Custom Shop had started in the 1960s at Kalamazoo, building one-offs to customers' requirements, although non-standard orders had been taken since the company's earliest days. The idea was revived in the 1980s at Nashville, with a small Custom area within the main plant from about 1983. The present Custom Shop started in a separate building nearby in 1993, continuing the traditional role of making custom orders and developing R&D ideas, as well as fulfilling special dealer orders and contributing its own upscale models to the line. It comes under the auspices of the Custom/Art/Historic division that caters for one-offs, individual "art" guitars, and top-of-the-line reissues. At the time of writing, around 80 people work in the Custom Shop.

The idea of reissuing classic models is hardly a new one for the Gibson Les Paul line. We've already met several examples in this book, not least the company's reaction to the new popularity of the old Les Paul design in the 1960s and the reissue of two models in 1968. We also learned how more reissues followed sporadically in the 1970s, reproducing the spirit if not the precise detail of the originals.

A number of US dealers then began to custom-order limited runs, because it was clear to them that there was a gap between the "correct" vintage vibe that some of their customers wanted from a Les Paul and the kind of thing that

UNACCUSTOMED

1990-91 in context

Gibson go Les-Paul-reissue crazy: gold-tops, Customs, Standards ... and a Classic.

Soviet Union dissolved; republics form Commonwealth of Independent States (91).

Gulf War erupts as Iraq invades Kuwait.

Gary Moore turns it up a notch with blistering *Still Got The Blues* album (90). Stevie Ray Vaughan killed, aged just 35.

World Wide Web is new system devised to link Internet sites (90).

New South African president releases Nelson Mandela from prison (90), and parliament repeals apartheid laws (91).

◀ Gary Moore: still with the Les Paul blues

▲ 1991 Custom Plus

FIFTY YEARS OF THE GIBSON LES PAUL

THE NINETIES

◀ 1991 Deluxe Plus Bass

1992 40th Anniversary ▶

More anniversaries, more reissues, new basses ... Gibson was decidedly busy in the Les Paul department as the new decade got underway, and seemed poised to make sense of all it had learned in the 1980s. The Deluxe Plus Bass (far left) was one of three levels of the new Les Paul four-stringers, and the first such models since the Signature Bass was dropped at the end of the 1970s. The odd 40th Anniversary (near left) was a "black gold-top" with gold-plated hardware that baffled anyone searching for its historical basis. Gibson also began to offer some Les Paul models with varying grades of figured tops, tagging them as Plus or Double Plus according to quality. So it was that guitar fans lined up for the unusual sight of a figured-top Custom, like the Custom Plus pictured here (main guitar). Reissues continued, with a moody shot in the 1991 catalogue (below) of a figured Standard.

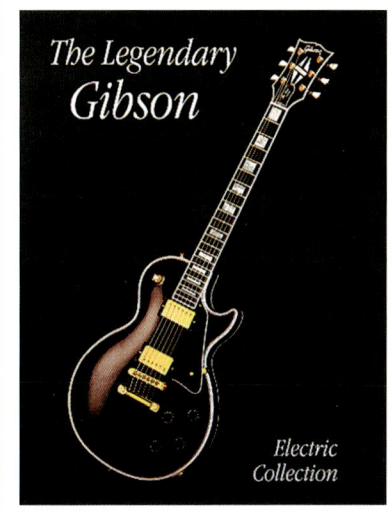

FIFTY YEARS OF THE GIBSON LES PAUL

Gibson were pulling off the production line at the time. They wanted the "correct" narrower headstock, the "correct" thin binding in the cutaway, the "correct" shape of top carve, plus a host of other tiny details. In fact, they wanted a Standard exactly like Gibson used to make – and until 1976 Gibson didn't even have a Standard officially on its list.

As we've seen, the first serious attempt by Gibson at any kind of accuracy in reproducing an old-style Les Paul came with the Heritage Standard models of 1980 – which were good for the time, but still not startling. More dealers became aware of the demand from a particular clientele for the right look – aside from any considerations of playability – and began ordering further small runs of better-spec Standards from Gibson. At last, in 1983, the company reacted and produced the first official Gibson Les Paul Reissues, as you will have read in the 1980s chapter.

> "We had to retrieve all the old Les Paul features. It was as if they'd been scattered across the Gibson plant floor, and were still here ... somewhere."

Since then, the company's efforts have gradually widened and improved, concentrating on the principal 1950s classics: the Standards, the gold-tops, the Customs and, to a lesser extent, the Juniors and Specials. Of these, it's the sunburst 1958-60 Standard that has generated the most activity. That's no great surprise. After all, this hallowed model pulls increasingly remarkable amounts of money among guitar collectors, and is rightly considered by guitarists as one of the prime benchmarks of the great solidbody electric instrument. With today's prices for a fine original around $25,000 and often a good deal upward, a small but lucrative market has developed for ever-more-accurate Gibson repros at a (relatively) more affordable rate.

Tom Murphy became an important person within the team that developed the Reissues. He'd been at Gibson since 1989, and a few years later moved from the finish repair department to the Custom area. As a player, he'd been attracted by several of Gibson's attempts to recapture the holy grail over the years. "I'd had two of the reissues made for Texas dealer Jimmy Wallace, for example," Murphy recalled, "and I would fantasise that I was getting a really good copy of an old Les Paul. But I'd soon get disenchanted and wonder why I thought they were going to be anything close to the original. They never cut it! Without having any vast knowledge of construction, I found that something just wasn't right with the overall feel. I wished someone at Gibson who knew would fix it. Don't they have any old Les Pauls they can look at? Then I thought, well, I guess mother nature never intended for us to have those guitars again. Now, I don't know why I thought it was that complicated." Once at Gibson, Murphy began to appreciate the practical considerations necessary to produce a good, acceptable reissue.

J T Riboloff in the Custom Shop had found that a lot of players who asked him to build special one-off Les Pauls were requesting the slimmer-profile neck associated with the 1960 Standard. Gibson boss Henry Juszkiewicz noted the interest caused when an example was shown at a NAMM show and told Riboloff to start work on a production version. This duly appeared in 1990, and the guitar was called the Les Paul Classic. "One of my main things," said Riboloff, "was to try to get the stock instrument to be just as cool as the custom ones. That's really how the Les Paul Classic came about."

Juszkiewicz had decided that the Classic needed to stand out from the rest of the line, and so insisted on a 1960 logo imprinted on the guitar's pickguard, emphasising the inspiration for its slim neck and "correct" size headstock. Riboloff's original intention had been to make the Classic with a rather plain top and faded finish, resembling some of the less visually spectacular Standards that players like Jimmy Page would still occasionally take on stage. Later variants with more extreme figured tops were added, such as the Classic Premium Plus.

But among all this retrospection, the sound of the Classic was definitely modern, thanks to some very powerful coverless humbuckers. A year later, in 1991, the Standard Reissue was revised and split into two models, effectively the Standard 59 Flametop Reissue and the Standard 60 Flametop Reissue. This is where the proper, modern Reissue starts. These models adopted the "correct" details of the Classic, as well as more traditional-sounding humbuckers, as developed by Riboloff.

REJIGGING THE REISSUES

Juszkiewicz and his colleagues had owned Gibson now for several years. There was a new awareness of the company's historical importance and that some old achievements were still highly valued by many players and collectors. Beginning in 1991, Riboloff worked on some commendable reissues of Gibson's revered oddball 1950s classics, the Flying V and the Explorer, as part of the company's Historic programme.

The accuracy of Riboloff's work set Murphy thinking that perhaps the same thing really could be done with the Les Paul models. "It was like; when are we going to admit it and totally re-do the reissue Les Paul?" recalled Murphy. As it turned out, it wouldn't be too long. He pointed to the significant arrival of a marketing manager who actually owned a 1960 Standard and, for once, understood the arguments. "He spoke the language," explained Murphy, evidently in awe of such an achievement among marketing folk. Murphy was invited to plant-management meetings, and presented a list of around 25 important changes that should be made to the Reissue.

Gibson people set to work in an attempt to replicate more closely than ever the magic of an original sunburst Standard. Management supported the costly experiments. The "new" Reissue would have more accurate body carving, the smaller-size vintage-style headstock, a re-tooled fat neck profile, holly veneer for the headstock face with a silkscreened logo, the most attractive figured maple for the top, a slight reduction in neck pitch, proper routing of the control cavity, an early-style Tune-o-matic bridge, and the reinstatement of a longer, wider neck tenon or "tongue" at the neck/body joint. "It was a matter of retrieving all those things," said Murphy. "It was almost as if they'd been thrown out and scattered across the plant floor, swept under a table. They were here … somewhere. I won't take credit for designing the 59 Les Paul," Murphy smiled. "That was done when I was nine years old. But I will take credit in unearthing and finding some of these old key things."

HISTORIC IMAGE

1992-95 in context

Gibson launches the Historic series (92) and improves the Standard reissues (93).

Fighting escalates in Bosnia and Croatia (95) and NATO planes bomb Bosnian Serb targets. Ceasefire declared in October.

Bill Murray repeats *Groundhog Day* (93).

Neil Young builds on the grunge cred of his 1990 album *Ragged Glory* by inviting Pearl Jam to back him on *Mirror Ball* (95).

Ceasefire called in Northern Ireland (94) by main Republican and Protestant groups.

Mosaic is first software to put World Wide Web in easy reach of computer users (93).

◀ Neil Young: godfather of grunge; Les Paul man

▲ 1993 Standard 59 Flametop Reissue

FIFTY YEARS OF THE GIBSON LES PAUL

THE NINETIES

◀ 1999 Classic Plus

1993 Studio Lite / MIII ▶

Some lessons were apparently hard to learn. Whenever Gibson had in the past tried to sell a Les Paul with new, complex controls, the model had failed to win affection. But that didn't stop the company trying again in the early 1990s with the MIII models. There were Classic and Studio Lite (far right) variants, each with a humbucker/single-coil/humbucker pickup layout and a five-way switch designed to give a variety of tones. Players said no thanks, we prefer simplicity. Both models had gone from the line by 1994.

The single Standard reissue model had split into two in 1991 – the Standard 59 Flametop Reissue, and the Standard 58 Figuredtop Reissue. Two years later Gibson formalised its plans for marketing the past by launching the Historic Collection, sharpening the accuracy of its reissues. The revered 59 Reissue was a major focus for these efforts, and pictured here (main guitar) is the instrument used in the publicity poster, appropriately signed by Gibson staff (top).

FIFTY YEARS OF THE GIBSON LES PAUL

Matthew Klein in the Custom Shop helped to establish the new shape for the revised Reissue's body carving – the "form" as it's known – by measuring every hundred-thousandth of an inch of the carving on some original Standards in order to construct a grid from which the production form was developed. Riboloff reckons he examined maybe 25 different Standards from the 1958-60 era. "They were all different," he laughed, pointing by way of example to the fact that no two headstocks were anything like the same. "The machine heads would be slightly further north or south, the scroll was shorter, and the logo would be different," he said, exasperated. "They were soft-tooled back then, and so every one is different. Really, there is no super-correct one to reissue. So with these 25 to hand, we took the best attributes of each instrument – cosmetics, carving and all – and combined them."

YOUR CHOICE: FLAMETOP, FIGUREDTOP OR PLAINTOP?

Edwin Wilson in the Custom Shop offered further insight into Reissue lore. "We have never claimed that the Reissue was issued as a replica," he said. "What we have continually said is that it is a work in process." He observed how some Reissue customers become obsessed with particular details, but stressed that from a production point of view Gibson have to consider the instrument as a whole. Take neck pitch as an example. There is much debate about the exact number of degrees that this should be. And yet it is another of those variables that differs among original Standards. There is no such thing as the "correct" measurement. "Since 1992 we have blueprinted numerous Les Pauls from 1952 to 1960," said Wilson, "and as with all handmade instruments there are variations from instrument to instrument. But the one thing that we have confirmed is that the neck pitch on 1959 and 1960 Standards ranges from four degrees to five-and-a-half degrees, with four being the majority."

Riboloff said the escalating retail price of the Reissue was another factor in concentrating their efforts. "It got to the point where we wanted it to be more of a replica rather a reissue," he suggests. Keith Medley in R&D built the prototypes, and the results were proudly displayed to the public for the first time at the 1993 NAMM show. (The first two prototypes ended up with Slash and Bryan Adams.) The "new" revised and improved Les Paul Standard 59 Flametop Reissue had arrived, along with a similarly ravishing 60, and a new Goldtop 57 Reissue. Already in the Reissue line were the Goldtop 56 and a brace of Black Beautys (Gibson's name for reissued Customs). Further improvements to details have been made since 1993 and more Reissue models added to the line, including the Standard 58 Plaintop (1994), Standard 58 Figuredtop (1996), Goldtop 54 (1997), Goldtop 52 (1998), and SG/Les Paul Custom (1998). Another model that might be considered a reissue came along in 1992 with the return of the small-humbucker Deluxe, last seen in the 1980s. Riboloff left Gibson in 1998.

With all this attention to detail and, at 2002 prices, the possibility to own a "correct" $7500 Standard 59 Flametop Reissue as opposed to a $25,000-plus original, how might a novice tell them apart? Or, for that matter, an experienced player not conversant with the constructional details of the late-1950s solidbody electric guitar in the Kalamazoo region? The answer is a die-stamped inked number that should be seen in the control pocket of all modern Gibson Les Paul Reissues (that's the hole left in the back of the body after you take off the panel). There on the lower ledge is stamped R9 for the Standard 59 Reissue, R8 for the 58, and R0 for the 60; R6 for the Goldtop 56 Reissue, and R7 for the 57.

When pressed, Tom Murphy thought that the electronics of the Reissue might be the only area that is now left for any improvement. Not that they're bad now, he emphasised – far from it, he said, given all the detailed research on materials and construction that has been done. The Reissues sound superb. But it's fairly safe to say that no one really knows why the genuine old pickups sound the way they do. "And that's sort of the beauty of it, right?" said Murphy. "Maybe mother nature's going: OK, go have all the fun you want, but I'm going to keep this one thing – because you're not supposed to have all that stuff. I have said many times to people: this is not a 1959 Les Paul. It's a 2002 Les Paul or whatever. That's not to misunderstand what it's supposed to refer to, and what they want. But it's not a '59!"

Gibson's April 1993 pricelist showed seven basic Les Paul guitars: Studio $899; Special $949; Studio Lite $1099; Studio Lite/MIII $1199; Standard $1599; Classic $2199; and Custom $2199. There were also three basic Les Paul basses: Special $1049; Deluxe $1599; and Standard $1649. The Historic Collection list showed six basic Les Paul models: Standard 59 Reissue $5059; Standard 60 Reissue $5059; Goldtop 56 Reissue $2549; Goldtop 57 Reissue $2549; Black Beauty 54 Custom Reissue $2399; and Black Beauty Custom 57 Reissue $2399.

LET'S NOT FORGET ORVILLE
Gibson has settled upon 1894 as the year its founder, Orville Gibson, began making instruments commercially, although there's no evidence to pinpoint such a date. He probably began making instruments in his spare time during the 1880s, when he was in his late 20s. The nearest that Walter Carter gets in *Gibson Guitars, 100 Years Of An American Icon* to a date for Orville setting up his operation is "by 1896", the first year that Orville merits a listing in the local Kalamazoo business directory as a manufacturer of musical instruments. But today you will see the line "since 1894" in plenty of Gibson publicity material, so we must accept this now as the de facto start year. With this in mind, Gibson celebrated their centennial in 1994, issuing a series of limited-edition instruments to mark the occasion.

There were 12 special Centennial models produced during 1994 – one per month – and each was limited to a maximum of 101 instruments, serial numbered 1894 to 1994, and costing around $8500 each. Among these were three Les Pauls: the Classic Centennial, the Custom Black Beauty 57 3-Pickup Centennial, and the Standard Centennial. They were all decked out with fancy inlay and luxury gold and diamond appointments, as might be expected, including a portrait of Orville on the headstock and an inscribed pickguard. We can only assume that Orville smiled as he looked down from his prime spot in Guitar Heaven. A further series of decorated upscale Les Pauls came along a couple of years later – the $2990 Catalina and Elegant and the $7999 Ultima.

WINNING THE PAULS

1996 in context

Gibson helps to save the planet with the new forest-friendly Smartwood models.

TWA airliner explodes off Long Island, New York, killing 228 people.

Oasis continue to reshape 60s pop for a 90s audience, basking in the popularity of 1995's superb *Morning Glory?* album.

British beef imports suspended in 19 countries amid crisis over link between "mad cow disease" and human CJD.

Yasser Arafat elected president of Palestine.

Noel Gallagher, Oasis, acquiescent with sunburst ▸

FIFTY YEARS OF THE GIBSON LES PAUL

THE NINETIES

1998 Smartwood Standard ▶

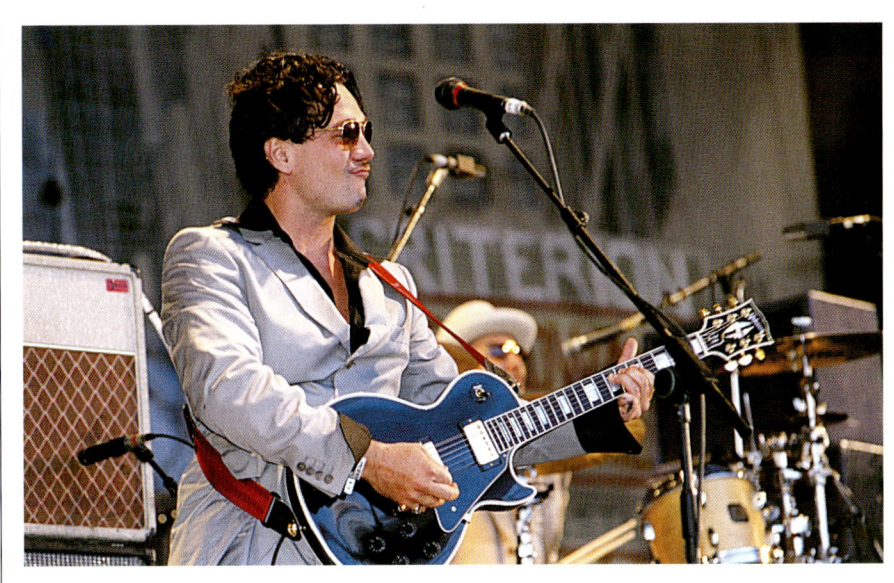

Fun Lovin' Criminals released their debut album in 1996, *Come Find Yourself*, with the Les Paul Custom of Huey Morgan (above) amid the inspiring mix of hip-hop, rock and blues. It was also the year that Gibson became eco-aware, launching the Smartwood Standard model (left) made from certified Smartwood, timber that has been harvested in an environmentally friendly manner, effectively strengthening the forests from which it came. Gibson claimed that this was the first example of a guitar manufacturer producing a cost-effective model made from Smartwood.

▲ 1997 Joe Perry

For that stadium-rocking sound guaranteed to keep you in the music business long beyond predictions of a natural sell-by date, the Joe Perry signature model launched in 1996 (main guitar) had a number of unusual features requested by the Aerosmith guitarist. Plenty of black-plated chrome enhances the suitably moody appeal of the "translucent blackburst" finish, and there is an active mid-boost circuit to shape the guitar's tone.

FIFTY YEARS OF THE GIBSON LES PAUL

FIFTY YEARS OF THE GIBSON LES PAUL

Where the Centennials had a circular portait of Orville on the headstock, these had a pearl Custom Shop banner. All three had the Florentine's hollowed "sound chambers" in the body for weight-saving. The Catalina came in opaque black, red or yellow finishes, while the Elegant had top-quality flame maple and abalone fingerboard markers. The Ultima was one of the fanciest Les Pauls for some time, with swathes of abalone, pearl and gold, and four optional fingerboard flourishes: flames, tree-of-life, butterflies, or harps. The Catalina was gone from the line by 1998, the Ultima two years later, while the Elegant Quilt, a figured-top version, was still on the catalogue at the time of writing.

Further down at a relatively affordable level was the Studio – the basic model first seen back in the early 1980s that still provides many players with their first experience of a Gibson Les Paul. It remains a straightforward, less expensive alternative to the regular Standard, and consistently comes near the top of Gibson's sales charts. Independent polls have confirmed the Studio as a Gibson bestseller. Surveys in 1998 of $700-plus electrics in *Music & Sound Retailer* magazine in the US, for example, pitched the $1400 Les Paul Studio at number four in its top ten, with the $2520 Standard in fifth place. Fender's all-conquering Stratocaster was at number one, in its American Standard guise.

GET YOUR EPIPHONE LES PAUL HERE
But it's with its sister brand, Epiphone, that Gibson has really scored in offering a line of affordable Les Pauls. Since 1970, with a few exceptions, Epiphones were made for Gibson by various oriental factories, and in 1988 the first proper set-neck Les Paul models had been added to the Epi line, the Korean-made Standard and Custom. More recently, many more have been added, with finishes ranging from exotic and transparent to sparkle, and a seven-string version followed a fashion among hardcore rockers around the turn of the millennium. There's an f-holed hollowbody model, the ES, plus signature models for Kiss's Ace Frehley and for Slash, as well as an unbound version, the 100. The price range is presently about $600 to $1100.

It was this formula of copying the best-known Gibson models that has made the Epiphone line such a success to the present day, and it should be marked up as another of the smart business moves made by Gibson's new owners. As Fender has done with its Squier brand, Gibson copied itself using the benefit of cheaper overseas production – and sold store-loads of guitars.

During the 1990s, there were two themes that seemed to be everywhere in the guitar industry. One was retro. Everyone wanted to look backwards for an old-style look. Gibson was, of course, well situated for such a view, having a glorious past to draw upon. The other theme was the signature guitar. This was a model authorised by a famous player and with personal specifications or visuals – and usually a combination of the two.

Gibson was also in a good position for this trend. After all, the Les Paul model itself was the original signature electric guitar. Les Paul had endorsed the company's very first solidbody back in 1952 – but since then, no other musician's name had ever appeared alongside Mr Paul's on a production model. Fender had now re-popularised the idea of the signature model, starting with their

THE NINETIES LES PAUL

Eric Clapton Stratocaster in 1988. Gibson followed by going for an equally big name among the legion of famous Les Paul players, honouring Led Zeppelin's Jimmy Page with the first signature-edition Les Paul, launched in 1995.

The Jimmy Page Les Paul lasted in the line until 1999, and accommodated the guitarist's request for an unusual neck shape and fret height. Page wanted the feel of his favourite "No.1" Standard (pictured on page 35) which meant low, low frets and a neck profile thinner at the seventh fret than the first, fattening again toward the 12th fret. Visually, the guitar appeared as a basic Les Paul Standard with a good, lightly figured top, gold-plated hardware, and Pagey's which-way-is-up autograph logo on the pickguard. But the guitar's major oddity was a series of switching options, again based on your man's original 1950s Standard.

The pickups were the powerful types used on the Classic, but they were combined with a push-pull switch on each of the four control knobs. Depending on your requirements, this could seem like a wonderfully expansive range of tonal possibilities … or just simply too many choices. In this way the Page Les Paul neatly highlights the major advantage and disadvantage of a signature instrument – whoever the artist, whatever the manufacturer. The advantage for a fan is that if you like the player concerned, you might feel a little closer to their style by owning one of these guitars. The disadvantage for a musician is that it's unlikely that one player's specific requirements will match your own. It goes back to Les Paul himself constantly modifying the guitars that Gibson sent to him. Players adapt instruments to suit themselves, quite rightly oblivious to what anyone else might like.

More signature Les Pauls have followed the Page. Aerosmith's Joe Perry saw his moody "blackburst" arrive in 1996, and the following year there were models for Ace Frehley of Kiss and Slash of Guns N'Roses, both with suitable graphics around the instrument. Ozzy Osbourne's guitar wiz Zakk Wylde saw his Les Paul go to market in 1999, unmistakeable with its circular bullseye finish, though there was briefly a plain Rough Top alternative.

> Gibson chose one of the biggest names among the legion of famous Les Paul players when it honoured Jimmy Page with the first signature-edition Les Paul in 1995. Page wanted the new guitar to have the feel of his favourite old "number one" Standard.

CAREFUL WITH THAT AXE

Today, it seems as if almost everyone is concerned with environmental issues, and the use and abuse of timber is often high on the list of those who lobby for changes in the way that people exploit the earth's natural resources. In the past, wood was largely considered as something that was simply available for the taking. The consequences of such an attitude were never much considered, or at least not so publicly as they are today. Over-cutting and deforestation – literally the stripping of forests from the ground – are worrying modern trends, especially in tropical regions, and illegal trade in "banned" woods is rife.

Some guitar-makers too have become concerned with the ecological impact of their business, while others figure that guitar-making barely dents world timber

CUTS BOTH WAYS

1997-99 in context

Gibson makes a Les Paul with carved-top body and twin cutaways (97), the DC.

Microsoft is biggest company in US (98).

Serbs massacre ethnic Albanians (99) in Kosovo; NATO forces attack.

Welsh stadium punks the Manic Street Preachers suggest 'If You Tolerate This Your Children Will Be Next' (98).

The oldest person in the world, Jeanne Caldwell, dies aged 122. Also dead: Frank Sinatra, Dusty Springfield, John Denver.

Cinema admissions in the US (97) are the highest for nearly 40 years.

James Dean Bradfield, Manic Street Preachers ▸

▲ 1998 DC Standard

It's difficult to imagine that Gibson did not look at the success of PRS – a US-based operation making double-cutaway, figured-carved-top guitars with strong Gibson influences – and aim the new Les Paul DC lines of 1997 and 1998 at a similar audience. As is often the case with Gibson, there were three levels: the DC Studio, DC Pro, and DC Standard (main guitar), with only the latter surviving in today's catalogue, renamed as the Standard Double Cut Plus.

THE NINETIES

Signature models loom larger than ever on the modern guitar scene, with a famous name seemingly worth its weight in original PAF pickups. Slash of Guns N'Roses was treated to a rare limited-run Gibson model with suitable graphics (Japanese ad, left) before moving to the budget Epiphone brand. It's impossible to miss the Bullseye model for Ozzy Osbourne's Zakk Wylde (below right), though a plainer Roughtop version was also sold for a while. The swelegant Elegant models (below left) were among several recent Les Pauls that have hollowed chambers inside the body to reduce weight.

◀ 1998 Elegant

1999 Zakk Wylde ▶
Bullseye

FIFTY YEARS OF THE GIBSON LES PAUL

stocks, and carry on regardless. For the small, independent craft maker turning out a handful of custom instruments, probably only a few trees would ever need to be cut down to provide them with enough raw materials to last for their entire career. With the big guitar makers, however, it's arguable that their consumption of wood is of greater importance.

Some of the scarcer guitar-making woods have already been outlawed from use. Most famously, in 1992 Brazilian rosewood – the hallowed fingerboard timber and acoustic-guitar material used in countless old vintage gems – was banned from international trade. Pre-1992 stocks are occasionally available for expensive instruments, but most guitar and most makers, Gibson included, now use rosewood from other sources, as well as the various alternatives. In truth, Brazilian rosewood represents more of an emotional loss than a practical hindrance in the guitar world.

> "There are a bunch of musicians who have one thing in common: we love guitars and we care about the future of the planet."
> Jackson Browne, 1997

SMARTWOOD FOR STING

In 1996, Gibson claimed to be the first guitar manufacturer to "craft a cost-effective model composed entirely of certified Smartwood". Smartwood is the Rainforest Alliance's name for its scheme to produce regular quantities of certified exotic woods in a way that strengthens the forests that supplied them – whether the end products are guitars, flooring, cabinets, picture frames or paper. The Rainforest Alliance is an international non-profit conservation organisation that aims to promote responsible timber use.

Gibson's new certified-wood model was the $3399 Les Paul Smartwood Standard. It had a maple top harvested by Menominee Tribal Enterprises in Wisconsin, US, and for its back and neck used chetchen, one of those rosewood alternatives – this one harvested by the Sociedad de Productures Forestales Ejidales co-operative in Mexico. (A number of other makers investigated the idea, and the Martin company produced its SWD Smartwood acoustic guitar a few years later, using spruce, cherry and katalox woods.)

A prototype of the Smartwood Standard was presented to singer-songwriter Jackson Browne who played it at a series of benefits for the Rainforest Alliance. Browne said, "These Smart Sounds concerts are a great chance to see a bunch of musicians who have one thing in common: we love guitars and we care about the future of the planet." Gibson took another opportunity to publicise the Smartwood idea when Sting was given the company's Les Paul Award at the 15th Annual Technical Excellence & Creativity Awards in New York in January 2000. Les Paul and Henry Juszkiewicz presented Sting with a suitably inscribed Les Paul Smartwood Standard.

Gibson went further in its use of Smartwood with a line of six more Les Pauls, the Smartwood Exotic models, which retailed at about $1500 and were launched during 1998. The new Smartwoods had certified mahogany backs and curupay fingerboards, while their tops made from rare and beautiful tropical woods – either ambay guasa, banara, cancharana, guasa, peroba, or taperyva – each harvested from a sustainable forest in Paraguay. A portion of revenue from the Exotics was donated to the Rainforest Alliance.

CUT AND THRUST

PRS Guitars, started by Paul Reed Smith in the mid 1980s, had shaken up the solidbody electric guitar market during the 1990s, its most famous player Carlos Santana spearheading an increasing number of PRS devotees. Smith's design clearly revealed his love of early Gibson Les Paul and Fender Stratocaster styles, melding a Standard-like carved, figured maple top and humbuckers with Strat-style offset cutaways and through-body stringing.

Gradually, PRS was attracting some players who previously might have opted naturally for a Les Paul or a Stratocaster. Looking at Gibson's new double-cutaway Les Paul DC Pro and DC Studio models of 1997, it seems that the growing demand for a double-cutaway carved-top guitar did not go un-noticed in Nashville. The DCs ("Double Cutaway") started with a Custom Shop model, the Pro, effectively merging the late 1950s Junior/Special double-cut shape with the Standard's carved top – which Gibson had done before, with limited success, in the 1980s, for the Double-Cutaway XPL (a model otherwise beyond the scope of this book because Gibson did not actually name it as a Les Paul).

In another weight-saving exercise, the new DC's mahogany back was hollowed out to leave a central "block", with a carved maple cap added on top. Matthew Klein in the Custom Shop was responsible for the Pro. "If you took a regular single-cut Les Paul, went to the bandsaw and cut out a different horn area, you'd have the DC," he said. "The top carving is exactly the same, but the outside shape gives a little more fret access."

Adding to the feeling that the DC was a reaction to PRS offerings, the Pro came with 24 frets, a straight-string-pull headstock design, and a two-knobs-and-selector control layout, as well as options of a longer scale-length and wrapover bridge – all features of Smith's instruments. But, of course, this one had the Gibson name and the Les Paul logo on the headstock.

It soon became clear that the DC model could become a viable production model manufactured in the main plant, and the DC Studio was born later in 1997, retailing at $1400. It retained the construction of the Pro, but with a standard headstock, plain top, unbound body and "short"-scale only. A fancier production version, the DC Standard, debuted in 1998, effectively halting sales of the $3200 Pro, dropped soon afterward. More recently the DC Studio and DC Standard were replaced by the similar Standard Lite and Standard Double Cut Plus.

"Just because they designed a guitar 700 years ago doesn't mean it can't feel dead right now."

2000s

Sonny Mayo, Amen ▸

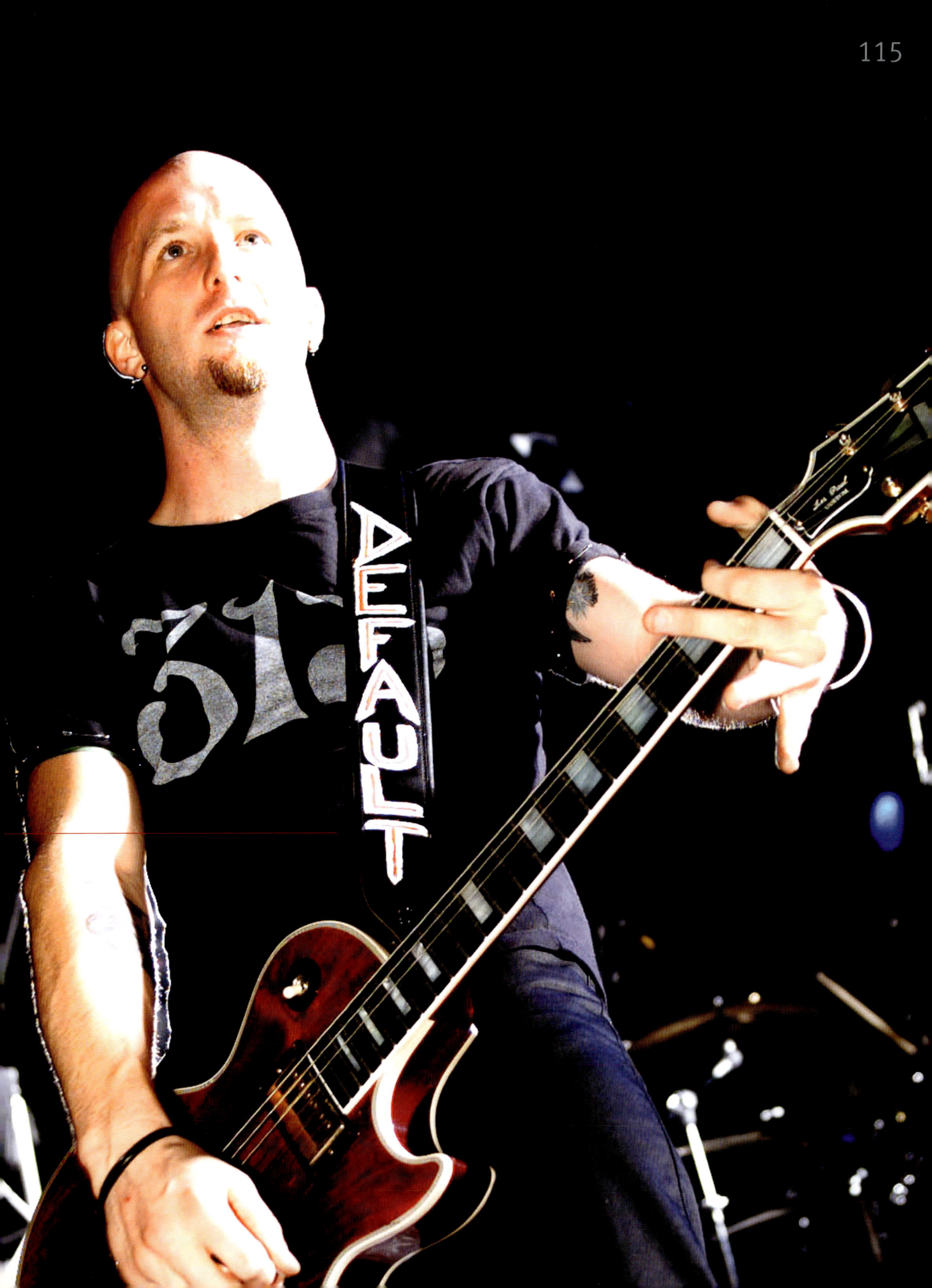
DEFAULT

By the turn of the 21st century it seemed that one fashion here to stay was the signature guitar – an instrument authorised by a famous player and made to their individual specifications. The anti-hero stance of many 1990s grunge players now appeared like a distant memory as more and more legendary guitarists lined up to have their name on a personalised instrument.

Gary Moore was the first musician to be honoured with a Les Paul signature model in the new millennium. Known for his early work with Thin Lizzy in the 1970s but more recently revered for some blistering blues revivals, Moore is also much envied among Les Paul fanciers as the owner of Peter Green's original Standard, sold to him by the Fleetwood Mac man many years ago (see page 39). Moore has even underlined the debt with a personal tribute record, *Blues For Greenie*. For his Gibson signature model, Moore opted for a workmanlike, player's instrument that echoed the Green guitar. It was an unbound Standard that had coverless humbuckers and no pickguard. Further signature Les Pauls have also been added to the line recently, including a Peter Frampton Custom with three coverless humbuckers and custom-wired switching, and the Dickey Betts 57 Goldtop based on the ex-Allman Brothers guitarist's vintage instrument.

WHO PLAYS PAUL?

Les Pauls continued to attract guitarists at all levels through the 1990s and into the 2000s. But the picture is less clear-cut than in earlier decades, where certain players could be easily identified as firm fans of the Les Paul, often to the exclusion of other models. It's now much more common for a player to shift around more from model to model and brand to brand. If anything, this is because there are now so many viable alternatives. Simply, there are more good guitars to choose from today, and for some players it doesn't make much sense to keep still for too long.

Competition continued to be aimed at Gibson's Les Paul models by the PRS company. As we've seen, Paul Reed Smith's clever distillation of Gibson and Fender features into a double-cutaway carved-top design of his own even led Gibson to retaliate directly with its double-cutaway DC models of the late 1990s, still on the catalogue in 2002 as the Standard Lite and Standard Double Cut Plus. And PRS had been stealing some publicity thunder when it used ex-Gibson boss Ted McCarty as a consultant and in advertising. (Another retired key ex-Gibson man, Seth Lover, had appeared in ads for pickup manufacturer Seymour Duncan. Note that Lover died in 1997, and Ted McCarty in 2001.)

A further irony came with PRS's launch of its Singlecut model in 2000. The ad copy for the new model left little doubt about its intentions: "Ted McCarty introduced the single cutaway, carved-top solidbody to the world in 1952. We learned a lot from Ted while we were working on ours." At the time of writing, the PRS Singlecut was the subject of litigation between Gibson and PRS.

To some players, Gibson's available guitar finishes had often seemed conservative, summed up most obviously by the supreme old-fashioned look: a sunburst top with flame-figured maple showing through. To aficionados this is the classic Les Paul look; to other, mostly younger observers it reeks of everything that is musty and behind the times. Some kinds of retro, went the thinking, are just not cool. So every now and then, Gibson has tried offering the Les Paul in new, bright finishes. The last few years have been no exception. In 2000 it was sparkle finishes for the Standard, in diamond, blue or green. For those who subscribe to the cyclical theory of fashion, it is necessary only to look at page 59 of this book to see a blue sparkle Les Paul Deluxe from the mid 1970s. This time around, Gibson claimed that because the sparkle flake is embedded into the guitar's lacquer it would therefore add "a silky sustain to the tone". And there we were thinking it just looked nice and shiny.

Another looker came along the following year when the Studio was offered in a special blue teal "flip flop" finish. This was a good one: as you moved the guitar at different angles, the colours changed, in the case of blue teal going through shades of greens and blues. It was based on something called Variocrom-effect pigment technology, developed by BASF, a company better known to musicians for recording media.

Also firmly in the flashy visual department – but this time right up at the most expensive end of the Gibson line – was the wild X-Men Wolverine Les Paul, a Custom/Art/Historic production dedicated to the comic-book superhero and limited to a run of just 50. Each of the X-Men guitars had suitably over-the-top vinyl press-on graphics on the body.

ACOUSTIC AND UNOBSTRUCTED

The Custom/Art/Historic division was still housed separately, a few doors along from the main factory in Nashville, and some interesting new models appeared from there during 2001. The Class 5 was a variant on the Reissue models produced at the Custom Shop, this one with a 1960 Standard flavour.

No one we spoke to seemed quite sure of where the model name comes from. Perhaps it's almost a Classic, we suggested, so it's shortened to "Class"? And that "5" might relate to the fashion among some makers for categorising flamed tops according to their intensity from one A (least impressive) to five or more As, written as AAAAA (meaning pretty spectacular) and so on. Certainly the Class 5 models do have great tops.

More clearly defined by its name was the hollowbody Les Paul Acoustic. This is an immediately striking guitar. Imagine a flamed maple Les Paul body with nothing on it at all. That's right – nothing. No pickups, no metal bridge, no controls, no pickguard … just the strings stretching across from the neck to a seemingly invisible anchor point in the midst of the maple. You have just visualised the Les Paul Acoustic. Remember that prophecy by Les Paul in 1971 about a piezo-like pickup?

Of course, the Acoustic model really does have a bridge and there is a pickup, but both are carefully hidden within the overall maple look, and the controls are on the side of the body. It was developed in the Custom Shop by Mickey McGuire, who has a good pedigree in guitar-making: he's the son of Mike McGuire who founded the custom guitar maker Valley Arts in the 1970s. McGuire Jr's idea was to take a hollowed-out Les Paul's mahogany rear and add a flat-back maple cap, carved on top like a regular Les Paul except for an area around the bridge. The maple left there was hand-shaped into a kind of four-sided

THE POWER OF THE PAUL

2000 in context

Gibson launch more signature Pauls, from Peter Frampton and Gary Moore.

Internet stock boom ends as markets plunge and investors regain their sight.

Aerosmith spend most of 2000 making *Push To Play* album, and early following year are inducted to Rock Hall of Fame.

Friends TV cast sign new contract that brings them $750,000 each per episode.

Concorde crashes near Paris, killing 113.

Presidential election in US is closest for years; George Bush wins after disputed recounts and Supreme Court ruling.

◀ Joe Perry (left) and Steve Tyler of Aerosmith

▲ 2000 Standard Raw Power

FIFTY YEARS OF THE GIBSON LES PAUL

THE NOUGHTIES

And so the Les Paul endorsement contracts continued to be signed, almost 50 years after Les Paul himself inked that significant piece of Gibson headed paper. Peter Frampton put his name on the line for a fair copy of his long-favoured Custom (left), complete with special-wired switching, while Gary Moore disposed of binding for his chunky signature model (below). No sign yet of a deal for Blur's Graham Coxon (pictured left) whose second solo album appeared during 2001 alongside the band's unmissable greatest-hits compilation.

◂ 2000 Peter Frampton

◂ 2000 Gary Moore

The latest in a long, long line of Les Paul Standard variations is this Raw Power model (main guitar), distinguished by its straightahead plain top and a natural "satin" finish. It's an anti-Standard, a guitar that says "turn me up to 11 and to hell with the ear muffs". Other new Les Pauls included the hollow-body Acoustic, with no pickups visible but a bug in the bridge for acoustic-like amplified sounds.

FIFTY YEARS OF THE GIBSON LES PAUL

pyramid, rounded off a little to make a bridge, with a Baggs "acoustic" piezo pickup worked in. The result is a Les Paul that one insider said gives a mix of the sound of maple with a cutting acoustic-like tonality.

THE NUMBERS GAME

Readers of this book hardly need reminding that 2002 marks 50 years since the introduction of the Gibson Les Paul. The company staged a number of celebrations, not least some special 50th Anniversary models. But an early manifestation came in August 2001 with an event at the Iridium jazz club in New York City, where Les himself, well into his 80s, was joined by noted Paul players Slash and Al DiMeola. Gibson CEO Henry Juszkiewicz presented Les with a Custom Shop Goldtop 52, specially engraved with this message: "Celebrate the legend. Revel in the legacy. Gibson pays tribute to the one and only Les Paul." Les also received a proclamation from New York City declaring August 13th to be that year's Les Paul Day. Juszkiewicz said: "Les Paul is not only America's most popular guitar player. He is a leading innovator in guitar and electronic design. He has been experimenting with electric guitars for as long as there have been electric guitars." Perhaps Les still had this last thought echoing in his ears when he got home and installed low-impedance pickups on the brand new 52?

> Some original guitars are now so expensive that Gibson offers not-quite-so-expensive "aged" Les Paul models, designed to give a new guitar the lived-in look.

Back in the Custom Shop, the Les Paul Reissues were, as usual, being gently tweaked to bring them closer than ever to the original instruments of the late 1950s and early 1960s. No detail was too small for attention. Take the serial number for example, which on original-period Pauls is ink-stamped on to the rear of the headstock. As any Les Paul forger will tell you, it is very hard to get close to the typeface and style and ink-colour of the original numerals. Gibson faced the same problem. Reissue guru Tom Murphy takes up the story. "At first, in the early 1990s, I'd asked our normal stamp supplier for a smaller typeface, because we'd had odd-shaped, bulky numbers through the 1980s," he said.

"We ended up realising that the original style number was not produced any more, so we went 'below' it: smaller, with a more aesthetically pleasing look, in the right style but not the right size," Murphy continued. "That wasn't received greatly by the real buffs. So now we've fixed that. We stumbled on a way to put those numbers on a stamp, in another configuration. So from 1999 the number style changed again, and we're very happy with it. It's not exactly perfect, but it's now the right font, in the right height and width."

Murphy had left Gibson in 1994 to set up his Guitar Preservation company, and now combines that with work for Gibson as a freelance. At his own workshop he has built on his speciality for refinishing and restoring old guitars. Gradually, he found that it was natural to "age" the finished job, blending in the new areas to sit more comfortably with the original worn guitar. He found customers at Guitar Preservation who welcomed this, and also several at Gibson's Custom Shop. Murphy wasn't alone in developing this technique, of course. Many guitar repairers now include ageing techniques in their set of skills. But why has it become so much in demand today? He thinks it's down to the scarcity of vintage guitars today. Years ago there was a good supply of original instruments about. "If a guitar was refinished because of someone's ignorance, like I did many times, or attempted as part of a repair, it denigrated the guitar. But back then there was an alterative," Murphy said. "In those days there would be an original instrument available at a reasonable price."

Back when a particular original vintage model might sell for, say, $400 while a refinished one was just $100, it was an easy and relatively cheap decision to go for the original. Even when the original became $2000 and the refinished one $800, you'd probably still want to buy the original. "But as the availability of the original instruments diminished and the prices skyrocketed," said Murphy, "the viability and the option of restoring an old one has now become more necessary, out of practicality. And it's more accepted, because we've all had to say well, it's not that big a deal if the paint has been redone on a Strat body or whatever. I'm a purist as much as anyone else. I'd rather they were all original guitars. But you can't always have that now."

BORN OLD AND GETTING NO YOUNGER
Tom Murphy developed his ability to make a repaired and/or restored guitar "look right" by using ageing techniques. Fender had introduced its aged Relic series in 1995 after Keith Richards complained that some replicas made for him by the company's Custom Shop for a Stones tour would look better if, as the guitarist put it, they "bashed them up a bit". There followed a line of new Strats and Teles with wear-and-tear distress marks added to the finish and the hardware, intended to make the guitars look as if they'd been knocked around on stage and on the road for years. The success of Fender's Relic scheme was obviously noted at Gibson HQ in Nashville; a few years later Murphy was doing the same thing to selected models in the Les Paul Reissue line. He prefers to call it a "broken-in" feel rather than an aged look.

The first to benefit was the Standard 59 Reissue Aged model, which officially started life as part of the Custom Shop line in 1999. The paint colours were made to appear faded, the nickel parts on the instrument such as the pickup covers were realistically tarnished, the lacquer "skin" was cracked and effectively dulled. Remarkably, the guitar really did look old and worn.

Like Fender and its Relics, Gibson aimed to recreate the almost indefinable allure of a vintage guitar but in a new instrument – and at a stiff price, of course. The Aged 59 at present lists at $10,155, about $3250 more than the regular Reissue. Added to the Aged line during the last few years have been the Goldtop 56 and 57 models, while the recent Dickey Betts signature Goldtop 57 also received Murphy's breaking-in treatment.

Murphy said that the Aged Reissues profit from a combination of techniques that he arrived at to simulate wear on small areas of the guitar. What's the secret of getting the aged look? "I can't tell you that," he laughed. "I can tell you it's done by hand, though – but that's only because it's the only way it can be done. I swear if we could do it with a laser we'd have the laser version and the hand-

BACK TO THE FUTURE

2001-02 in context

Gibson marks 50 years of the Les Paul with a special edition gold-top model (02).

Attacks in US (01) destroy twin Trade Center towers leaving 3,000-plus dead. US-led coalition bombs Afghanistan.

Nouveau mods Ocean Colour Scene put out fine *Mechanical Wonder* album (01).

Philip Morris tobacco firm pays $3billion damages to 40-year Marlboro smoker.

Russian nuclear sub *Kursk* raised (01) after sinking a year before killing 118 crew.

Twelve EU countries abandon their own notes and coins and adopt the euro (02).

◄ Steve Cradock of Ocean Colour Scene

Now here's irony. What's the most desired model in the entire 50-year history of the Les Paul line? Of course, it's that old sunburst Standard, of which only 1,700 or so were made between 1958 and 1960. And so it is that the Gibson company today spends vast amounts of time and money to edge closer and closer to the detail of that long-ceased production run – and now even makes versions aged to look just like an old one (main guitar).

FIFTY YEARS OF THE GIBSON LES PAUL

THE NOUGHTIES

◀ 2001 Standard 58 Figuredtop Reissue

2001 Junior Special Plus ▶

▼ 1999 Standard 59 Flametop Reissue Aged

▲ 2001 Class 5

The newest models and the lastest bands (like A Perfect Circle, above) are always the hardest to talk about in this kind of book – it's impossible to know which will last and which will fade into obscurity. But Gibson's muddle over the Junior and Special models surely must be revised soon. What exactly is a "Junior Special Plus"? Well, it's that guitar above. You work it out. And why is the Class 5 (below) so called? Feels like a '60 Reissue to us. So why not be straightforward with the name – like that lovely Standard 58 (top left)?

FIFTY YEARS OF THE GIBSON LES PAUL

done version. But we can't. And it would be great if we had a magic box to put them in, a time machine or something where we could just switch it on to, let's say, winter in Minnesota, 1959. But we can't do that." Not yet, anyway.

WELCOME TO THE 21ST CENTURY GIBSON EXPERIENCE
Gibson's July 2001 pricelist showed 17 basic Les Pauls: Junior Lite $998; Junior $1152; Special $1229; Smartwood $1537; Junior Special Plus $1614; Studio $1691; Studio Gothic $1922; Standard Double Cut Plus $2152; Studio Plus $2383; Classic $2537; Standard Raw Power $2845; Deluxe $2922; Gary Moore $2922; Standard $3075; Standard Plus $3614; Custom $3998; Premium Plus $4382. The June 2001 Custom list had three basic Custom Authentic Reissues: Goldtop 58 $3880; Standard Figuredtop 58 $5895; Custom 68 $3900; plus 19 basic Reissues: Junior 57 single or double cut $2080; Special 60 single or double cut $3348; SG/Les Paul Standard $4159; Custom 54 $4671; Custom 57 $4525; Goldtop 52 $4279; Goldtop 54 $4517; Goldtop 56 $4517; Goldtop 57 $4582; Goldtop 57 Darkback $4582; Custom 57 $4671; SG/Les Paul Custom $4938; Oxblood 54 $5084; Standard Figuredtop 58 $5700; Standard 59 Flametop $7500; Standard 60 Flametop $7500; Goldtop 56 Aged $7680; Goldtop 57 Aged $7706; Standard 59 Flametop Aged $10,155; and nine other basic models: Mahogany Classic $4568; Zakk Wylde Bullseye $4900; Class 5 $4925; X-Men Wolverine $5000; Custom 68 Figuredtop $5062; Acoustic $5350; Elegant Quilt $5778; Peter Frampton $5802; Dickey Betts Goldtop 57 $8866.

From the outside, the division of Gibson's current lines can seem confusing. It's arguable that 45 basic Les Pauls on a pricelist are overwhelming for customers trying to choose the right model for their needs. Gibson claims that its electric guitar production is clearly defined into three divisions or levels: Gibson Custom Shop (more accurately the long-winded Custom/Art/Historic division) which provides the limited-run, high-end models; Gibson USA, or the normal factory, for regular production; and the Epiphone brand for less expensive versions of Gibson classics. Gibson is offering a Les Paul for every kind of player, runs the argument.

There is sometimes movement across these barriers, of course. The Joe Perry signature Les Paul, for example, began as a limited-run Custom model and then moved to Gibson USA after the initial run had sold out. This is logical, says Gibson. But there is little logic apparent in naming a new-for-2001 model the "Les Paul Junior Special Plus". A potential buyer with a modicum of historical awareness might well argue that a Junior is a Junior is a single-pickup Junior and a Special is a Special is a twin-pickup Special. The "Junior Special Plus" turns out to be a Special … and a Special with humbuckers. Perhaps Gibson should run a competition to give it a better name? Or maybe the thinking is that young players don't care about the history. Under 40 and reading this book? How long have you been a rebel, exactly?

The modern Gibson company not only aims to offer every kind of guitar, but also appears to aspire to that dreadful modern invention, the "lifestyle" company. Harley Davidson has always been the model, it seems. A typical Harley dealer in the US has three or four motorcycles (back-ordered for months), racks and racks of Harley clothing for men, women and children, and a restaurant. Gibson's Bluegrass Showcase and Memphis Showcase were steps in that direction. Both aim to be customer-friendly retail, performance, restaurant and manufacturing facilities, and both were at the time of writing doing OK.

Walter Carter, Gibson's Historian and Publicity Director, naturally looks to a healthy future for the company and its Les Paul models. "Going back to the early days, we had the catchphrase 'Everyone A Gibsonite'," he says. "Gibson has always thought of an instrument as something more – something along the lines of a Gibson experience or a Gibson lifestyle. The scope of that concept has grown tremendously over the last hundred years, from mandolin clubs to rock'n'roll around the world, and Gibson will continue to build on the idea of Gibson as a part of our everyday lives. I think we'll see more variations on the Les Paul to match the individual preferences of guitarists, and at the same time Gibson will protect and preserve the integrity of the Les Paul."

HAPPY BIRTHDAY TO YOU
At the start of the 21st century, the Gibson group of companies enjoyed annual revenues of around $200million and had 1200 employees. And 2002 saw that famous anniversary. Fifty years is a long time in guitar history. In fact the Gibson Les Paul is just about the longest-running electric guitar still in production today, only beaten by the Fender Telecaster, which is some two years older. Gibson often uses a neat advertising line alongside its Les Paul models: "The Standard since '52." But a lot has changed in those 50 years. Perhaps the most significant difference between the early 2000s and the early 1950s is that there are many more good electric guitars around now in competition with Gibson and Fender, who for years were considered as The Invincible Two.

No longer are guitarists dependent upon a choice only between those venerable names. Many, many other brands now offer well made, excellent playing, good sounding, attractively priced instruments. But the best new Gibson Les Pauls still stand out, and still they can be supreme instruments that make you want to play on into the small hours. It must be apparent to Gibson that, among today's greatly increased guitar market, the company is uniquely placed to serve up its own true, traditional flavour – but with all the benefits of the improvements made in modern manufacturing. As we've seen throughout this book, that tradition can also be a hindrance when Gibson comes to ask players to accept new designs. But the Gibson Les Paul looks set for many new adventures in the hands of succeeding generations of musicians and in the care of its creators. Here's to another 50 years.

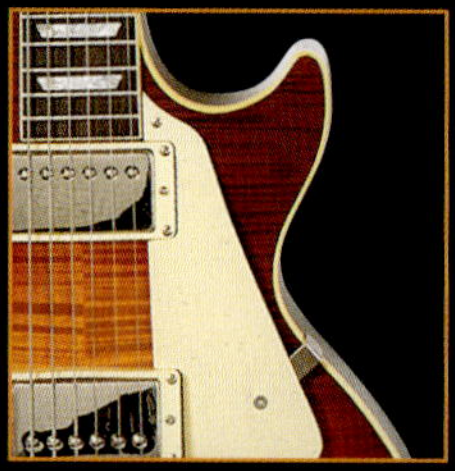

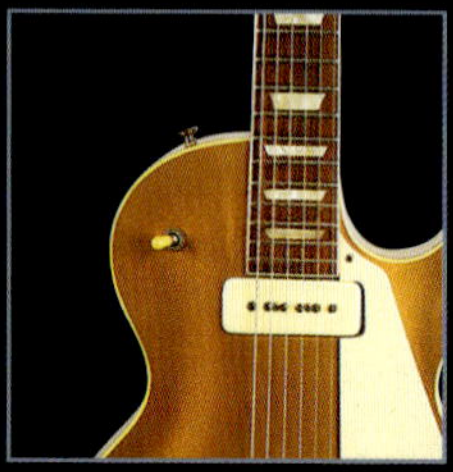

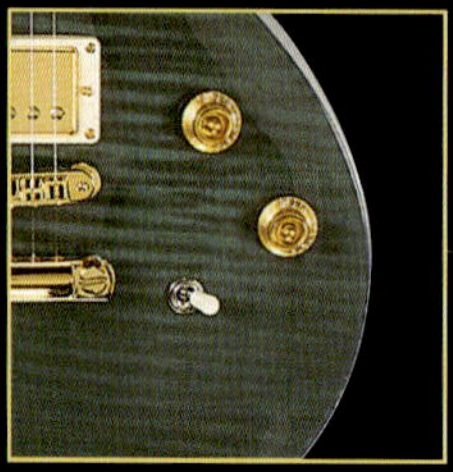

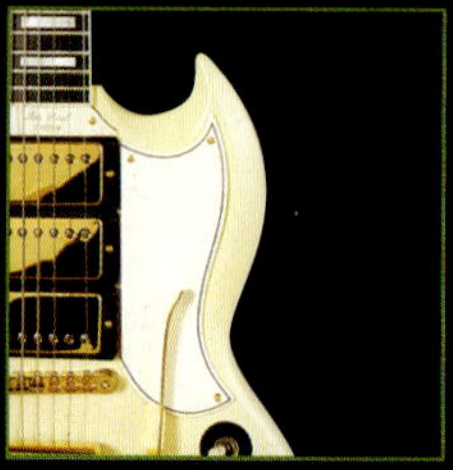

reference section

How to use the reference listing

The main Reference listing offers a simple, condensed format to convey a huge amount of information about every Gibson Les Paul model, and the following notes are intended to help you use this unique inventory.

Individual entries in the Reference listing contain all or some of the following:

- Model name
- Date or range of dates in production
- Brief one-sentence identification
- Reference to another model entry
- List of specification points
- Variations
- General comments
- Gibson production totals

At the head of each entry is the model name in bold type, listed in alphabetical order. This is followed by a date or range of dates showing the production period of the instrument. These dates, and any other dates shown within the Reference Section, are approximate. In many cases it is virtually impossible to pinpoint with total accuracy the period during which a model was in production at the factory. Gibson's promotional catalogues usually bear dates, but the content is often decided far in advance and does not always reflect what is being made when the catalogue eventually is issued. Similarly, Gibson's dated pricelists itemise the models that the company are selling at any one time, and not necessarily the guitars that were then in production.

Gibson's lists of the numbers of guitars "shipped" (ie leaving the factory) sometimes show guitars mad in years beyond the range we give for production. we assume that where only a small quantity of guitars is shown for a model otherwise produced in reasonably substantial numbers, these are either samples (made before the start of a production period) or leftovers being sold off (after production has ceased). Naturally we have gone to some lengths to list the most accurate dates possible for the production periods and changes made to Gibson's Les Paul models. But please treat them as approximate, for that all is that they can be.

In italics, following the model name and production dates, is a brief one-sentence identification of the guitar in question. This is intended to help you recognise a specific model at a glance. To enable you to do this we have noted elements of the guitar's design that are unique to that particular model.

For some guitars there may be a sentence below this reading "Similar to …

except:" or "As ... except:". This will take the form of a reference to another model entry. The description will list any major differences between the two models.

The list of specification points, separated into groups, provides details of the model's features. In the order listed the points refer to:

- Neck, fingerboard, headstock
- Body
- Pickups
- Controls
- Pickguard
- Bridge*
- Hardware finish.

*Note that Bigsby vibrato tailpieces were and are available as an option on many models, but that this option is not recorded in the reference listing.

Of course, not every model will need all seven points. And to avoid repetition in the specification points, we have considered a number of features to be common to all Gibson Les Paul models. They are:

- Plastic truss-rod cover unless stated
- Metal tuner buttons unless stated
- 22 frets unless stated
- Scale length approximately 24.6" unless stated
- Single-cutaway body unless stated
- Side-mounted jack (socket) unless stated
- Nickel- or chrome-plated hardware unless stated

Some models were made in a number of variations, and where applicable these are listed after the specification points, in italics. And other general comments are also made in this position.

At the end of each entry or group of entries we sometimes show Available Production figures. These are taken from official Gibson records showing the number of guitars shipped from (ie leaving) the Kalamazoo factory each year. They were totalled each month by Shipping Department staff and subsequently entered into a yearly report. These figures shown in the listing should be treated with caution: the calculations were tallied by hand, and human error is very evident. The figures we've used here continue to 1979, but we could find no figures for Kalamazoo from 1980 to its closure in 1984, and no figures for any Nashville production since its opening in 1975 until the late 1980s – these are apparently lost in a computer file somewhere. Figures are again being kept by the new owners of Gibson, but for commercial reasons they will not release them to us.

All this information is designed to tell you more about your Gibson Les Paul guitar. By using the general information and illustrations earlier in the book, combined with the knowledge obtained from this reference section, you should be able to build up a very full picture of your instrument and its pedigree.

Gibson Les Paul reference listing

ACE FREHLEY

ACE FREHLEY 1997-2000 *Three white-coil pickups, Ace Frehley graphic on headstock.* Similar to CUSTOM, except:
- Lightning-bolt markers; signature inlaid at 12th fret; Ace playing card on truss rod cover; Frehley face on headstock.
- Bound carved-top body; flamed maple top cap; cherry sunburst.
- Three uncovered pickups with white coils.
- Four controls (two volume, two tone) plus three-way selector.
- Chrome-plated hardware.

ACOUSTIC

ACOUSTIC 2001-current *No visible pickups, acoustic-style pin bridge, figured top.*
- Bound rosewood fingerboard; crown markers, pearl "Gibson" logo on headstock, plastic tuner buttons.
- Bound carved-top body; figured maple top; trans blue, trans black, or tangerine burst.
- Electronics from Gibson Chet Atkins SST model, piezo pickup.
- Two controls (volume, tone) mounted on rim.
- No pickguard.
- Rosewood bridge with bridge pins.
- Nickel-plated hardware.

ARTISAN

ARTISAN 1976-82 *Ornate fingerboard markers.*
- Bound ebony fingerboard, ornate markers; script Gibson logo and ornate inlay on headstock; "Artisan" on truss-rod cover.
- Bound carved-top body; sunburst, brown or black.
- Two or three metal-cover humbucker pickups.
- Four controls (two volume, two tone) plus three-way selector.
- Black laminated plastic pickguard.
- Six-saddle bridge plus separate bar tailpiece with six fine-tuning knobs.
- Gold-plated hardware.

Some without fine-tuners on tailpiece.

AVAILABLE PRODUCTION TOTALS for Artisan models: 1976/2; 1977/1469; 1978/641; 1979/108. Figures not available for 1980s.

ARTIST

ARTIST 1979-81 *Block fingerboard markers, "LP" headstock inlay, three controls and three mini-switches.*
- Bound ebony fingerboard, block markers; "LP" inlay on headstock; metal truss-rod cover; brass nut.
- Bound carved-top body; sunbursts or black.
- Two metal-cover humbucker pickups.
- Three controls (volume, bass, treble) plus three-way selector, three mini-switches; active circuit.
- Black laminated plastic pickguard.
- Six-saddle bridge plus separate bar tailpiece with six fine-tuning knobs.
- Gold-plated hardware.

AVAILABLE PRODUCTION TOTAL for Artist model: 1979/234. Figures not available for 1980 and 1981.

BANTAM

Early name for Elite and Florentine models; see later ELITE and FLORENTINE entries.

BLACK BEAUTY

See later CUSTOM entry.

CATALINA

CATALINA 1996–98 *Opaque colours, pearl Custom Shop logo on headstock.* Similar to STANDARD, except:
- Ebony fingerboard with compound radius; pearl crown markers; pearl Custom Shop logo inlaid on headstock.
- Black, yellow or red.
- Nickel-plated hardware

CLASS 5

CLASS-5 2001-current *Figured top, black knobs.*
Similar to STANDARD 59 FLAMETOP REISSUE, except:
- Tone chambers to lighten weight (not visible).
- Non-traditional finishes (amber, cranberry, tangerineburst, trans blue, trans black).

CLASSIC

CLASSIC 1990-current *"Classic" on truss-rod cover.*
- Bound rosewood fingerboard, crown markers; "Les Paul Model" on headstock; "Classic" on truss-rod cover; plastic tuner buttons.
- Bound carved-top body; sunbursts or colours (gold only 1998).
- Two coverless humbuckers.

REFERENCE SECTION

- Four controls (two volume, two tone) plus three-way selector.
- Cream plastic pickguard with "1960" logo.
- Six-saddle bridge plus separate bar tailpiece.
- Nickel-plated hardware.

CLASSIC CELEBRITY 1992 *"Celebrity" on pickguard.*
Similar to CLASSIC, except:
- Bound ebony fingerboard.
- Black only.
- Two coverless humbuckers.
- White plastic pickguard with "Celebrity" logo.
- Gold-plated hardware.

Limited run of 200 units.

CLASSIC CENTENNIAL 1994
Gold-top, production of no more than 101, 4-digit serial number on tailpiece with first digit (1) in diamonds.

CLASSIC MAHOGANY 2000-current
Mahogany top cap, zebra-coil pickups (one black coil, one white). Similar to CLASSIC, except:
- Mahogany top cap; natural, trans red or sunbursts.
- "Zebra" pickup coils (one black, one white coil).

CLASSIC/MIII 1991-92 *Additional central single-coil pickup; bound fingerboard.*
Similar to CLASSIC, except:
- Sunburst only.
- Two coverless humbuckers plus one central six-polepiece single-coil pickup.
- Two controls (volume, tone) plus five-way selector and mini-switch.
- No pickguard.

CLASSIC PLUS 1992-95, 1999-2000
CLASSIC PREMIUM PLUS 1993-97, 1999-current
CLASSIC BIRDSEYE 1993
CLASSIC PREMIUM BIRDSEYE 1993
CLASSIC QUILT TOP 1998
All similar to CLASSIC, except:
- Varying grades of figured maple carved-top (Premium Plus better than Plus, Premium Birdseye better than Birdseye).
- No pickguard on earliest, then pickguard with inscribed "1960" included in case but not mounted, then pickguard mounted.

CUSTOM

CUSTOM NORMAL MODELS
chronological order

CUSTOM "FIRST VERSION" 1954-57
Block fingerboard markers, split-diamond headstock inlay, "Les Paul Custom" on truss-rod cover, two plastic-cover pickups.
- Bound ebony fingerboard, block markers; split-diamond inlay on headstock; "Les Paul Custom" on truss-rod cover.
- Bound carved-top body; black only.
- Two plastic-cover six-polepiece single-coil pickups (neck unit with oblong polepieces; bridge unit with round polepieces).
- Four controls (two volume, two tone) plus three-way selector.
- Black laminated plastic pickguard.
- Six-saddle bridge plus separate bar tailpiece.
- Gold-plated hardware.

CUSTOM "SECOND VERSION" 1957-61 *Humbucker pickups.*
Similar to "FIRST VERSION", except:
- Three metal-cover humbucker pickups.

Some with two humbucker pickups. Shape changed in 1961: see later SG/LES PAUL CUSTOM entry. Also 35th Anniversary version with appropriate inlay on headstock (1989-90): see later 35th ANNIVERSARY entry.

CUSTOM "THIRD VERSION" 1968-current *Two humbuckers.*
Similar to "SECOND VERSION", except:
- Sunbursts, natural or colours.
- Two metal-cover humbucker pickups.

Also three-humbucker version (various periods). Also versions with nickel-plated hardware (1976-83, 1996) or chrome-plated hardware (1983-87). Also maple fingerboard version (1975-81). Also 20th Anniversary version with appropriate inlay at 15th fret (1974): see later 20th ANNIVERSARY entry.

AVAILABLE PRODUCTION TOTALS
for Custom models made at Kalamazoo: 1954/94; 1955/355; 1956/489; 1957/283; 1958/256; 1959/246; 1960/189; 1961/513 (includes some "SG/Les" Custom models); 1968/433; 1969/2353; 1970/2612; 1971/3201; 1972/4002; 1973/7232; 1974/7563; 1975/7448; 1976/4323; 1977/3133; 1978/10,744; 1979/1624. Figures not available for large Nashville production started 1975, nor for 1980s & 1990s.

CUSTOM OTHER MODELS
alphabetical order

CUSTOM BLACK BEAUTY 54
1991-current *Reissue based on "FIRST VERSION". Optional Bigsby.*

CUSTOM BLACK BEAUTY 57
1991-current *Reissue based on rare two-humbucker "SECOND VERSION". Optional Bigsby*

FIFTY YEARS OF THE GIBSON LES PAUL

FIFTY YEARS OF THE GIBSON LES PAUL

CUSTOM BLACK BEAUTY 57 3-PICKUP 1991-current *Reissue based on "SECOND VERSION" with optional Bigsby. Also with optional controls of three volume, one master tone (1999). Also 35th Anniversary version with appropriate inlay on headstock (1989-90): see later 35th ANNIVERSARY entry*

CUSTOM BLACK BEAUTY 57 3-PICKUP CENTENNIAL 1994 *With four-digit serial number on tailpiece and first digit (1) of diamonds.*

CUSTOM BLACK BEAUTY 82 1982-83 *Combines features of Custom and Standard, multi-ply body binding, unbound ebony fingerboard with crown inlay, gold-plated hardware.*

CUSTOM LITE 1987-89 *Contoured, thinner body; block fingerboard markers.*
- Bound ebony fingerboard, block markers; split-diamond inlay on headstock.
- Bound carved-top thinner body with contoured back; sunburst, black or pink.
- Two metal-cover humbucker pickups.
- Three controls (two volumes, one tone) plus three-way selector (two controls plus three-way selector 1989) and mini-switch.
- Black laminated plastic pickguard.
- Six-saddle bridge plus separate bar tailpiece.
- Gold-plated hardware (black-plated 1989).
- Six-saddle locking bridge/vibrato unit option.

CUSTOM LITE SHOWCASE EDITION 1998 *Similar to CUSTOM LITE, except plastic-cover EMG pickups, active electronics, gold top, gold-plated hardware; production: 250*

CUSTOM PLUS 1991-96 Similar to CUSTOM "THIRD VERSION", except:
- Fancier grade of figured maple carved-top; sunbursts.
- No pickguard.

CUSTOM/400 1991-92 *Split-block fingerboard markers, Custom Shop Edition logo on rear of headstock.* Similar to CUSTOM "THIRD VERSION", except:
- Bound ebony fingerboard, split-block markers; "Custom Shop Edition" logo on rear of headstock.
- Bound carved-top body; black only.
- Gold-plated hardware.

Name derives from Custom-style appointments and Gibson Super 400-style fingerboard markers.

CUSTOM 54 LTD EDITION 1972-73 *Reissue based on "FIRST VERSION", identifiable by serial number prefixed with LE.*

AVAILABLE PRODUCTION TOTALS for Custom 54 Ltd Edition models: 1972/60; 1973/1090; 1975/3; 1977/1.

CUSTOM 68 FIGUREDTOP 2000-current Similar to CUSTOM "SECOND VERSION", except:
- Figured maple top; antique natural, butterscotch, heritage cherry sunburst or triburst.

MAHOGANY CUSTOM 1998 Similar to CUSTOM "SECOND VERSION", except:
- 1-piece mahogany body (no top cap); faded cherry.
- Three metal-cover humbucker pickups.

CUSTOM SHOP

Special one-off custom orders were available from Gibson's original factory in Kalamazoo from its earliest days, but a bona fide Custom Department wasn't officially established until the 1960s. There was a Custom Shop at the current Nashville factory from 1983 until 1988, and then from 1993 as a seperate division and under a seperate roof just along from the main plant, at the time of writing known as the Custom/Historic/Art division. The Custom Shop's purpose has been and is to manufacture special models, custom-order one-of-a-kinds, and limited edition production runs in relatively small quantities. These have included exclusive guitars for dealers such as Guitar Trader, Leo's, Jimmy Wallace, Norman's Rare Guitars and others. Some Custom Shop instruments have been elaborate versions of stock items, employing higher quality timbers, better hardware, or impressive finishes – for example some models extravagantly inlaid with pearl by Greg Rich, or the Web-Slinger One with John Ronita's Spiderman artwork. Custom Shop guitars sometimes carry an identifying logo on the back of the headstock. (See also listings for SPOTLIGHT SPECIAL and CUSTOM/400 models).

DC

DC PRO 1997-98 *Double-cutaway carved-top body, non-standard headstock with straight string-pull (no "Les Paul" on headstock or truss rod cover).*
- Unbound ebony fingerboard, dot markers; 24¾" scale-length (25½" scale optional); headstock with straight string pull.
- Bound carved-top body with shape of SPECIAL "SECOND VERSION"; flamed

maple top; sunbursts or translucents.
- Optional pickup and bridge configurations: two plastic-cover single-coil pickups with wraparound bridge, two metal-cover humbucker pickups with wraparound bridge or with separate bridge and tailpiece.
- Two controls (volume, tone) plus three-way selector.
- Nickel-plated hardware.

DC STANDARD 1998-current *Double-cutaway carved-top body, crown markers, standard Gibson headstock (no "Les Paul" on headstock or truss rod cover).*
- Bound rosewood fingerboard, crown markers; 24¾" scale-length; standard Gibson headstock shape.
- Unbound carved-top body with shape of Special "SECOND VERSION"; maple top (flamed from 2001); sunbursts or colours (sparkle finishes only in 2000, trans finishes only from 2001).
- Two metal-cover humbucker pickups.
- Two knobs (tone, volume) plus selector switch
- Wraparound tailpiece (separate bridge and tailpiece from 1998).
- Chrome-plated hardware (in 2000 chrome with lemonburst, gold with tangerineburst; gold-plated from 2001).

Standard Double Cut Plus from 2001.

DC STUDIO 1997-98 *Unbound double-cutaway carved-top body, dot markers.*
- Unbound rosewood fingerboard, dot markers; 24¾" scale-length; standard Gibson headstock shape.
- Unbound carved-top body with shape of Special "SECOND VERSION"; sunbursts or colours.
- Two metal-cover humbucker pickups.
- Two knobs (tone, volume) plus selector switch
- Wraparound tailpiece (separate bridge and tailpiece from 1998).
- Chrome-plated hardware.

DELUXE

DELUXE 1969-84, 1992-97, 1999-current *"Deluxe" on truss-rod cover.*
- Bound rosewood fingerboard, crown markers; "Les Paul Model" on headstock; "Deluxe" on truss-rod cover; plastic tuner buttons (later metal).
- Bound carved-top body; sunbursts, natural or colours.
- Two mini-sized metal-cover humbucker pickups.
- Four controls (two volume, two tone) plus three-way selector.
- Cream plastic pickguard.
- Six-saddle bridge plus separate bar tailpiece.

Earliest examples with plastic-cover six-polepiece single-coil pickups. Some mini-humbucker-equipped examples with extra plastic ring around pickup covers.

AVAILABLE PRODUCTION TOTALS for Deluxe models made at Kalamazoo: 1971/4466; 1972/5194; 1973/10,484; 1974/7367; 1975/2561; 1976/172; 1977/413; 1978/4450; 1979/413. Figures not available for 1969, 1970, and 1980s, nor for any Nashville production.

DELUXE HALL OF FAME EDITION 1991 Similar to DELUXE, except gold finish all around (sides, back, back of neck).

DELUXE BASS

DELUXE PLUS BASS 1991-95 *20 frets, crown markers, black-plated hardware.*
- Unbound ebony fingerboard, crown markers; 20 frets, 34" scale-length; ornate "flower pot" inlay on headstock (omitted from 1993); "Les Paul" on truss-rod cover.
- Bound slab body; various colours.
- Two plain-cover humbucker pickups.
- Four controls (volume, bass, treble, balance); active circuit.
- No pickguard.
- Four-saddle bridge/tailpiece.
- Black-plated hardware.

DELUXE PREMIUM PLUS BASS 1993-95 Similar to DELUXE PLUS BASS, except:
- Fancier grades of figured maple carved-top.

Also five-string version (1993-95).

DICKEY BETTS

DICKEY BETTS 57 GOLDTOP 2001 *Similar to GOLD-TOP 57 REISSUE, except aged by Gibson employee Tom Murphy; replica Dickey Betts strap and faux alligator hardshell case included.*

DOUBLE CUTAWAY XPL

This model is beyond our coverage since the guitar does not bear the Les Paul name (despite references to the contrary in Gibson literature).

ELEGANT

ELEGANT 1996-2000 *Abalone crown markers, figured top.*
- Bound ebony fingerboard with compound radius, abalone pearl crown markers, pearl "Gibson" logo on headstock, metal tuner buttons.
- Bound carved-top body with sound chambers (not visible); figured maple top; natural, stains or sunbursts.
- Two covered six-polepiece humbucker pickups.
- Four controls (two volumes, two tones) plus three-way selector switch.

FIFTY YEARS OF THE GIBSON LES PAUL

- No pickguard.
- Six-saddle bridge plus separate bar tailpiece.
- Nickel-plated hardware.

ELEGANT QUILT 1997-98 & 2001-current
ELEGANT DOUBLE QUILT 1997
ELEGANT SUPER DOUBLE QUILT 1997
Progressively heavier quilt figuration in maple top.

ELITE DIAMOND SPARKLE

ELITE DIAMOND SPARKLE 1995-97
Diamond soundholes.
- Bound ebony fingerboard, pearl rectangular markers, split-diamond headstock inlay.
- Bound carved-top body, diamond soundholes, sparkles.
- Two metal-cover humbucker pickups.
- Four knobs (two tone, two volume) plus selector switch.
- Six-saddle bridge plus separate tailpiece.
- Gold-plated hardware.
Earliest named Bantam Elite.

EPIPHONE

Gibson acquired the Epiphone brandname in 1957 and started making Epiphone guitars in 1959. They ceased all production of Epiphone in the USA in 1970, having started around 1968 to transfer the brandname to instruments made in Japan. In the late 1980s these were succeeded by Epiphone models made in Korea. Epiphone introduced a Korean-built Les Paul Standard in 1988, and at the time of writing offers a range of seven Les Paul models: Black Beauty, Custom, Custom Flame, Standard, Studio, 56 Goldtop, and 100 (no binding, dot markers).

FLORENTINE

FLORENTINE PLUS 1995-98 *Similar to FLORENTINE STANDARD (below), except flamed maple top, trans colours (earliest named Bantam Elite Plus). Some with "diamond" soundholes, sparkle finish.*

FLORENTINE STANDARD 1995-98
F-holes in top.
- Bound ebony fingerboard, pearl rectangular markers, split-diamond headstock inlay.
- Bound carved-top body, f-holes, sunburst.
- Two metal-cover humbucker pickups.
- Four knobs (two tone, two volume) plus selector switch.
- Six-saddle bridge plus separate tailpiece.
- Gold-plated hardware.
Earliest named Bantam Elite.

GARY MOORE

GARY MOORE 2000-current
Zebra-coil neck pickup, black-coil bridge pickup, "Gary Moore" on truss rod cover.
Similar to STANDARD, except:
- Unbound carved-top of figured maple; lemonburst.
- Unbound rosewood fingerboard; "Gary Moore" on truss rod cover.
- Two uncovered humbucker pickups (black-white coils in neck position, black coils in bridge positon).
- No pickguard.
- Nickel-plated hardware.

GOLD-TOP

GOLD-TOP NORMAL MODELS
chronological order

GOLD-TOP "FIRST VERSION"
1952-53 *Crown fingerboard markers, two plastic-cover pickups, bridge/tailpiece on long "trapeze" anchor.*
- Bound rosewood fingerboard, crown markers; "Les Paul Model" on headstock; plastic tuner buttons.
- Bound carved-top body; gold only.
- Two plastic-cover six-polepiece single-coil pickups.
- Four controls (two volume, two tone) plus three-way selector.
- Cream plastic pickguard.
- Wrap-under bar bridge/tailpiece on long "trapeze" anchor.
Some early examples do not have a bound fingerboard. Most examples do not have a serial number. Some with all-gold body (rather than normal gold top with brown back and sides) and gold back of neck.

GOLD-TOP "SECOND VERSION"
1953-55 *Angled one-piece bridge/tailpiece.*
Similar to "FIRST VERSION", except:
- Wrap-over bar bridge/tailpiece.
Some with all-gold body and back of neck.

GOLD-TOP "THIRD VERSION"
1955-57 *Six-saddle bridge plus separate bar tailpiece, two plastic-cover pickups.*
Similar to "SECOND VERSION", except:
- Six-saddle bridge plus separate bar tailpiece.

GOLD-TOP "FOURTH VERSION"
1957-58 *Two humbuckers, six-saddle bridge plus separate bar tailpiece.*
Similar to "THIRD VERSION", except:
- Two metal-cover humbucker pickups.
Finish changed to sunburst in 1958: see later STANDARD entry.

GOLD-TOP "FIFTH VERSION"
1968-69 *Based on "THIRD VERSION" (bridge and separate tailpiece), but wide binding in cutaway. Confusingly referred to in Gibson literature as "Standard" model.*

REFERENCE SECTION

GOLD-TOP "SIXTH VERSION"
1971-72 *Based on "SECOND VERSION" (one-piece bridge/tailpiece), but with Gibson logo on pickups. Some examples with extra plastic ring around pickup covers. Also referred to in literature as "Standard 58".*

AVAILABLE PRODUCTION TOTALS for gold-top models: 1952/1716; 1953/2245; 1954/1504; 1955/862; 1956/920; 1957/598; 1958/434 (includes some "Sunburst" models); 1968/1224; 1969/2751; 1971/25; 1972/1046; 1973/4; 1974/1. Figures not available for 1980s, 1990s and 2000s.

GOLD-TOP OTHER MODELS
alphabetical order

GOLD-TOP 52 REISSUE
1998–current *Based on "FIRST VERSION".*

GOLD-TOP 54 REISSUE
1997–current *Based on "SECOND VERSION".*

GOLD-TOP 56 REISSUE
1990–current *Based on "THIRD VERSION", except plastic-covered humbucker pickups (visually identical to single-coils) through 1996, then single-coils.*

GOLD-TOP 56 REISSUE AGED
2001-current *Aged hardware.*

GOLD-TOP 57 DARKBACK REISSUE
2000-current *Dark-stained back.*

GOLD-TOP 57 MARY FORD 1997
Based on "FOURTH VERSION", except gold-stenciled leaves on pickguard, custom armrest.

GOLD-TOP 57 REISSUE 1983-90, 1993–current *Based on "FOURTH VERSION"*

GOLD-TOP 57 REISSUE AGED
2001-current *Aged hardware, optional reissue case and amplifier.*

40th ANNIVERSARY *See later 40th Anniversary entry.*

HERITAGE

HERITAGE STANDARD 80 1980-82
"Heritage Series Standard-80" on truss-rod cover; extra four-figure number on back of headstock.
- Bound rosewood fingerboard, crown markers; "Les Paul Model" on headstock; "Heritage Series Standard-80" on truss-rod cover; four-figure number on back of headstock in addition to normal serial number.
- Bound carved-top body; sunbursts.
- Two metal-cover humbucker pickups.
- Four controls (two volume, two tone) plus three-way selector.
- Cream plastic pickguard.
- Six-saddle bridge plus separate bar tailpiece.

HERITAGE STANDARD 80 AWARD
1981 *pearl trapezoid inlay, gold-plated hardware*
Similar to HERITAGE STANDARD 80, except:
- Bound ebony fingerboard.
- Gold-plated hardware.
- Oval pearl medallion on back of peghead with limited edition ranking.

HERITAGE STANDARD 80 ELITE
1980-82 *"Heritage Series Standard-80 Elite" on truss-rod cover; additional four-figure serial number on back of headstock.*

Similar to HERITAGE STANDARD 80, except:
- Bound ebony fingerboard; "Heritage Series Standard-80 Elite" on truss-rod cover.
- Quilted maple carved-top.

JIMMY PAGE

JIMMY PAGE 1995-99 *Flamed top, signature on pickguard*
Based on STANDARD, except:
- Push/pull knobs for phasing and coil-tapping (no visible difference).
- Faded cherry sunburst.
- Locking nut added to bridge height adjustment after first 500.
- Page signature on pickguard
- Gold-plated hardware.

JOE PERRY

JOE PERRY 1996–2000 *Black stain finish on flamed top; white pearloid pickguard.*
Similar to STANDARD, except:
- Unbound rosewood fingerboard; decal logo on headstock.
- Unbound carved-top of figured maple; blackburst.
- Two uncovered humbucker pickups; four controls (two volume, two tone, push/pull tone knob to activate mid-boost) plus selector.
- White pearloid pickguard.
- Black hardware.

JUMBO

JUMBO 1970-71 *Round soundhole.*
- Rosewood fingerboard, dot markers; "Les Paul Jumbo" on truss-rod cover.
- Bound single-cutaway Jumbo acoustic body; natural.
- One round-end plastic-cover low-impedance humbucker pickup.
- Four controls (volume, treble, bass, "Decade") plus bypass switch.

- Black plastic pickguard.
- Height-adjustable one-piece bridge with string-anchor pins in wooden surround.

Requires special lead with built-in impedance-matching transformer to match normal amplification impedance.

AVAILABLE PRODUCTION TOTALS
for Jumbo models: 1971/43; 1972/3; 1973/3. Figures not available for 1970.

JUNIOR SINGLE-CUTAWAY

JUNIOR SINGLE-CUTAWAY NORMAL MODELS
chronological order

JUNIOR "SINGLE-CUT" 1954-58 *Slab single-cutaway body, one pickup.*
- Unbound rosewood fingerboard, dot markers; "Les Paul Junior" on headstock; plastic tuner buttons.
- Unbound slab body; sunburst. (For beige examples, see later TV entry.)
- One plastic-cover six-polepiece single-coil pickup.
- Two controls (volume, tone).
- Black or tortoiseshell plastic pickguard.
- Wrap-over bar bridge/tailpiece.

JUNIOR "SINGLE-CUT THREE-QUARTER" 1956-58 *Shorter 19-fret neck.*
Similar to "SINGLE-CUT", except:
- Shorter neck (with 19 frets) and scale-length (2" less than normal).

JUNIOR SINGLE-CUTAWAY OTHER MODELS
alphabetical order

JUNIOR (JR.) SPECIAL *see OTHER MODELS in later SPECIAL SINGLE-CUTAWAY entry.*

JUNIOR (JR.) SPECIAL HUM (or HB) *see OTHER MODELS in later SPECIAL SINGLE-CUTAWAY entry.*

JUNIOR (JR.) SPECIAL PLUS *see OTHER MODELS in later SPECIAL SINGLE-CUTAWAY entry.*

JUNIOR II *see OTHER MODELS in later SPECIAL SINGLE-CUTAWAY entry.*

JUNIOR 54 1986-92 *Based on "SINGLE-CUT" but six-saddle bridge plus separate bar tailpiece; sunburst, cherry or white.*

JUNIOR 57 1998-current *Based on "SINGLE-CUT" but six-saddle bridge plus separate bar tailpiece; sunburst, cherry or TV yellow.*

JUNIOR DOUBLE-CUTAWAY

JUNIOR DOUBLE-CUTAWAY NORMAL MODELS
chronological order

JUNIOR "DOUBLE-CUT" 1958-61 & 1997-98 *Slab double-cutaway body, one pickup.*
- Unbound rosewood fingerboard, dot markers; "Les Paul Junior" on headstock; plastic tuner buttons.
- Unbound slab double-cutaway body; cherry. (For yellow examples, see later TV entry.)
- One plastic-cover six-polepiece single-coil pickup.
- Two controls (volume, tone).
- Black or tortoiseshell plastic pickguard.
- Wrap-over bar bridge/tailpiece.

Shape changed in 1961: see later SG/LES PAUL JUNIOR entry. Some examples in sunburst.

JUNIOR "DOUBLE-CUT THREE-QUARTER" 1958-61 *Shorter 19-fret neck.*
Similar to "DOUBLE-CUT", except:
- Shorter neck (with 19 frets) and scale-length (2" less than normal.

AVAILABLE PRODUCTION TOTALS
for Junior models: 1954/823; 1955/2939; 1956/3129; 1957/2959; 1958/2408; 1959/4364; 1960/2513; 1961/2151 (includes some "SG/Les Paul" Junior models). And for Junior 3/4 models: 1956/18; 1957/222; 1958/181; 1959/199; 1960/96; 1961/71.

JUNIOR DOUBLE-CUTAWAY OTHER MODELS
alphabetical order

JUNIOR LITE *see OTHER MODELS in later SPECIAL entry.*

JUNIOR 58 1987-95 & 1998-current *Based on "DOUBLE-CUT" but six-saddle bridge plus separate bar tailpiece; nickel-plated hardware and plastic-cover humbucker pickup (appears identical to single-coil) 1990-92 only.*

KORINA

KORINA 1996 *Korina (wood) back and neck.*
Similar to STANDARD, except:
- Figured maple top, korina back and neck.
- Nickel-plated hardware.

KM

KM 1979 *"Les Paul KM" on truss-rod cover.*
Similar to STANDARD, except:
- "Les Paul KM" on truss rod cover.
- Sunbursts or natural.
- Two coverless cream-coil humbucker pickups;

REFERENCE SECTION

- Larger rectangular six-saddle bridge plus separate bar tailpiece.

Made in Kalamazoo (=KM) after Les Paul production moved to Nashville.
Early examples with "Custom Made" plastic plate on body face below tailpiece.

AVAILABLE PRODUCTION TOTAL for KM model: 1979/1052.

K-II

K-II 1980 *Carved-top double-cutaway body, two humbucking pickups, "K-II" on truss rod cover.*

LES PAUL BASS

LES PAUL BASS "FIRST VERSION" 1969-70 *24 frets, dot markers, most controls not on panel.*

- Unbound rosewood fingerboard, dot markers; 24 frets, 30.5" scale-length; "thistle"-style inlay on headstock.
- Bound carved-top body; brown.
- Two round-end plastic-cover low-impedance humbucker pickups.
- Three controls (volume, bass, treble) plus three-way selector, all on body; phase slide switch and tone selector on small panel.
- No pickguard.
- Four-saddle bridge/tailpiece with integral damper; plus metal cover.

Requires special lead with built-in impedance-matching transformer to match normal amplification impedance.

LES PAUL BASS "SECOND VERSION" *(also known as LES PAUL TRIUMPH BASS)* **1971-79** *24 frets, block markers, all controls on panel.*

- Bound rosewood fingerboard, block markers; 24 frets, 30.5" scale-length; split-diamond inlay on headstock.
- Bound carved-top body; brown or white.

- Two round-end plastic-cover low-impedance humbucker pickups.
- Three controls (volume, bass, treble) plus three-way selector, phase slide switch, tone selector, impedance slide switch, and jack socket, all on black laminated plastic panel; built-in impedance-matching transformer.
- No pickguard.
- Four-saddle bridge/tailpiece; plus metal cover.

AVAILABLE PRODUCTION TOTALS for Bass and/or Triumph Bass models: 1971/321; 1972/768; 1973/959; 1974/526; 1975/208; 1976/171; 1977/101; 1978/80; 1979/44. Figures not available for 1969 and 1970.

LP XRI/XRII/XRIII

LP XRI 1981-82 *"XR-I" on truss-rod cover.*

- Unbound rosewood fingerboard, dot markers; "Les Paul Model" on headstock; "XR-I" on truss-rod cover.
- Unbound carved-top body; sunbursts.
- Two coverless humbucker pickups.
- Four controls (two volume, two tone) plus three-way selector and mini-switch.
- No pickguard.
- Six-saddle bridge plus separate bar tailpiece.

LP XRII 1981-82 *"XR-II" on truss-rod cover.* Similar to LP XRI, except:
- "XR-II" on truss-rod cover.
- Bound slab body; sunbursts or natural.
- Two mini-sized metal-cover humbucker pickups.

LP XRIII 1982 *"XR-III" on truss-rod cover.*
- Possibly red only.

No other information available for this model.

NORTH STAR

NORTH STAR 1978 *Star inlay on headstock.*
Similar to STANDARD, except:
- Multi-layer (Custom-style) body binding.
- "North Star" on truss rod cover, star inlaid in headstock.

OLD HICKORY

OLD HICKORY 1998 *"Old Hickory" on fingerboard*
- Bound, carved-top tulip poplar body from tree felled by 1998 tornado in Nashville.
- Two metal-cover humbucker pickups.
- Bound hickory fingerboard; "Old Hickory" fingerboard inlay; image of Pres. Andrew Jackson("Old Hickory")on peghead.

ORVILLE

The forename of the founder of the American company was used by Gibson on a range of Japanese-made guitars, launched in 1988, which officially copy Gibson's most famous designs. While the cheaper guitars carry only the Orville logo, the higher priced versions are branded Orville By Gibson. This latter range bear the "Les Paul" logo when appropriate, and models include the Custom, Standard and Junior. The Orville By Gibson instruments are equipped with US-made Gibson pickups. At the time of writing these high-quality, accurate repros are sold only on the Japanese market; Gibson do not see a market for them elsewhere.

PERSONAL

PERSONAL 1969-72 *Two angled pickups, block markers, gold hardware.*
- Bound ebony fingerboard, block

markers; split-diamond inlay on headstock.
- Bound carved-top body; brown.
- Two angled round-end plastic-cover low-impedance humbucker pickups.
- Five controls (volume, bass, treble, Decade, microphone volume) plus three-way selector, all on body; phase slide switch and tone selector on small panel. Microphone input socket on upper left side of body.
- Black laminated plastic pickguard.
- Gold-plated hardware.

Requires special lead with built-in impedance-matching transformer to match normal amplification impedance.

AVAILABLE PRODUCTION TOTALS
for Personal models: 1971/95; 1972/49; 1973/2. Figures not available for 1969 and 1970.

PETER FRAMPTON

PETER FRAMPTON 2000-current
Three uncovered humbucking pickups, "Peter Frampton" on 12th fret marker. Similar to CUSTOM "THIRD VERSION"
- "Peter Frampton" on 12th fret marker.
- Three uncovered humbucker pickups.
- Custom-wired selector switch (no visible difference).
- No pickguard
- Strap-locking endpin.

PRO DELUXE

PRO DELUXE 1976-82 *Bound ebony fingerboard with crown markers.*
- Bound ebony fingerboard, crown markers; "Les Paul Model" on headstock; "Pro" on truss-rod cover.
- Bound carved-top body; sunbursts or colours.
- Two plastic-cover six-polepiece single-coil pickups.
- Four controls (two volume, two tone) plus three-way selector.
- Cream plastic pickguard.
- Six-saddle bridge plus separate bar tailpiece.

PRO SHOWCASE EDITION

PRO SHOWCASE EDITION 1988
Gold-top, production 250.

PROFESSIONAL

PROFESSIONAL 1969-71 *Two angled pickups, crown markers, nickel-plated hardware.*
- Bound rosewood fingerboard, crown markers.
- Bound carved-top body; brown.
- Two angled round-end plastic-cover low-impedance humbucker pickups.
- Four controls (volume, bass, treble, Decade) plus three-way selector, all on body; phase slide switch and tone selector on small panel.
- Black laminated plastic pickguard.

Requires special lead with built-in impedance-matching transformer to match normal amplification impedance.

AVAILABLE PRODUCTION TOTALS
for Professional models: 1971/116; 1973/2; 1977/11; 1978/1399 (probably a misprint); 1979/6. Figures not available for 1969 and 1970.

RECORDING

RECORDING "FIRST VERSION" 1971-77 *"Les Paul Recording" on truss-rod cover; all controls on panel.*
- Bound rosewood fingerboard, block markers; split-diamond inlay on headstock; "Les Paul Recording" on truss-rod cover.
- Bound carved-top body; sunburst, brown or white.
- Two angled round-end plastic-cover low-impedance humbucker pickups.
- Four controls (volume, bass, treble, Decade) plus three-way selector, tone selector, phase slide switch, low/high impedance slide switch, and jack socket, all on laminated black plastic panel; built-in impedance-matching transformer.
- Black laminated plastic pickguard.
- Six-saddle bridge plus separate bar tailpiece.

RECORDING "SECOND VERSION" 1977-79 *"Les Paul Recording" on truss-rod cover; selector by neck pickup.* Similar to "FIRST VERSION", except:
- Sunburst, brown, white or black.
- Bound ebony fingerboard.
- Four controls (volume, bass, treble, Decade) plus phase slide switch and tone selector, all on laminated black plastic panel; three-way selector on body; one jack socket on side of body for normal high-impedance output, plus second jack socket on body face for low-impedance output.

AVAILABLE PRODUCTION TOTALS
for Recording models made at Kalamazoo: 1971/236; 1972/1314; 1973/1759; 1974/915; 1975/204; 1976/352; 1977/362; 1978/180; 1979/78. Figures not available for any Nashville production.

SG/LES PAUL CUSTOM

SG/LES PAUL CUSTOM 1961-63
Bevelled-edge two-cutaway body; three pickups.
- Bound ebony fingerboard, block markers; split-diamond inlay on headstock; "Custom" on truss-rod cover.
- Bevelled-edge two-cutaway body; white only.
- Three metal-cover humbucker pickups.

REFERENCE SECTION

- Four controls (two volume, two tone) plus three-way selector; jack socket on body face.
- White laminated plastic pickguard, plus small white plastic plate reading "Les Paul Custom".
- Six-saddle bridge plus separate sideways-action vibrato tailpiece.
- Gold-plated hardware.

Some examples with standard-action vibrato tailpieces, some of which have inlaid decorative block in body face masking holes intended for sideways-action vibrato unit.
Also 30th Anniversary version with appropriate inlay on headstock (1991-92): see later 30th ANNIVERSARY entry.

AVAILABLE PRODUCTION TOTALS
for "SG/Les Paul" Custom models: 1961/513 (includes some Les Paul Custom models); 1962/298; 1963/264 (includes some SG Custom models).

SG/LES PAUL CUSTOM REISSUE
1987-90 & 98-current *Reissue based on original version, but with six-saddle bridge plus separate bar tailpiece; optional Maestro vibrato (long cover but not side-pull).*

SG/LES PAUL JUNIOR

SG/LES PAUL JUNIOR 1961-63
Bevelled-edge two-cutaway body; one pickup.
- Unbound rosewood fingerboard, dot markers; "Les Paul Junior" on headstock; plastic tuner buttons.
- Bevelled-edge two-cutaway body; cherry.
- One plastic-cover six-polepiece single-coil pickup.
- Two controls (volume, tone); jack socket on body face.
- Black laminated plastic pickguard.

- Wrap-over bar bridge/tailpiece; optional separate vibrato tailpiece.

AVAILABLE PRODUCTION TOTALS
for "SG/Les Paul" Junior models: 1961/2151 (includes some Les Paul Junior models); 1962/2395; 1963/2318 (includes some SG Junior models).

SG/LES PAUL SPECIAL "REISSUE"
Based on 1961-63 SG Special, this model (2000-current) is not a Les Paul model. Contrary to some photos, and the name, the instrument does not have "Les Paul" on truss rod cover or headstock – and so is outside the scope of this book.

SG/LES PAUL STANDARD

SG/LES PAUL STANDARD
1961-63 *Bevelled-edge two-cutaway body; two humbucker pickups.*
- Bound rosewood fingerboard, crown markers; "thistle"-style inlay on headstock; "Les Paul" on truss-rod cover; plastic tuner buttons.
- Bevelled-edge two-cutaway body; cherry.
- Two metal-cover humbucker pickups.
- Four controls (two volume, two tone) plus three-way selector; jack socket on body face.
- Black laminated plastic pickguard.
- Six-saddle bridge plus separate sideways-action vibrato tailpiece.

Some examples with standard-action vibrato tailpieces, some of which have inlaid decorative block in body face masking holes intended for sideways-action vibrato unit.
Some examples in white or sunburst.

AVAILABLE PRODUCTION TOTALS
for "SG/Les Paul" Standard models: 1961/1662; 1962/1449; 1963/1445 (includes some SG Standard models).

SG/LES PAUL STANDARD REISSUE
2000-current *Reissue based on original version but with optional Maestro vibrato (long cover but not side-pull); optional aged hardware; faded cherry, white or TV yellow. Although reissues have been produced since 1986 under various names, including "62 SG Standard, "61 SG Standard and Les Paul/SG "61 Reissue (1993-95), the SG/Les Paul Standard Reissue (2000-current) is the only one with "Les Paul" on the truss rod cover.*

SG/LES PAUL STANDARD REISSUE – AGED 2001-current

SIGNATURE

SIGNATURE 1974-78 *Semi-acoustic with two f-holes and offset cutaways.*
- Bound rosewood fingerboard, crown markers; "Les Paul Signature" on headstock; plastic tuner buttons.
- Bound semi-acoustic thinline body with two f-holes and offset cutaways; gold or sunburst.
- Two rectangular plastic-cover low-impedance humbucker pickups.
- Two controls (volume, tone) plus three-position impedance rotary switch, two-way phase rotary switch, and three-way selector; one jack socket on side of body for normal high-impedance output, plus second jack socket on body face for low-impedance output; built-in impedance transformer.
- Cream plastic pickguard.
- Six-saddle bridge plus separate bar tailpiece.

Earliest examples with two round-end plastic-cover low-impedance humbucker pickups, and two side-mounted jack sockets.

AVAILABLE PRODUCTION TOTALS
for Signature models: 1973/3; 1974/1046; 1975/118; 1976/150; 1977/123; 1978/20; 1979/3.

SIGNATURE BASS

SIGNATURE BASS 1974-79
Semi-acoustic bass with two f-holes and offset cutaways.

- Unbound rosewood fingerboard, crown markers; 34½" scale-length, 20 frets; "Les Paul Signature" on headstock.
- Bound semi-acoustic thinline body with two f-holes and offset cutaways; gold top or sunburst.
- One rectangular plastic-cover low-impedance humbucker pickup.
- Two controls (volume, tone) plus three-position impedance rotary switch; one jack socket on side of body for normal high-impedance output, plus second jack socket on body face for low-impedance output; built-in impedance transformer.
- Cream plastic pickguard.
- Four-saddle bridge/tailpiece.

Earliest examples with one round-end plastic-cover low-impedance humbucker pickup, and two side-mounted jack sockets.

AVAILABLE PRODUCTION TOTALS
for Signature Bass models: 1973/3; 1974/428; 1975/26; 1976/44; 1977/45; 1978/23; 1979/58.

SILVER STREAK

SILVER STREAK 1982 *Similar to STANDARD, except: dot markers, all silver finish.*

SLASH

SLASH 1997 *Slash image carved into top, limited to 50, cranberry finish*

SM

SM 1980 *Dot markers, "SM" on truss rod cover, coil tap.*

- Bound rosewood fingerboard, dot markers; "SM" on truss rod cover.
- Multiple-bound carved-top body, silverburst.
- Two metal-cover humbucker pickups.
- Four controls (2 volume, 2 tone) plus selector and coil-tap switch
- Six-saddle bridge plus separate bar tailpiece.

SMARTWOOD

SMARTWOOD EXOTIC 1998-current
"Smartwood" on truss rod cover.
Similar to STANDARD, except:
- Wood certified by Rainforest Alliance.
- Curupay fingerboard, dot markers, "Smartwood" on truss rod cover.
- Gold-plated hardware.
- Top of ambay guasa, banara, taperyva, cancharana, peroba, or quasa wood.
- Natural finish, optional "SL" matte urethane finish.

SMARTWOOD STANDARD 1996-2000 *"Smartwood" on truss rod cover.*
Similar to STANDARD, except:
- Wood certified by Rainforest Alliance.
- Chechen fingerboard, pearl crown markers, "Smartwood" on truss rod cover.
- Gold-plated hardware.
- Natural finish.

SMARTWOOD BASS

SMARTWOOD BASS 1998 *20 frets, crown markers, chrome-plated hardware.*

- Unbound chechen fingerboard, crown markers; 20 frets, 34" scale-length; "Les Paul" on truss-rod cover.
- Unbound flat-top body; wood certified by Rainforest Alliance; sunbursts, black natural or emerald.
- Two plain-cover humbucker pickups.
- Four controls (volume, bass, treble, balance), active circuit.
- No pickguard.
- Four-saddle bridge/tailpiece.

SPECIAL BASS

SPECIAL BASS 1991-95 *20 frets, dot markers.*

- Unbound ebony fingerboard, dot markers; 20 frets, 34" scale-length; ornate "flower pot" inlay on headstock (omitted from 1993); "Les Paul" on truss-rod cover.
- Unbound slab body; black, cherry or yellow.
- Two plain-cover humbucker pickups.
- 1992 model three controls (volume, volume, tone), passive circuit; from 1993 four controls (volume, bass, treble, balance), active circuit.
- No pickguard.
- Four-saddle bridge/tailpiece.
- Black-plated hardware.

Also five-string version (1993-95).

SPECIAL SINGLE-CUTAWAY

SPECIAL SINGLE-CUTAWAY NORMAL MODELS
chronological order

SPECIAL "SINGLE-CUT" 1955-58, 1998 *Slab single-cutaway body, two pickups.*

- Bound rosewood fingerboard, dot markers; "Les Paul Special" on headstock; plastic tuner buttons.
- Unbound slab body; beige (SL urethane colours 1998 only).
- Two plastic-cover six-polepiece single-coil pickups.
- Four controls (two volume, two tone) plus three-way selector.
- Black laminated plastic pickguard.

- Wrap-over bar bridge/tailpiece.

Some early examples with brown plastic parts (knobs, pickguard etc).

SPECIAL "SINGLE-CUT" REISSUE
1989-current

Similar to SPECIAL "SINGLE-CUT", except:
- Metal tuner buttons (white plastic from 1998).
- Sunburst, cherry, yellow or black (faded cherry or TV yellow from 1998).
- Pickups, although visually similar to originals, are actually humbuckers (single-coils from 1998).
- Six-saddle bridge plus separate bar tailpiece (wraparound from 1998).

Originally and erroneously referred to in Gibson literature as Junior II. Also available (1998) with SL (Sans Lacquer) urethane finish and unbound fingerboard.

SPECIAL SINGLE-CUTAWAY OTHER MODELS
alphabetical order

JUNIOR SPECIAL 1999-current
Similar to SPECIAL "SINGLE-CUT", except humbucker pickups (at first not visibly different from single-coils), six-saddle bridge with separate tailpiece, unbound fingerboard, half-size crown markers (dots from 2001), contoured back of body.

JUNIOR SPECIAL HUM (or HB) 2001-current
Similar to SPECIAL "SINGLE-CUT", except metal-cover humbucker pickups; six-saddle bridge with separate tailpiece; unbound fingerboard, contoured back of body; chrome-plated hardware.

JUNIOR SPECIAL PLUS 2001-current
Similar to SPECIAL "SINGLE-CUT", except figured maple top cap; metal-cover humbucker pickups; six-saddle bridge with separate tailpiece; selector switch on upper bass bout; unbound fingerboard; gold-plated hardware; trans amber or trans red.

JUNIOR II 1989
Similar to SPECIAL "SINGLE-CUT", except humbucker pickups (not visibly different from single-coils) and six-saddle bridge with separate tailpiece (renamed SPECIAL in 1989: see "60 SPECIAL SINGLE-CUT").

SPECIAL 55 1974, 1977-80
Based on SPECIAL "SINGLE CUT": earliest examples with wrap-over bar bridge/tailpiece; majority have six-saddle bridge plus separate bar tailpiece. Sunbursts or colours. Earlier examples have plastic tuner buttons.

AVAILABLE PRODUCTION TOTALS for "Special 55" models made at Kalamazoo: 1974/1925; 1976/2; 1977/331; 1978/293; 1979/224. Figures not available for 1980, nor for any Nashville production.

SPECIAL 400 1985
Based on SPECIAL "SINGLE-CUT" except for 1 humbucker and 2 single-coil pickups; 2 knobs (master tone and master volume), 3 switches (on-off pickup selector), vibrato, most with ebony fingerboard.

SPECIAL DOUBLE-CUTAWAY

SPECIAL DOUBLE-CUTAWAY NORMAL MODELS
chronological order

SPECIAL "DOUBLE-CUT" 1959-60, 1998
Slab double-cutaway body, two pickups.
- Bound rosewood fingerboard, dot markers; "Les Paul Special" on headstock; plastic tuner buttons.
- Unbound slab double-cutaway body; yellow or cherry.
- Two plastic-cover six-polepiece single-coil pickups.
- Four controls (two volume, two tone) plus three-way selector.
- Black laminated plastic pickguard.
- Wrap-over bar bridge/tailpiece.

Later examples with neck pickup moved further down body, away from end of fingerboard; selector moved next to bridge (see pXX).
Model name changed to SG Special in 1960 when Les Paul logo removed.

SPECIAL "DOUBLE-CUT" REISSUE
1998-current *Similar to SPECIAL "DOUBLE-CUT", except: nickel-plated hardware; faded cherry or TV yellow finish (ebony, cinnamon or natural from 2001).*

SPECIAL "DOUBLE-CUT THREE-QUARTER" 1959-60
Shorter 19-fret neck. Similar to "DOUBLE-CUT", except:
- Shorter neck (with 19 frets) and scale-length (2" less than normal).
- Cherry finish only.

Model name changed to SG Special 3/4 in 1960 when Les Paul logo removed.

AVAILABLE PRODUCTION TOTALS for Special models: 1955/373; 1956/1345; 1957/1452; 1958/958; 1959/1821; 1960/1387 (includes some SG Special models). And for Special ¾ models: 1959/12; 1960/39 (includes some SG Special ¾ models).

FIFTY YEARS OF THE GIBSON LES PAUL

SPECIAL DOUBLE-CUTAWAY OTHER MODELS
alphabetical order

JUNIOR LITE 1999-current *Based on SPECIAL "DOUBLE-CUT" but with two "stacked" humbucker pickups (not visibly different from single-coils), six-saddle bridge with separate tailpiece, unbound fingerboard, half-size crown markers, contoured back of body.*

SPECIAL 58 1976-85, 1998-current *Based on SPECIAL "DOUBLE-CUT" but six-saddle bridge plus separate bar tailpiece; sunbursts or colours.*

AVAILABLE PRODUCTION TOTALS
for "Special 58" models made at Kalamazoo: 1976/162; 1977/1622; 1978/803; 1979/150. Figures not available for any Nashville production.

SPOTLIGHT SPECIAL

SPOTLIGHT SPECIAL 1983
Contrasting wood stripe down centre of body.
- Bound rosewood fingerboard, crown markers; "Les Paul Model" on headstock; "Custom Shop Edition" logo on rear of headstock; "83" plus three-figure number on back of headstock instead of normal serial number.
- Bound carved-top body with darker contrasting wood stripe down centre; natural or sunburst.
- Two metal-cover humbucker pickups.
- Four controls (two volume, two tone) plus three-way selector.
- No pickguard.
- Six-saddle bridge plus separate bar tailpiece.
- Gold-plated hardware.

STANDARD

STANDARD NORMAL MODELS
chronological order

STANDARD "FIRST VERSION"
1958-60 Similar to GOLD-TOP "FOURTH VERSION" (see listing in earlier GOLD-TOP section), except:
- Body with sunburst top.

For 1950s/1960s gold-top model, sometimes referred to as "Standard", see earlier GOLD-TOP entry.
For early-1960s SG-shaped version, see earlier SG/LES PAUL STANDARD entry.

AVAILABLE PRODUCTION TOTALS
for Standard "First Version" models: 1958/434 (includes some gold-top models); 1959/643; 1960/635.

STANDARD "SECOND VERSION"
1976-current *"Standard" on truss-rod cover.*
- Bound rosewood fingerboard, crown markers; "Les Paul Model" on headstock; "Standard" on truss-rod cover.
- Bound carved-top body; sunbursts, natural or colours.
- Two metal-cover humbucker pickups.
- Four controls (two volume, two tone) plus three-way selector.
- Cream plastic pickguard.
- Six-saddle bridge plus separate bar tailpiece.
- Chrome-plated hardware (gold optional in many years).

Also natural-finish version with gold-plated hardware (1991-92).
For 1980s STANDARD-80 models, see earlier HERITAGE entry.

AVAILABLE PRODUCTION TOTALS
for Standard "Second Version" models made at Kalamazoo: 1975/1; 1976/24; 1977/586; 1978/5947; 1979/1054. Figures not available for large Nashville production started in 1970s, nor for 1980s, 1990s and 2000s.

STANDARD OTHER MODELS
alphabetical order

CUSTOM SHOP STANDARD
1997-current *Similar to STANDARD "SECOND VERSION", except coverless pickups, one with zebra-coil, one with black-coil, inked number with first digit corresponding to last digit of year of manufacturer (as Les Paul Classic).*

STANDARD BIRDSEYE 1993-96
Similar to STANDARD "SECOND VERSION", except special figured maple top.

STANDARD CENTENNIAL 1994
Similar to STANDARD "SECOND VERSION", except brown sunburst, four-digit serial number on tailpiece.

STANDARD CMT 1986-89 *Similar to STANDARD REISSUE except wide binding in cutaway, metal jack-socket plate. CMT stands for "curly maple top".*

STANDARD DOUBLE-CUT PLUS *See earlier DC STANDARD entry.*

STANDARD LITE
1999-current *No binding, double-cutaway carved-top body, gold-plated hardware.*
- Unbound rosewood fingerboard, three-quarter-size crown markers; 24¾" scale-length; standard headstock.
- Unbound carved-top body with shape of Special "SECOND VERSION"; maple top cap; sunbursts or colours.
- Two metal-cover humbucker pickups.
- Two knobs (tone, volume), selector
- Wraparound tailpiece.
- Gold-plated hardware.

REFERENCE SECTION

STANDARD MAHOGANY 1993 *Similar to STANDARD "SECOND VERSION", except solid mahogany body (no top cap), plastic-covered single-coil pickups.*

STANDARD PLUS 1995-99 *Similar to STANDARD "SECOND VERSION", except figured maple top.*

STANDARD RAW POWER 2000-current *Similar to STANDARD "SECOND VERSION", except plain top, chrome-plated hardware, natural satin finish.*

STANDARD REISSUE 1983-90 *Reissue based on STANDARD "FIRST VERSION". Divided into 59 Flametop Reissue and 60 Flametop Reissue models in 1991.*

STANDARD SHOWCASE EDITION 1988 *Similar to STANDARD "SECOND VERSION", except black-cover pole-less EMG pickups, silverburst.*

STANDARD SPECIAL 1983 *Similar to STANDARD "SECOND VERSION", except ebony fingerboard, pearl inlay, gold-plated hardware, cardinal red finish.*

STANDARD TIE DYE 1996 *Similar to STANDARD "SECOND VERSION", except simulated tie-dye top finish (each instrument unique), production around 100.*

STANDARD 58 FIGUREDTOP REISSUE 1996-99, 2001-current *Reissue based on STANDARD "FIRST VERSION" from 1958 period. Figured maple top (but less figure than 59 Reissues). Cherry sunburst finish; then vintage red or butterscotch finish; butterscotch only from 2001.*

STANDARD 58 PLAINTOP REISSUE 1994-99 *Plain (un-figured) maple top.*

STANDARD 59 FLAMETOP REISSUE 1991-current *Reissue based on STANDARD "FIRST VERSION" from 1959 period with relatively fat neck profile. Progressively more "accurate" features, eg longer neck tenon, smaller peghead. "R9" stamped in control cavity from 1993. Also available with AAAAA "Killertop".*

STANDARD 59 FLAMETOP REISSUE AGED 1999-current *Tom Murphy (Gibson employee) distressed ("aged") features.*

STANDARD 59 PLAINTOP REISSUE 1999-2000 *Plain (un-figured) maple top.*

STANDARD 60 FLAMETOP/FIGUREDTOP REISSUE 1991-current *Reissue based on STANDARD "FIRST VERSION" from 1960 period with relatively slimmer neck profile; progressively more accurate features, ie longer neck tenon, smaller peghead. "R0" stamped in control cavity from 1993.*

STANDARD 82 1982 *Reissue made in Kalamazoo, "Standard 82" on truss rod cover.*

STANDARD 83 1983 *PAF Reissue pickups, pearl trapezoid inlay, nickel-plated hardware, natural and sunbursts.*

STANDARD BASS

STANDARD BASS 1992-95, 1999-current *20 frets, crown markers, chrome-plated hardware.*

- Unbound ebony fingerboard, crown markers; 20 frets, 34" scale-length; ornate "flower pot" inlay on headstock (omitted from 1993); "Les Paul" on truss-rod cover.
- Bound carved-top body; sunbursts or black.
- Two plain-cover humbucker pickups.
- 1992 model four controls (two volume, two tone), passive circuit; from 1993 four controls (volume, bass, treble, balance), active circuit.
- No pickguard.
- Four-saddle bridge/tailpiece.

STANDARD PREMIUM PLUS BASS 1993-95
Similar to STANDARD BASS, except:
- Fancier grades of figured maple carved-top.

Also five-string version (1993-95.

STUDIO

STUDIO 1983-current *"Studio" on truss-rod cover.*

- Unbound rosewood fingerboard (rosewood or ebony 1987-98, rosewood 1999-current), dot markers (crown markers 1990-98, three-quarter-size crown markers 1999-2000, full-size crown markers 2001-current); "Les Paul Model" on headstock; "Studio" on truss-rod cover; plastic tuner buttons (metal from 1990).
- Unbound carved-top body; sunburst, natural or colours.
- Two metal-cover humbucker pickups.
- Four controls (two volume, two tone) plus three-way selector.
- Cream or laminated black plastic pickguard.
- Six-saddle bridge plus separate bar tailpiece; optional bridge/vibrato unit.
- Optional gold-plated hardware (from 1986).

Also version with P-90 pickups, white finish, gold-plated, 1997 only.

STUDIO CUSTOM 1984-85
Similar to STUDIO, except:
- Gold-plated hardware.

STUDIO GEM 1996-97
Similar to STUDIO, except:
- Single-coil pickups with cream plastic covers.
- Gold-plated hardware.
- Rosewood fingerboard, crown markers.
- Gemstone finishes.

STUDIO GOTHIC 2000-current
Similar to STUDIO, except:
- Ebony fingerboard, moon-and-star marker at 12th fret.
- Black hardware.
- Flat black finish.

STUDIO PLUS 2001-current
Similar to STUDIO, except *figured top, translucent red or desert burst (brown) finish; gold-plated hardware.*

STUDIO STANDARD 1984-87
Similar to STUDIO, except:
- Bound rosewood fingerboard.
- Bound carved-top body.

STUDIO SYNTHESIZER 1985
Similar to STUDIO, except:
- Roland 700 synthesizer system

STUDIO LITE

STUDIO LITE "FIRST VERSION" 1988-90 *Unbound ebony fingerboard, dot markers.*
- Unbound ebony fingerboard, dot markers; "thistle"-style inlay on headstock.
- Unbound carved-top thinner body with contoured back; sunbursts or colours.
- Two plastic-cover humbucker pickups.
- Two controls (volume, tone) plus three-way selector and mini-switch.
- No pickguard.
- Six-saddle bridge plus separate bar tailpiece; optional bridge/vibrato unit (1988-89).
- Black-plated or gold-plated hardware.

STUDIO LITE "SECOND VERSION" 1990-98 *Unbound ebony fingerboard, crown markers.*
Similar to "FIRST VERSION", except:
- Crown markers.
- "Les Paul Model" on headstock.
- Lightweight carved-top flat-back body.
- Two coverless humbucker pickups.
- Two volumes, two tones, three-way selector.

Also version with three-piece figured maple top, amber or red (1991).

STUDIO LITE/MIII 1992-94
Similar to "SECOND VERSION", except:
- Two coverless humbuckers plus one central six-polepiece single-coil pickup.
- Two controls (volume, tone) plus five-way selector and mini-switch.

THE LES PAUL

THE LES PAUL 1976-79 *"The Les Paul" on truss-rod cover.*
- Bound ebony fingerboard, block markers; split-diamond inlay on headstock; "The Les Paul" on truss-rod cover.
- Bound carved-top body; natural or red.
- Two metal-cover humbucker pickups.
- Four controls (two volume, two tone) plus three-way selector.
- Wooden pickguard.
- Six-saddle bridge plus separate bar tailpiece.
- Gold-plated hardware.

Some examples with fine-tuning tailpiece. Most examples have carved wooden components (pickup surrounds, pickguard, knobs etc) rather than plastic.

AVAILABLE PRODUCTION TOTALS for The Les Paul models: 1976/33; 1977/10; 1979/11. Figures not available for 1978.

THE PAUL

Despite its apparent nominal connection, this model is beyond our coverage since it does not bear the full Les Paul name.

TRIUMPH BASS

See earlier LES PAUL BASS entry, under "SECOND VERSION".

TV

TV "SINGLE-CUT" 1955-58 *Slab single-cutaway body, one pickup, beige finish, "Les Paul TV Model" on headstock.*
- Unbound rosewood fingerboard, dot markers; "Les Paul TV Model" on headstock; plastic tuner buttons.
- Unbound slab body; beige.
- One plastic-cover six-polepiece single-coil pickup.
- Two controls (volume, tone).
- Black or tortoiseshell plastic pickguard.
- Wrap-over bar bridge/tailpiece.

A "three-quarter" short-scale version has been documented.

TV "DOUBLE-CUT" 1958-59 *Slab double-cutaway body, one pickup, yellow finish, "Les Paul TV Model" on headstock.*
- Unbound rosewood fingerboard, dot markers; "Les Paul TV Model" on headstock; plastic tuner buttons.
- Unbound slab double-cutaway body; yellow.
- One plastic-cover six-polepiece single-coil pickup.
- Two controls (volume, tone).
- Black or tortoiseshell plastic pickguard.
- Wrap-over bar bridge/tailpiece.

Name changed to SG TV in 1959 when Les Paul logo removed.

AVAILABLE PRODUCTION TOTALS
for TV models: 1954/5; 1955/230; 1956/511; 1957/552; 1958/429; 1959/543 (includes some SG TV models).

ULTIMA

ULTIMA 1996-2000 *Abalone top border, fancy fingerboard inlay.*

- Bound ebony fingerboard, four optional inlay patterns: flame, tree of life, harp, butterfly; Custom Shop logo inlaid on headstock; pearl tuner buttons.
- Bound carved-top body with abalone pearl border; flamed maple top; natural, stains or sunbursts.
- Two six-polepiece humbucker pickups.
- Four controls (two volumes, two tones) plus three-way selector.
- No pickguard.
- Six-saddle bridge plus separate bar tailpiece, optional trapeze tailpiece.
- Gold-plated hardware.

ZAKK WYLDE

ZAKK WYLDE BULLSEYE 1999-current *Bull"s-eye finish.*
Based on Custom "SECOND VERSION" except:

- Unfinished maple neck; engraved gold-plated truss rod cover; Zakk Wylde decal on back of headstock
- Two plastic-covered poleless EMG pickups.
- Black-white bull's-eye (concentric circles) top finish, white finish on back of body and peghead.
- No pickguard.

ZAKK WYLDE ROUGH TOP 1999-2000 Rough maple top (very little sanding), crown markers, nickel-plated hardware, natural finish.

20th ANNIVERSARY

CUSTOM 20TH ANNIVERSARY 1974 *Anniversary model based on CUSTOM "THIRD VERSION" (see listing in earlier CUSTOM section) but with "Twentieth Anniversary" inlaid into position marker at 15th fret. Sunburst or colours.*

25th ANNIVERSARY

CUSTOM 25TH ANNIVERSARY 1977 *Anniversary model based on CUSTOM "THIRD VERSION" (see listing in earlier CUSTOM section) – even though 1977 was 25th anniversary of Les Paul Standard – but with "25th Anniversary" engraved on tailpiece, "Les Paul" signature on pickguard, chrome-plated hardware, metallic silver.*

25/50 ANNIVERSARY 1978-79
"25 50" inlay on headstock.

- Bound ebony fingerboard, split-block markers; "Les Paul 25 50" on headstock; "Les Paul Anniversary" on gold-plated metal truss-rod cover; brass nut; four-figure number on back of headstock in addition to normal serial number.
- Bound carved-top body; sunburst, natural, red or black.
- Two metal-cover humbucker pickups.
- Four controls (two volume, two tone) plus three-way selector and mini-switch.
- Black laminated plastic pickguard.
- Six-saddle bridge plus separate bar tailpiece with six fine-tuning knobs.
- Gold-/chrome-plated hardware.

AVAILABLE PRODUCTION TOTALS
for 25/50 Anniversary models: 1978/1106; 1979/2305.

30th ANNIVERSARY

GOLD-TOP 30th ANNIVERSARY 1982-83 *Anniversary model based on GOLD-TOP "FOURTH VERSION" (see listing in earlier GOLD-TOP section) but with "Thirtieth Anniversary" inlaid into position marker at 19th fret, gold finish all-around, serial number with letter prefix A, B or C.*

SG/LES PAUL CUSTOM 30th ANNIVERSARY 1991-92 *Anniversary model based on SG/LES PAUL CUSTOM REISSUE (see listing in earlier SG/LES PAUL CUSTOM section) but split-diamond inlay on headstock has "30th Anniversary" in bar and "1961, 1991" in diamond sections. Yellow finish.*

35th ANNIVERSARY

35th ANNIVERSARY 1989-90
Anniversary model based on CUSTOM "SECOND VERSION" (see listing in earlier CUSTOM section) but with "35th Anniversary" in bar of split-diamond inlay on headstock.

40th ANNIVERSARY

40th ANNIVERSARY 1992-93
Similar to GOLD-TOP "THIRD VERSION" (see earlier GOLD-TOP section), except:

- Ebony fingerboard; "40th Anniversary" inlaid into position marker at 12th fret and on rear of headstock.
- Black finish.
- Pickups, although visually similar to single-coils, are actually humbuckers.
- Gold-plated hardware.

54 OXBLOOD

54 OXBLOOD 1998-current *Similar to GOLD-TOP 54 REISSUE, except oxblood finish.*

60 CORVETTE

60 CORVETTE 1995-97 *Similar to STANDARD, except top scooped out to simulate 1960 Chevrolet Corvette car body, Corvette-related appointments, automotive colours.*

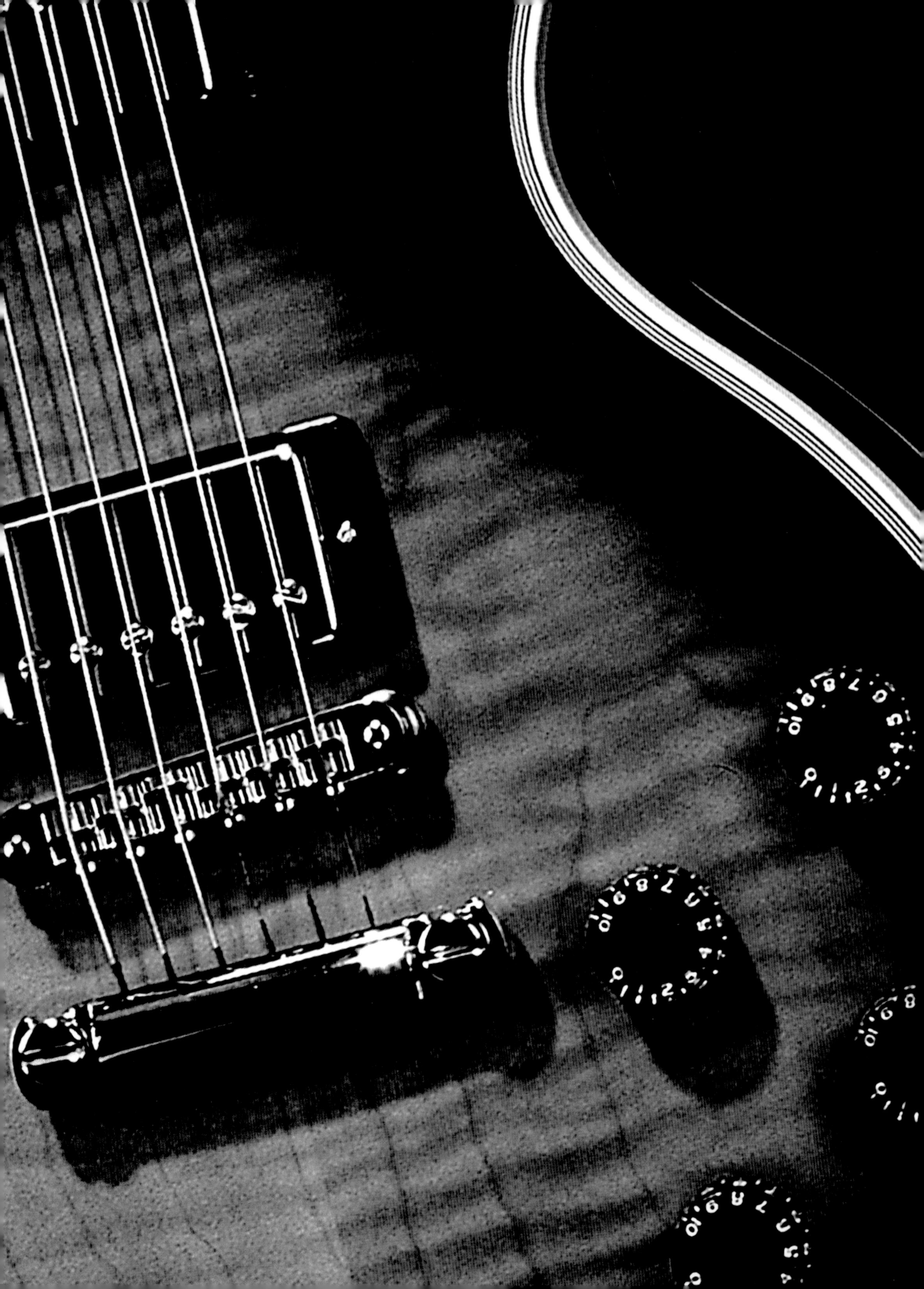

How to date Gibson Les Pauls

DATING GIBSON LES PAULS

As well as being satisfying, it can be important to work out the production date of an instrument. If a guitar can be accurately dated then you might be able to relate it to your personal history or to particular musical styles and famous players. These associations can of course have a significant bearing on value, and where Gibson Les Paul guitars are concerned the vintage is definitely important. Certain years are considered far more desirable than others for quality and performance – and so any clues that confirm an instrument's age are useful, to say the least.

In this book we're dealing with a relatively small selection of guitars from the vast range of instruments produced by the Gibson company during a 50-year period. Gibson made surprisingly few changes during much of this time that will now help a Les Paul owner easily and accurately date an instrument.

It's worth stressing that no single method provides foolproof, totally accurate dating. Gibson, like all mass-manufacturers of instruments, made numerous changes to production procedures, construction technicalities, and component styles. But many of these were introduced over a period of time rather than instantaneously. Often, existing parts would continue to be used, sometimes in combination with revised methods or new features, creating a variety of "transitional" guitars. Such instruments tend to cause confusion and blur the chronological picture. But by careful scrutiny of the following information it should be possible to date most Gibson Les Pauls to a relatively narrow time slot.

VINTAGE VERIFICATION

Instruments from Fender and other makers are often easier to date than those from Gibson, whose guitars yield fewer obvious clues. Many of Gibson's pointers require direct comparison between two or more instruments, or involve technical measuring equipment or specialised knowledge of the construction and workings of the company's electric guitars. It is essential to have a keen, trained eye, plus a very good memory, as some of the data relating to the age of Les Pauls are complex and confusing.

Just as with Fender and other high-profile US-made guitars, many Gibson instruments occupy prime positions in the vintage market. Certain Les Pauls are among the most desirable, and therefore reside at the very top of the big-money league. Other Les Paul models too command much interest and high values, and the year of manufacture has a great bearing on this. Sometimes a guitar's vintage even seems more important than the inherent quality and playability of an individual guitar. Conversely, there are other Les Pauls that have little appeal among players and collectors, mostly thanks to the low esteem in which a particular production period is held – and here, determining age can help you to know what to avoid.

Specific changes made to various Les Pauls have been included in the relevant entries in the main instrument listing. These details provide an accurate timescale for individual models, but there are a number of more general indicators of age. Of course, these are only of use if they are original to the instrument concerned. With so many broad similarities between groups of Les Paul models, even the replacement of something as apparently innocent as a truss-rod cover can give the impression that one model is actually another, even on relatively recent guitars. As usual, please beware of modifications made to mislead.

Note that "c" in front of a date stands for circa, meaning "about".

GIBSON HEADSTOCK LOGO

The Gibson brandname is proudly displayed on the headstock of all Les Pauls. The style and method of lettering has been modified in various small details over the years, and these can be related to certain periods. While many are extremely minor and can be very hard to spot or determine accurately, some are less subtle and of more immediate help.

From c1952 to c1968 the dot of the **i** in Gibson was not joined to the **G**, and the **b** and **o** were not continuously solid.

From c1968 the **i** lost its dot, and the **b** and **o** became continuously solid.

In 1972 the dotted **i** appeared again, but then came and went with confusing irregularity until c1981.

From 1981 the **o** and **n** were linked at the top, and not at the bottom as usual. However, the usual style was soon reintroduced, and the two versions have been used ever since.

HEADSTOCK ANGLE

From 1965 to 1973 the "tilt-back" angle of the headstock in relation to the neck was altered from a previously standardised 17 degrees to 14 degrees. In 1973 the angle of 17 degrees was reintroduced, but both have been employed since. Direct comparison between two instruments is necessary to determine the rather subtle difference of three degrees.

HEADSTOCK VOLUTE

A volute is a carved "heel" situated at the transition point between the rear of the neck and the angled headstock. The extra timber of the volute was intended to provide reinforcement in this potentially weak area. Gibson introduced the feature c1970, and kept it until c1981.

"MADE IN USA" HEADSTOCK LOGO

From 1970 to 1975 "Made In USA" was stamped into the rear of the headstock. A version of this logo on a decal (transfer) was applied from 1975 to 1977, but in 1977 stamping was reintroduced and has continued ever since.

GIBSON PICKUP LOGO

Plastic-covered P-90 and metal-covered humbucker pickups bore the Gibson logo from c1970 to c1972.

CONTROL KNOBS

Gibson have employed five distinct types of control knob on the Les Paul models over the years, and these do help to indicate production periods, although of course certain versions have since been re-introduced. The dates shown below refer to the original periods of use.

SPEED KNOB Smooth-side barrel shape, internal numbers, clear/coloured all-plastic. First used c1952 to c1955.

BELL KNOB Smooth-side bell shape, internal numbers, clear/coloured all-plastic. First used c1955 to c1960.

METAL-TOP KNOB Smooth-side larger bell shape, internal numbers, clear/coloured plastic with "Volume" or "Tone" inset on large metal top. First used c1960 to c1967.

DATING METHODS

WITCH-HAT KNOB Ribbed-side conical shape, numbered skirt, black plastic with "Volume" or "Tone" on small metal top. First used c1967 to c1975.

CONTROL POT CODES

Removing the control plate on the rear of a Les Paul's body will reveal the metal casings of the control potentiometers, usually called "pots". Some American-made pot casings carry code numbers which, when translated, provide a useful confirmation of the instrument's age. However, it should be noted that the pots could of course have been changed since the guitar was made.

On pots used in Les Pauls from 1952-95, the code consists of six or seven digits. The first three identify the manufacturer and can be ignored. The next one or two digits show the year: one shows the last digit of 195X; a pair indicates any year thereafter. The final two digits signify the week of the appropriate year.

In 1995, Gibson began using a new code consisting of a pair of alpha-numeric figures, followed by the numbers 440, followed by a hyphen and four final numbers. The first figure corresponds to the month (1 to 9 for January to September; letters X, Y and Z for October, November and December, respectively). The second figure corresponds to the last digit of the year.

BRIDGE

Gibson have used various types of bridges on Les Paul models since 1952. Some have been reintroduced since their first appearances; the dates shown below refer to the original periods of use.

WRAP-UNDER Combination unit with two long rod "anchors", as on the very first Les Paul Gold-tops. First used 1952 to 1953.

WRAP-OVER Stud-mounted successor to the above. First used 1953 to c1962.

RIDGED WRAP-OVER As the previous unit, but with a staggered, moulded ridge on the top. First used c1962 to c1971.

TUNE-O-MATIC A bridge with six saddles, individually adjustable for length. First used c1954 to c1961.

TUNE-O-MATIC RETAINER As above, but with a bridge-saddle retaining wire. First used c1961 to c1971.

TUNE-O-MATIC NYLON As above, but with white nylon bridge saddles replacing the metal type of the other versions. First used c1961 to c1971.

NEW TUNE-O-MATIC A heavier-duty version with no bridge-saddle retaining wire. Introduced c1971 and still in use.

RECTANGULAR TUNE-O-MATIC A large rectangular bridge (at times referred to as the Nashville Tune-o-matic) with six long-travel metal saddles. First used c1971 to c1982.

NASHVILLE WIDE-TRAVEL TUNE-O-MATIC Similar to earlier Tune-o-matics but with wider adjustability for saddles. First used 1977 to current.

TP-6 Six fine-tuner adjustments at bridge. First used 1978 to current.

SERIAL NUMBERS

Gibson has changed its system for serial-numbering of instruments several times, and only certain periods provide logical and orderly sequences. In these instances it is easy to give an accurate production date to a guitar once the appropriate system is understood. However, the company has also been guilty of using numbers which appear to have little basis in logic, often being applied out of sequence or, worse still, duplicated once or more. Such numbers provide confusion and very little else, and they should of course be disregarded for dating purposes – except perhaps to confirm a broad period indicated by clues from construction styles and component types.

The earliest Les Paul gold-tops had no serial numbers, but as production increased some examples were given a three-digit number stamped on the top edge of the headstock.

In 1953 a serial-numbering system was instituted specifically for the new Gibson solidbodies. At first this consisted of a five-digit number, ink-stamped on to the rear of the headstock. The first digit was slightly apart from the other four and signified the year of manufacture. In 1955, Gibson's increased output required the addition of a sixth digit (effectively in the "second" position, between the date code and the rest of the number) to some sequences. In both styles, the first digit always provides the date: 3 = 1953; 4 = 1954; 5 = 1955; 6 = 1956; 7 = 1957; 8 = 1958; 9 = 1959; 0 = 1960; 1 = 1961.

During 1961 inked-on numbering was replaced by a method using digits physically stamped right into the back of the headstock. At this time Gibson introduced a new serialisation system for all instruments. The numbers were supposed to be allocated in a strict sequence, but this didn't happen in practice – and the fun started. Many instruments from the 1960s carry duplicated serial numbers, used not only twice but sometimes as many as six or seven times on different guitars.

Similar problems afflicted manufacture for the first five years of the 1970s, with numerous duplications of sequences that had already appeared on 1960s and 1970s guitars. It's extremely difficult to provide a useful table of the numbers used during this 15-year period from 1961 to 1975, and any listing can provide only a very approximate guide, mainly serving to indicate some of the duplicated permutations.

SERIAL NUMBERS 1961-1975

Numbers	Indicates circa	Numbers	Indicates circa
100 to 61,000s	1961-62	332,000s to 368,000s	1965-66
61,000s to 70,000s	1962-64	348,000s to 349,000s	1965-66
71,000s to 99,000s	1962-64	368,000s to 370,000s	1966-67
000,000s	1967, 1973-75	380,000s to 385,000s	1966
100,000s	1963-65, 1970-75	390,000s	1967
100,000s to 144,000s	1963-64, 1967	400,000s	1965-68, 1974-75
147,000s to 199,000s	1963-65	401,000s to 409,000s	1966
200,000s to 290,000s	1964-65, 1973-75	420,000s to 438,000s	1966
300,000s	1965-68, 1974-75	500,000s	1965-66, 1968-69, 1974-75
301,000s to 305,000s	1965		
306,000s to 307,000s	1965, 1967	501,000s to 503,000s	1965
309,000s to 310,000s	1965, 1967	501,000s to 530,000s	1968
311,000s to 326,000s	1965, 1967	530,000s	1966
328,000s to 329,000s	1965	530,000s to 545,000s	1969
329,000s to 332,000s	1965, 1967-68	540,000s	1966

DATING METHODS

Numbers	Indicates circa	Numbers	Indicates circa
550,000s to 556,000s	1966	828,000s to 847,000s	1966, 1969
558,000s to 567,000s	1969	847,000s to 858,000s	1966
570,000s	1966	859,000s to 880,000s	1967
580,000s	1969	893,000s to 897,000s	1967
600,000s	1966-69, 1970-72, 1974-75	895,000s to 896,000s	1968
		897,000s to 898,000s	1967
601,000s	1969	899,000s to 920,000s	1968
605,000s to 606,000s	1969	900,000s	1968, 1970-72
700,000s	1966-67, 1970-72	940,000s to 943,000s	1968
750,000s	1968-69	945,000s	1968
800,000s	1966-69, 1973-75	947,000s to 966,000s	1968
801,000s to 812,000s	1966, 1969	959,000s to 960,000s	1968
812,000s to 814,000s	1969	970,000s to 972,000s	1968
817,000s to 819,000s	1969		
820,000s to 823,000s	1966	A + 6 digits	1973-75
820,000s	1969	B, C, D, E or F + 6 digits	1974-75
824,000s	1969		

In 1975 Gibson at last replaced this haphazard system with a simpler scheme that ran for three years. This used eight digits, the first two of which formed a coded date prefix: 99 = 1975; 00 = 1976; 06 = 1977. And instead of being stamped into the back of the headstock, serial numbers from this series were part of a decal (transfer) which also included the model name and "Made In USA".

In 1977 Gibson reverted to stamping the serial number into the rear of the headstock, and changed the serial number system yet again. The number remained at eight digits, but now the first and fifth indicated the last two numbers of the year of production.

> *For example:*
> 93291369 indicates 1991
> (first number 9 + fifth number 1)
> 02561647 is from 2001
> (first number 0 + fifth number 1).

For 1994 only, Gibson's Nashville plant (but not the Custom Division) changed the system to one in which the first two digits are always 94 to indicate the year of manufacture. In 1995 Gibson returned to the system in which the first and fifth digits denote the year. This system has proved to be successful and reliable, and is still in operation at the time of writing.

The various methods and systems of serial numbering outlined here cover most Gibson Les Pauls issued between 1952 and 2002. However, there are various unusual series, special prefixes and so on which are found on instruments in the Custom and Historic series, on limited editions, on vintage re-issue models, and others. As these are only relevant to specific models and offer no overall dating clues they have been excluded from this listing (but may sometimes be found mentioned elsewhere in the text). On some instruments made by Gibson a separate stamped "2" can be seen, usually below the serial number, and this indicates a factory "second". This is an instrument officially identified at some point in its production as having some cosmetic defect, usually minor and often very hard to detect.

FIFTY YEARS OF THE GIBSON LES PAUL

Model chronology

(*...) = also available earlier during year(s) shown

1952-53	**GOLD-TOP** 1st version (long trapeze)	1961-63	**SG/LES PAUL CUSTOM**
		1961-63	**SG/LES PAUL JUNIOR**
1953-55	**GOLD-TOP** 2nd version (angled 1-piece bridge)	1961-63	**SG/LES PAUL STANDARD**
		1968-current	**CUSTOM** 3rd version (2 humbuckers)
1954-57	**CUSTOM** 1st version (black pickups)	1968-69	**GOLD-TOP** 5th version (6-saddle bridge; sep t/piece)
1954-58	**JUNIOR SINGLE-CUT**		
1955-57	**GOLD-TOP** 3rd version (white p/ups; 6-saddle bridge)	1969-84, 1992-97, 1999-current	**DELUXE**
		1969-70	**LES PAUL BASS** 1st version (most controls not on panel)
1955-58, 1989-current	**SPECIAL SINGLE-CUT**		
1955-58	**TV SINGLE-CUT**	1969-72	**PERSONAL**
1956-58	**JUNIOR SINGLE-CUT THREE-QUARTER**	1969-71	**PROFESSIONAL**
		1970-71	**JUMBO**
1957-61	**CUSTOM** 2nd version (3 humbuckers)	1971-72	**GOLD-TOP** 6th version (angled 1-piece bridge)
1957-58	**GOLD-TOP** 4th version (humbuckers)	1971-77	**RECORDING** 1st version (all controls on panel)
1958-61, 1997-98	**JUNIOR DOUBLE-CUT**	1971-79	**TRIUMPH/LES PAUL BASS** (BASS 2nd version: all controls on panel)
1958-61	**JUNIOR DOUBLE-CUT THREE-QUARTER**		
1958-60, 1976-current	**STANDARD**	1972-73	**CUSTOM 54 LTD EDITION**
1958-59	**TV DOUBLE-CUT**	1974	**CUSTOM 20TH ANNIVERSARY**
1959-60, 1998-current	**SPECIAL DOUBLE-CUT**	1974-78	**SIGNATURE**
1959-60	**SPECIAL DOUBLE-CUT THREE-QUARTER**	1974-79	**SIGNATURE BASS**
		1974, 1977-80	**SPECIAL 55** (single-cut)

MODEL CHRONOLOGY

1976-82	ARTISAN
1976-82	PRO DELUXE
1976-85, 1998-current	
	SPECIAL 58 (double-cut)
1976-current	STANDARD (*58-60)
1976-79	THE LES PAUL

1977	CUSTOM 25TH ANNIVERSARY
1977-79	RECORDING 2nd version (selector by neck pickup)
1977-80	SPECIAL 55 (single-cut) (*74)

1978	NORTH STAR
1978-79	25/50 ANNIVERSARY

1979-81	ARTIST
1979	KM

1980-82	HERITAGE STANDARD 80
1980-82	HERITAGE STANDARD 80 ELITE
1980	K-II
1980	SM

1981	HERITAGE STANDARD 80 AWARD
1981-82	LP XRI
1981-82	LP XRII

1982-83	CUSTOM BLACK BEAUTY 82
1982-83	GOLD-TOP 30th ANNIVERSARY
1982	LP XRIII
1982	SILVER STREAK
1982	STANDARD 82

1983-90, 1993-current	
	GOLD-TOP 57 REISSUE (humbuckers)
1983	SPOTLIGHT SPECIAL
1983-90	STANDARD REISSUE
1983	STANDARD SPECIAL
1983	STANDARD 83
1983-current	STUDIO

1984-85	STUDIO CUSTOM
1984-87	STUDIO STANDARD

1985	SPECIAL 400
1985	STUDIO SYNTHESIZER

1986-89	STANDARD CMT
1986-92	JUNIOR 54 (single-cut)

1987-89	CUSTOM LITE
1987-95, 1998-current	
	JUNIOR 58 (double-cut)
1987-90, 1998-current	
	SG/LES PAUL CUSTOM REISSUE

1988	PRO SHOWCASE EDITION
1988	STANDARD SHOWCASE EDITION
1988-90	STUDIO LITE 1st version (dot markers)

1989-90	35th ANNIVERSARY
1989-current	SPECIAL SINGLE-CUT REISSUE (* 55-58)

1990-current	CLASSIC
1990-current	GOLD-TOP 56 REISSUE (white pickups)

FIFTY YEARS OF THE GIBSON LES PAUL

1990-98	STUDIO LITE 2nd version (crown markers)	1993-95	DELUXE PREMIUM PLUS BASS
1991-92	CLASSIC/MIII	1993-current	GOLD-TOP 57 REISSUE (humbuckers) (* 83-90)
1991-current	CUSTOM BLACK BEAUTY 54	1993-96	STANDARD BIRDSEYE
1991-current	CUSTOM BLACK BEAUTY 57 (2 pickups)	1993	STANDARD MAHOGANY
1991-current	CUSTOM BLACK BEAUTY 57 3-PICKUP	1993-95	STANDARD PREMIUM PLUS BASS
1991-96	CUSTOM PLUS	1994	CLASSIC CENTENNIAL
1991-92	CUSTOM/400	1994	CUSTOM BLACK BEAUTY 57 3-PICKUP CENTENNIAL
1991	DELUXE HALL OF FAME EDITION	1994	STANDARD CENTENNIAL
1991-95	DELUXE PLUS BASS	1994-99	STANDARD 58 PLAINTOP REISSUE
1991-92	SG/LES PAUL CUSTOM 30th ANNIVERSARY	1995-97	ELITE DIAMOND SPARKLE
1991-95	SPECIAL BASS	1995-98	FLORENTINE STANDARD
1991-current	STANDARD 59 FLAMETOP REISSUE	1995-98	FLORENTINE PLUS
1991-current	STANDARD 60 FLAMETOP REISSUE (slim neck)	1995-99	JIMMY PAGE
		1995-97	STANDARD PLUS
		1995-97	60 CORVETTE
1992	CLASSIC CELEBRITY	1996-98	CATALINA
1992-95, 1999-2000	CLASSIC PLUS	1996-2000	ELEGANT
1992-97, 1999-current	DELUXE (* 69-84)	1996-2000	JOE PERRY
		1996	KORINA
1992-95, 1999-current	STANDARD BASS	1996-2000	SMARTWOOD STANDARD
1992-94	STUDIO LITE/MIII	1996	STANDARD TIE DYE
1992-93	40th ANNIVERSARY gold-top	1996-99, 2001-current	STANDARD 58 FIGUREDTOP REISSUE
		1996-97	STUDIO GEM
1993	CLASSIC BIRDSEYE	1996-2000	ULTIMA
1993	CLASSIC PREMIUM BIRDSEYE	1997-2000	ACE FREHLEY
1993-97, 1999-current	CLASSIC PREMIUM PLUS	1997-current	CUSTOM SHOP STANDARD

MODEL CHRONOLOGY

1997-98	DC PRO
1997-98	DC STUDIO
1997	ELEGANT DOUBLE QUILT
1997-98, 2001-current	ELEGANT QUILT
1997	ELEGANT SUPER DOUBLE QUILT
1997-current	GOLD-TOP 54 REISSUE (based on 2nd version)
1997	GOLD-TOP 57 MARY FORD
1997-98	JUNIOR DOUBLE-CUT (*58-61)
1997	SLASH
1998	CLASSIC QUILT TOP
1998	CUSTOM LITE SHOWCASE EDITION
1998-current	DC STANDARD
1998-current	GOLD-TOP 52 REISSUE (based on 1st version)
1998-current	JUNIOR 57
1998-current	JUNIOR 58 (double-cut) (*87-95)
1998	MAHOGANY CUSTOM
1998	OLD HICKORY
1998-current	SG/LES PAUL CUSTOM REISSUE (* 87-90)
1998	SMARTWOOD BASS
1998-current	SMARTWOOD EXOTIC
1998	SPECIAL 58 (* 76-85)
1998-current	SPECIAL DOUBLE-CUT (*59-60)
1998-current	54 OXBLOOD
1999-2000	CLASSIC PLUS (* 92-95)
1999-current	CLASSIC PREMIUM PLUS (* 93-97)
1999-current	DELUXE (* 69-84, 92-97)
1999-current	JUNIOR LITE dbl-cut Special
1999-current	JUNIOR SPECIAL sgl-cut Special
1999-current	STANDARD BASS (* 92-95)
1999-current	STANDARD LITE carved-top Special
1999-current	STANDARD 59 FLAMETOP AGED REISSUE
1999-2000	STANDARD 59 PLAINTOP REISSUE
1999-current	ZAKK WYLDE BULLSEYE
1999-2000	ZAKK WYLDE ROUGHTOP
2000-current	CLASSIC MAHOGANY
2000-current	CUSTOM 68 FIGUREDTOP
2000-current	GARY MOORE
2000-current	GOLD-TOP 57 DARKBACK REISSUE
2000-current	PETER FRAMPTON
2000-current	SG/LES PAUL STANDARD REISSUE
2000-current	STANDARD RAW POWER
2000-current	STUDIO GOTHIC
2001-current	ACOUSTIC
2001-current	CLASS 5
2001	DICKEY BETTS 57 GOLDTOP
2001-current	ELEGANT QUILT (* 97-98)
2001-current	GOLD-TOP 56 REISSUE AGED
2001-current	GOLD-TOP 57 REISSUE AGED
2001-current	JUNIOR SPECIAL HUM/HB
2001-current	JUNIOR SPECIAL PLUS
2001-current	SG/LES PAUL STANDARD REISSUE AGED
2001-current	STANDARD 58 FIGUREDTOP REISSUE
2001-current	STUDIO PLUS

(*...) – also available earlier during year(s) shown

Index

Les Paul guitar models are listed under their individual names; for example, Les Paul Customs appear under Custom.
Page numbers between 130 and 145 indicate the A-to-Z directory of models in the reference section.
An *italic* page number indicates an illustration.

A

Acoustic model 117, 130
"aged" new models 121
all-gold model 27, *27*
Allman, Duane *66*, 73
alnico *see* pickups
Aria 76
Artisan model 74, *75*, 130
Artist model 74, *75*, 77, 130

B

balsa wood 91, 96
Bantam model 96, 130
Barnes, George 21
Bass model 60, 137
Beck, Jeff 49, 52, 92
Beecher, Frannie 33
Bellson, Julius 16
Berlin, Maurice 9, 13, 16, 17, 48, 53, 54
Berryman, David 88
Betts, Dickey 73, *see also* Dickey Betts 57 Goldtop model
Bigsby tailpiece 129
Black Beauty *see* Custom model
Bloomfield, Mike 49
Blues Breakers album (Mayall) 49
body "sandwich" (from 1969) 55
Bolan, Marc 71, *71*, 73
Bolen, Bruce 48, 52, 53, 72, 80, 85
bookmatching 36
Bradfield, James Dean *110*
Braunstein, Phil 17

bridge (/tailpiece) 17, 24, 27, 28, 149
Browne, Jackson 112
Burge, Chuck 76, 77, 80
Butts, Ray 32

C

Caldwell, Doc 21
Caldwell, Toy 73
Carlucci, Marc 16, 53
Carter, Walter 125
Casady, Jack 71
Catalina model 108, 130
Centennial models 105
Charvel 92
cherry red finish 36
Chicago Musical Instrument Company *see* CMI
chromite *see* balsa
Clapton, Eric *43*, 48-49, 92
Clark, Steve 91, *91*
Class 5 model 117, *123*, 130
Classic model 100-101, *103*, 130
Classic other models
    Birdseye/Premium Birdseye models 131
    Celebrity model 131
    Centennial model 131
    Mahogany model 131
    MIII model 97, 131
    Premium/Premium Plus models 131
    Quilt Top model 131
"Classical Guitar" model 64
"clunker" guitars *7*, 8, 9, 20
CMI 9
colour *see* finish; sunburst
control knobs 148-149
"copy" guitars 76
Coxon, Graham 119, *119*
Cradock, Steve 122
Cream (group) 49
Crosby, Bing 9

cross-banding 56
curly wood 37
Custom/Art/Historic division 97, 117, 124
Custom models *18/19*, 19, *19*, *22*, 25, 28, 32, 33, 48, 52, 54, *58*, 59, 60, 65, 73, *74*, 77, *82*, 90, *115*, 116, *119*, 131
Custom other models
    Black Beauty 54 model 131
    Black Beauty 57 models 131-132
    Black Beauty 82 model 132
    Lite models 92, 132
    Mahogany model 132
    Plus model *98*, 132
    20th Anniversary model 68, 145
    25th Anniversary model 145
    35th Anniversary model *90/91*, 145
    54 model 65, 132
    68 Figuredtop model 132
    400 model 132
Custom Shop 85, 97, 117, 120, 124, 132

D

Daniels, Charlie 73
dating methods 147-151
DC models *110/111*, 113, 132-133
DeArmond 28
Decade control 60
Deluxe model 56, 57, 59, *59*, 75, 104, 133
Deluxe Plus/Premium Plus Bass model 97, *99*, 133
Deurloo, Jim 56, 57, 84
Dickey Betts 57 Goldtop model 116, 133
DiMeola, Al 120
Double Cutaway XPL model 113, 133
Duchossoir, André 65

E

ECL 54
Elegant models 108, *111*, 133-134
Elite Diamond Sparkle model 134

INDEX

Epiphone brand 8, 20, 57-58, 71, 88, 96, 108, 111, 124, 134
ES-295 model 21
ES-300 model 6, 8

F

factory seconds 151
factories
    amps/strings/pickups 45
    Kalamazoo 9, 37, 44, 53, 57, 68, 69, 72, 76, 80, 81, 84
    Nashville 68-69, 72, 81, 84, 97
Fender 12, 13, 28, 55, 92, 108, 121, 125
fiddleback wood 37
figured wood 36-37, 40
finish (colour) 21, 25, 28, 29, 36, 40, 116-117
flame(d) wood 37
flip-flop finish 117
Florentine models 96, 134
Ford, Carol 17
Ford, Mary (Colleen Summers) 7, 8, 12, 17, 19, 39, 44, 135
Frampton, Peter 74, 119, see also Peter Frampton model
Frehley, Ace 82, see also Ace Frehley model
"fretless wonder" 25
Fripp, Robert 58, 60
Fuller, Walt 29

G

Gallagher, Noel 106
Gary Moore model 116, 119, 134
Gibbons, Billy 49, 86, 96
Gibbons, Bobby 28
Gibson, Orville 105, 137
gold-top models 11, 14/15, 13-24, 15, 15, 26, 26, 26/27, 27, 27, 32, 33, 34, 36, 37, 38, 54, 56, 57, 58, 59, 66, 73, 134-135
gold-top other models
    30th Anniversary model 83, 83, 145
    40th Anniversary 145
    52 Reissue model 120, 135
    54 Reissue 135
    56 Reissue Aged model 135
    56 Reissue model 105, 135
    57 Darkback Reissue model 135
    57 Mary Ford 135
    57 Reissue Aged model 135
    57 Reissue model 85, 104, 105, 135
Gossard, Stone 97
Green, Peter 39, 49, 59, 116
Gretsch 25, 32, 55, 68, 96
Gruhn, George 65
Guild 96
Guitar Slim 33
Guitar Trader (dealer) 80

H

Haley, Bill 33
Harmony 13
Hart, Guy 13
Havenga, Clarence 16
Haynes, Tiger 21
headstock angle/pitch 148
headstock logo 148
Henrickson, Marv 16
Heritage Guitars (company) 84
Heritage Series Standard models 82/83, 80-81, 83, 135
Hooker, John Lee 33, 34
Howe, Steve 65
Howerdel, Billy 123
Howlin' Wolf 33, 38
Huis, John 16, 45
humbucker/humbucking see pickups

I

Ibanez 76, 92

J

Jackson 92
Jimmy Page model 109, 135
Joe Perry model 106/107, 109, 118, 124, 135
Jones, Mick 76
Jones, Phil 96, 97
Jones, Steve 76
Jumbo model 64, 67, 135
Junior double-cutaway models 30/31, 31, 33, 75, 76, 136
Junior single-cutaway models 22/23, 23, 23, 25, 33, 76, 136
Junior other models
    Lite model 142
    Special Hum/HB model 141
    Special model 141
    Special Plus model 123, 124, 141
    three-quarter model 29, 33, 136
    54 model 136
    57 model 136
    58 model 136
    II model 141
Juszkiewicz, Henry 88

K

Kamin, Wally 17
Kath, Terry 60
Kay 13
Killman, Ken 40, 69
King, Freddie 11, 33, 48
Klein, Matthew 96, 104
KM model 76, 136
knobs see control knobs
Korina model 136
Kossoff, Paul 67, 67
Kramer 88
K-II model 137

L

Lamb, Marv 84
Leo's (dealer) 80
Les Paul amplifier (GA-40) 21
Les Paul award 112
Les Paul & Mary Ford Show (TV) 12, 28
Les Paul/SG models see SG/Les Paul
Les Paul Show (radio) 12
limed finish 28
Locke, Marty 72, 84
"log" guitar 6/7
logo position 148
Lover, Seth 25, 28, 29, 32, 40, 116
low-impedance models 57, 59, 60, 64, 68
Lowe, Mundell 21
LP XR models 137
Lucas, Nick 20 see also Nick Lucas model

M

"Made In USA" logo 148
mahogany 21, 25, 55, 89, 96
maple 21, 25, 36, 37, 40, 55
Marker, Wilbur 16
Marley, Bob *70*, 76
Matthews, Roger 73
Mayo, Sonny *115*
McCarty, Ted 13, 16, 17, 28, 45, 116
McGuire, Mickey 117
Medley, Keith 104
Moats, J P 85
model chronology 152-155
model directory A-to-Z 130-143
Moog 77
Moore, Gary *98*, 116, 119, *see also* Gary Moore model
Morgan, Huey *107*
Mottola, Tony 21
Muddy Waters *14*, 33
Mure, Billy 21
Murphy, Tom 28, 100, 101, 120-121
MIII models 96-97

N

National 13
neck construction 56, 80, 81
Nick Lucas model 20
Norlin Industries 54, 81
North Star model 137

O

Old Hickory model 137
Orville brand 137

P

PAF *see* pickups
Page, Jimmy 35, 49, 52, 61, *63*, 73, 92, 109, *see also* Jimmy Page model
patent 32
Paul, Les (Lester Polfus) 6, 7, *7*, 8, 9, 12, 15, *15*, 16, 17, *19*, 20, 21, *22*, 24, 39, 44, 45, 52, 53, 57, 61, 64, 72, 76, *83*, 88, 108, 120
Perkins, Carl *26*, 33
Perry, Joe 107, *118*, *see also* Joe Perry model

Personal model *59*, 60, 137-138
Peter Frampton model 116, *119*, 138
pickups
    alnico 25
    bobbin colours 40
    Gibson logo 148
    humbucking 26, 29, 32, 49, 56, 57, 59
    low-impedance 57, 67
    PAF 32
    P-90 24, 25
    zebra (bobbins) 40
pot codes 149
prices (US list): 1950 13; 1952 20; 1954 25; 1955 29; 1957 32-33; 1959 40; 1963 45; 1968 54; 1969 57, 60; 1971 64; 1974 68; 1976 72, 73; 1980 81; 1983 85; 1985 85; 1987 92; 1989 93; 1993 105; 1994 105; 1996 105; 1997 113; 1998 108, 113; 2001 124.
Pro Deluxe model *71*, 72, 138
Pro Showcase Edition model 138
production figures 129
Professional model 60, 138
Propp, Les 72
PRS Guitars 110, 113, 116
P-90 *see* pickups

R

Ralphs, Mick 76
Raw Power model *see* Standard Raw Power
RD models 77
Recording models 64, 66, *66/67*, 68, 138
reference section 128-155
reissues 53-54, 65, 73, 85, 100-101, 104-105, 120-121
Rendell, Stan 48, 53, 72
Riboloff, J T 89, 96, 100
Richards, Keith *2*, 19, 39, 49, *50*,
Richrath, Gary 93
Ronson, Mick 73

S

Santiago, Joey *90*
Satriani, Joe 92
Schneider, Dick 72

Schneider, Donnie 72
serial numbers 105, 120, 149-151
SG/Les Paul 44-45, 50, 51
    Custom models 50, *50/51*, *51*, 87, 138
    Junior model *51*, 139
    Standard models *51*, 139
    30th Anniversary model 145
Shaw, Tim 77, 89
Signature model 68, *70/71*, 139
Signature Bass model 68, *71*, 140
Silver Streak model 140
Slash *79*, 93, 111, 120
Slash model 93, 109, *111*, 140
SM model 140
Smartwood models 107, *107*, 112, 140
Smartwood Bass model 140
Smith, Paul Reed 113
solidbody guitar 8, 12-13
Special Bass model 97, 140
Special double-cutaway models *30/31*, 31, 36, 76, 141-142
Special single-cutaway models 23, *23*, 28, 70, 76, 140-141
Special other models
    three-quarter model *31*, 141
    55 model 141
    58 model 142
    400 model 141
Spotlight Special model 83, *83*, 84-85, 142
Standard model (1958-60) *2*, *34/35*, 35, *35*, 36-41, *38/39*, 39, *39*, *43*, 46, *46*, *46/47*, *47*, 47, 48, 49, *50*, *59*, 61, *63*, 65, 73, 80, *86*, 93, 100, 101, 104, 122, 142
Standard model (from 1970s) 73, 93, 142
Standard other models
    Bass models 97, 143
    Birdseye model 142
    Centennial model 143
    CMT model 142
    Custom Shop model 142
    Double Cut Plus model 113, 133
    Heritage *see* Heritage Series
    Lite model 113, 142
    Mahogany model 143
    Plus model 143

INDEX

Standard other models (continued)
    Raw Power model *118/119*, 119, 143
    Showcase Edition 143
    Special model 143
    Tie Dye model 143
    82 model 81, 143
    83 model 143
Standard official Reissue models
    Reissue model (1983-90) 85, *86/87*, 87, 89, *91*, *99*, 143
    58 Figuredtop Reissue model 105, *123*, 143
    58 Plaintop Reissue model 143
    59 Flametop Reissue model (from 1991) 101, *102/103*, 103, 104, 105, 143
    59 Flametop Reissue Aged model 121, *122/123*, 143
    59 Plaintop Reissue model 143
    60 Flametop Reissue model (from 1991) 101, 104, 105
    60 Plaintop Reissue model 143
Stevens, Norton 54, 81
Stills, Steve 64-65
Sting 112
Strings & Things (dealer) 73
Studio model 85, 109, 143
Studio other models
    Custom model 144
    Gem model 144
    Gothic model 144
    Lite models *see below*
    Plus model 144
    Standard model 144
    Synthesizer model 144
Studio Lite models 91, *91*, 92, 96, 144
Studio Lite/MIII model 97, *103*, 144
Sumlin, Hubert 33, *39*
sunburst finish 25, 36, 40
"superstrat" guitar 92, 93
Supro 13
synthesisers 77

T

tailpiece *see* bridge
The Les Paul model 72, 74, *74/75*, 144
The Paul model 144
Thunders, Johnny 75, *75*, 76
tigerstripe wood 37
timber *see* figured; mahogany; maple
Tite, Jim 54
Townshend, Pete 75, *75*
Triumph Bass model 64, *67*, 137
Tune-o-matic bridge 28, 149
TV double-cutaway model *31*, 31, 36, 144
TV finish 28, 29, 36
TV single-cutaway model 23, *23*, 28, 144

U

Ultima model 108, 145
"unburst" finish 40
US-1 model 93, 96

V

Valco 13
Voltz, Mike 96
volute 56, 80, 81, 148

W

Wallace, Jimmy (dealer) 80
Walsh, Joe 73, 93
Waring, Fred 8
Washburn 96
Waters, Muddy *see* Muddy Waters
Wechter, Abe 72, 77
West, Leslie 76
Wheeler, Tom 65
Whitford, Brad 80
Wilson, Edwin 104
Wolverine model 117
wood *see* figured; mahogany; maple
Wylde, Zakk 111, *see also* Zakk Wylde model

X

X-Men Wolverine model 117

Y

Yamaha 76
years of production 128, 152-155
Young, Neil *102*

Z

Zakk Wylde models 109, 111, *111*, 145
Zappa, Frank 65
zebra *see* pickups
Zebrowski, Gary 88

20th Anniversary (Custom) model 68, 145
25th Anniversary (Custom) model 145
25/50 Anniversary model 74, *74/75*, 76, 145
30th Anniversary (gold-top) model 83, *83*, 145
30th Anniversary (SG/Les Paul Custom) model 145
35th Anniversary (Custom) model *90/91*, 145
40th Anniversary model 99, *99*
50th Anniversary models 120
54 Oxblood model 145
60 Corvette model 145

ACKNOWLEDGEMENTS

OWNERS' CREDITS
Guitars photographed came from the following individuals' and organisations' collections, and we are most grateful for their help. The owners are listed here in the alphabetical order of the code used to identify their instruments in the Key below.
BB Bruce Bowling; **CB** Clive Brown; **CC** Chinery Collection; **CM** Country Music Hall of Fame; **DN** David Noble; **GA** Garry Malone; **GG** Gruhn Guitars; **GJ** Ged Johnson; **GL** Gibson London; **GM** Gary Moore; **GN** Gibson Nashville; **HK** Hiroshi Kato; **JC** John Coleman; **JP** Jimmy Page; **JS** John Smith; **MJ** Mike Jopp; **MN** Marc Noel-Johnson; **MW** Mick Watts; **PD** Paul Day; **PM** Paul McCartney; **PU** Paul Unkert; **RH** Rick Harrison; **SA** Scot Arch; **SC** Simon Carlton; **SH** Shane's; **TA** Terry Anthony.

KEY TO INSTRUMENT & AMP PHOTOGRAPHS
The following key is designed to identify who owned which guitars when they were photographed. After the relevant page number(s) we list: the model followed by the owner's initials in **bold type** (see Owners' Credits above).
6/7: Log **CM**. 14/15: gold-top **JS**. 15: gold-top black pickups **CC**; gold-top lefty **TA**. 18/19: painted Custom **AR**; 54 Custom **DN**. 19: proto Custom **CC**. 22/23: Junior **DN**. 23: TV model **CB**; Special **CB**. 26: 57 gold-top **CC**. 26/27: gold-top lefty **PM**. 27: 54 gold-top **GJ**; all-gold **GG**. 30/31: Junior **CB**; Special **PU**. 31: TV\model **SC**; Special three-quarter **SH**. 34/35: 58 Standard **AR**. 35: Page Standard **JP**. 38/39 Richards Standard **MJ**. 39: cherry Standard **CC**; Green Standard **GM**. 46: 60 standard **CC**. 46/47: 60 lefty **PM**. 47: unburst Standard **DN**. 50/51: white custom **DN**. 51: Junior **SC**; Standard **DN**; Custom **SA**. 58: gold-top **MN**. 59: Personal **HK**; Deluxe blue **CC**; Deluxe sunburst **BB**. 66/67: Recording **PD**. 67: Jumbo **CC**. 70/71 Signature **GA**. 71: Pro Deluxe **SC**; Signature Bass **RH**. 74/75 The Les Paul **GA**; 25/50 model **GA**. 75: Artist **GA**; Artisan **GA**. 82/83: Heritage **MW**. 83: Spotlight **GA**. 86/87: Standard Reissue **DN**. 87: Custom **GN**. 90/91 Anniversary **DN**. 91: Studio Lite **GA**. 98/99 Custom Plus **RH**. 99: Bass **GL**; Anniversary **JC**. 102/103: Flametop Reissue **CC**. 103: Classic **GN**; MIII **GL**. 106/107: Perry **GL**. 107: Smartwood **GN**. 110/111 DC model **GN**. 111: Elegant **GN**; Wylde **GN**. 118/119: Raw Power **GL**. 119: Frampton **GN**; Moore **GN**. 122/123: Flametop Aged **GL**. 123: Figuredtop **GL**; Plus **GL**; Class 5 **GL**.

Picture correction On page 58 the Custom shown is a 1956 model, not 1968 as captioned. On page 14 Muddy Waters did indeed have a gold-top, only he loved it so much he kept it just out of view.

Principal guitar photography was by Miki Slingsby. A small number of additional guitar pictures were taken by Garth Blore, Nigel Bradley and Matthew Chattle or supplied by Gibson Guitars.

Memorabilia illustrated in this book, including advertisements, catalogues, photographs, is drawn from the Balafon Image Bank. Originals came from the collections of Tony Bacon, Scott Chinery, Paul Day, National Jazz Archive (Loughton), The Music Trades, Alan Rogan, and Steve Soest.

Artist pictures supplied by Redfern's, London.

THANKS (in addition to those named in Owners' Credits above and in Original Interviews below): Julie Bowie; Dave Burrluck (Guitarist); André Duchossoir; Roger Giffin; Dave Gregory; Dave Hunter; Mel Lambert; Brian Majeski (The Music Trades); Stuart Maskell; Don Merlino; David Nathan (National Jazz Archive); Julian Ridgeway (Redfern's); Steve Soest (Soest Guitar Repair).

SPECIAL THANKS to Paul Day for his contributions to the vintage Gibson Les Paul Book, on which this work is based, and especially the original reference section, as well as for his continuing help and guidance; and to Walter Carter for updating the reference section and all manner of valuable assistance, official and otherwise.

ORIGINAL INTERVIEWS used in this book were conducted by Tony Bacon as follows: Jeff Beck, January 1984 and March 1993; Bruce Bolen, January 1993; Jim Deurloo, October 1992; Robert Fripp, March 1991; Henry Juszkiewicz, March 1993; Matthew Klein, January 2002; Marv Lamb, October 1992; Seth Lover, October 1992; Ted McCarty, October 1992; Tom Murphy, December 2001; Les Paul, March 1989 and March 1993; Stan Rendell, December 1992; J T Riboloff, March 1993; Tim Shaw, February and March 1993. The sources of previously published quotations are generally given where they occur in the text.

BOOKS
Tony Bacon *The History Of The American Guitar* (Balafon/Friedman Fairfax (2001); *50 Years Of Fender* (Balafon/Miller Freeman 2000).
Tony Bacon (ed) *Echo & Twang* (Backbeat 2001); *Feedback & Fuzz* (Miller Freeman 2000); *Electric Guitars: The Illustrated Encyclopedia* (Thunder Bay 2000).
Tony Bacon & Barry Moorhouse *The Bass Book* (Balafon/Miller Freeman 1995).
Tony Bacon & Paul Day *The Fender Book* (Balafon/Miller Freeman 1998); *The Gibson Les Paul Book* (Balafon/Miller Freeman 1993); *The Ultimate Guitar Book* (DK/Knopf 1991).
Walter Carter *Gibson Guitars: 100 Years Of An American Icon* (GPG 1994).
A.R. Duchossoir *Gibson Electrics* (Hal Leonard 1994); *Guitar Identification* (Hal Leonard 1990).
Hugh Gregory *1000 Great Guitarists* (Balafon/Miller Freeman 1994).
George Gruhn & Walter Carter *Gruhn's Guide To Vintage Guitars* (Miller Freeman 1999).
Guitar Player Magazine *The Guitar Player Book* (GPI 1983).
Guitar Trader *Vintage Guitar Bulletin Volume 1* (Bold Strummer 1991).
Terry Hounsome *Rock Record 7* (Record Researcher 1997).
Steve Howe & Tony Bacon *The Steve Howe Guitar Collection* (Balafon/Miller Freeman 1994).
Joseph F Laredo *Les Paul: The Complete Trios Plus* – booklet with CD set (Decca 1997).
Colin Larkin (ed) *The Guinness Encyclopedia Of Popular Music* (Guinness 1992).
Stephen K Peeples *Les Paul: The Legend and the Legacy* – booklet with CD box-set (Capitol 1991).
Pete Prown & H.P. Newquist *Legends Of Rock Guitar* (Hal Leonard 1997).

Rittor Music *The Beauty Of The Burst* (Rittor 1996).
Jay Scott & Vic Da Pra *Burst: 1958-60 Sunburst Les Paul* (Seventh String Press 1994).
Mary Alice Shaughnessy *Les Paul, An American Original* (Morrow 1993).
M.C. Strong *The Great Rock Discography* (Canongate 1995).
Tom Wheeler *American Guitars* (HarperPerennial 1990).
Joel Whitburn *Pop Memories 1890-1954* (Record Research 1986).

We also consulted various back issues of the following magazines: *The Amplifier*; *Beat Instrumental*; *Billboard*; *Disc International*; *Down Beat*; *Gibson Gazette*; *Guitar Player*; *Guitar World*; *Making Music*; *Melody Maker*; *The Music Trades*; *Music World*; *One Two Testing*; *Vintage Guitar*.

LISTENING to Les Paul can be a wonderful experience. We recommend *The Legend And The Legacy* 1948-58 (four CDs, Capitol 1991) and *The Trio's Complete Decca Recordings Plus* 1936-47 (two CDs, Decca 1997). We find the later Columbia material less interesting – and it's scattered over many CDs.

TRADEMARKS Throughout this book a number of registered trademark names are used. Rather than put a trademark or registered symbol next to every occurrence of a trademarked name, we state here that we are using the names only in an editorial fashion and that we do not intend to infringe any trademarks.

RETAIL PRICES quoted in the text are in US dollars and generally are drawn from Gibson's official pricelists through the years. Note that these prices have not applied and do not apply elsewhere in the world, where higher local-currency equivalents may prevail. We sometimes provide approximate conversions into today's buying power, based on information from the US Department Of Labor and the British Government Statistics Office.

Updates? The author and publisher welcome any new information for future editions. Write to: Les Paul 50, Backbeat UK, 115J Cleveland Street, London W1T 6PU, England. Or email us at lespaul@backbeatuk.com

"I've traced a hell of a lot of rock'n'roll, little riffs and things, back to Les Paul. He's the father of it all. If it hadn't been for him, there wouldn't have been anything, really." Jimmy Page, 1977